Providing Relationships and Sex Education for Special Learners

C000153315

Paul Bray wonderfully champions the rights of those with learning disabilities to have access to the very best teaching and learning in this vital part of their lives. [...]They need this education now and those of us engaged with their lives owe it to them to provide the very best.

David S Stewart, OBE D.Litt.h.c. DL, Nottingham

Effective Relationships and Sex Education (RSE) provision is a right for all learners, yet it often proves challenging for educators and caregivers, particularly those teaching learners with additional needs.

This book provides practical guidance for teachers and Special Educational Needs Coordinators (SENCOs) who require the knowledge, skills and confidence to deliver effective RSE to young people with Special Educational Needs. It offers both specific support tailored to pupils with Profound & Multiple Learning Difficulties (PMLD) and Severe Learning Difficulties (SLD), Down's Syndrome and Autism, as well as broad support to embed a whole-school approach in mainstream and special settings. Chapters guide the reader through a range of key topics, with advice, strategies and ready-to-use resources to teach RSE in a positive and respectful way.

This much-needed book will be invaluable for education professionals, residential care providers, and anybody looking to support young people with Special Educational Needs as they learn about relationships and sex. It will also help schools to meet statutory requirements covering the delivery of Relationships and Sex Education.

Paul Bray has 24 years of teaching and senior leadership experience in mainstream and special educational needs schools. He is the founder of INSIGHT training and support Community Interest Company (CIC) that offers support for those with additional needs, their families and professionals. After completing his Masters, Plymouth Marjon University invited Paul to teach on the BA SEND degree course. He is also a member of their Professional Advisory Group.

nasen is a professional membership association that supports all those who work with or care for children and young people with special and additional educational needs. Members include SENCOs, school leaders, governors/trustees, teachers, teaching assistants, support workers, other educationalists, students and families.

nasen supports its members through policy documents, peer-reviewed academic journals, its membership magazine *nasen Connect*, publications, professional development courses, regional networks and newsletters. Its website contains more current information such as responses to government consultations.

nasen's published documents are held in very high regard both in the UK and internationally.

For a full list of titles see: https://www.routledge.com/nasen-spotlight/book-series/FULNASEN

Other titles published in association with the National Association for Special Educational Needs (nasen):

Brilliant Ideas for Using ICT in the Inclusive Classroom, 2ed
Sally McKeown and Angela McGlashon
2015/pb: 978-1-138-80902-4

Curricula for Teaching Children and Young People with Severe or Profound and Multiple Learning Difficulties: Practical strategies for educational professionals
Peter Imray and Viv Hinchcliffe
2013/pb: 978-0-415-83847-4

Time to Talk: Implementing outstanding practice in speech, language and communication
Jean Gross
2013/pb: 978-0-415-63334-5

Promoting and Delivering School-to-School Support for Special Educational Needs: A practical guide for SENCOs
Rita Cheminais
2013/pb 978-0-415-63370-3

Dyslexia and Inclusion: Classroom Approaches for Assessment, Teaching and Learning, 2ed
Gavin Reid
2012/pb: 978-0-415-60758-2

The Equality Act for Educational Professionals: A simple guide to disability and inclusion in schools
Geraldine Hills
2012/pb: 978-0-415-68768-3

Using Playful Practice to Communicate with Special Children
Margaret Corke
2012/pb: 978-0-415-68767-6

Language for Learning in the Secondary School: A practical guide for supporting students with speech, language and communication needs
Sue Hayden and Emma Jordan
2012/pb: 978-0-415-61975-2

Providing Relationships and Sex Education for Special Learners: An Essential Guide for Developing RSE Provision
Paul Bray
2022/pb: 978-1-138-48747-5

Providing Relationships and Sex Education for Special Learners

An Essential Guide for Developing RSE Provision

Paul Bray

Routledge
Taylor & Francis Group

LONDON AND NEW YORK

First published 2022
by Routledge
2 Park Square, Milton Park, Abingdon, Oxon OX14 4RN

and by Routledge
605 Third Avenue, New York, NY 10158

Routledge is an imprint of the Taylor & Francis Group, an informa business

British Library Cataloguing-in-Publication Data
A catalogue record for this book is available from the British Library

Library of Congress Cataloging-in-Publication Data
Names: Bray, Paul (Special education teacher) author.
Title: Providing relationships and sex education for special learners : an essential guide for developing RSE provision / Paul Bray.
Description: Abingdon, Oxon ; New York, NY : Routledge, 2021. | Series: Nasen spotlight | Includes bibliographical references and index.
Identifiers: LCCN 2021001226 (print) | LCCN 2021001227 (ebook) | ISBN 9781138487468 (hardback) | ISBN 9781138487475 (paperback) | ISBN 9781351043144 (ebook)
Subjects: LCSH: Sex instruction for people with mental disabilities.
Classification: LCC HQ30.5 .B74 2021 (print) | LCC HQ30.5 (ebook) | DDC 306.7087--dc23
LC record available at https://lccn.loc.gov/2021001226
LC ebook record available at https://lccn.loc.gov/2021001227

ISBN: 978-1-138-48746-8 (hbk)
ISBN: 978-1-138-48747-5 (pbk)
ISBN: 978-1-351-04314-4 (ebk)

Typeset in Helvetica
by KnowledgeWorks Global Ltd.

Access the Support Material: www.routledge.com/9781138487475

For my amazing, beautiful children; Harrison, Ava and Izaak. Life is full when filled with love. x x x

Contents

Lists of figures

List of abbreviations

SEN = Special Educational Needs

SEND = Special Educational Needs and Disability

SLD = Severe Learning Difficulties

LD = Learning Disability

PMLD = Profound and Multiple Learning Difficulties

ASD = Autistic Spectrum Disorder

PDA = Pathological Demand Avoidance

RSE = Relationships and Sex Education

SRE = Sex and Relationships Education

DfE = Department for Education

DoH = Department of Health

Foreword

'And what I assume you shall assume

For every atom belonging to me as good belongs to you'.

Walt Whitman in his lines reminds us to have equal respect for ourselves and others and Paul Bray in *Providing Relationships and Sex Education for Special Learners* wonderfully champions the rights of those with learning disabilities to have access to the very best teaching and learning in this vital part of their lives.

Being a sexual being is a part of our humanity. Someone may determine whether someone has the ability to enter a sexual relationship under capacity legislation but they cannot determine someone's sexual expression. Education is therefore essential for all and Paul is not afraid to tackle the real issues facing the young people, their parents and carers and staff in school and other settings.

For parents this can be an issue they may wish to ignore and the book is sensitive to the support and guidance for families. Young people are vulnerable but keeping them in ignorance does not make them safer and referencing international research, Paul establishes the importance of imparting knowledge not just for keeping people safe but so they can enjoy happy and fulfilling lives.

From one's own experience of training in schools in the UK, I know the importance of support and professional development for school staff. With lack of national guidance and little training in this area of education, staff can feel anxious and may avoid teaching RSE to pupils with additional needs. Having such a book as this will empower staff and give them the confidence to proceed.

Clearly there is a wide range of pupils with learning disabilities and different strategies will need to be deployed to ensure that pupils get the appropriate teaching. Some will pick some messages quickly; others may need weeks if not months of re-enforcement. The chapter on ASD will be of use to many who are looking for ways to teach RSE to these young learners who find concepts such as private and public difficult to understand.

Parents and staff often struggle with finding the right curriculum or resource for the child's level of understanding or their age and the book guides the reader with practical advice, sharing strategies and ideas which others in the field have found useful.

For some young people who require more personal and intimate care, Paul raises the issue of dignity, privacy and respect for these students. Parents and staff who are working with youngsters in these situations often feel unsure or worry about what others may think and they need to be given an opportunity to express their concerns.

Having been engaged in RSE and young people with SEND for the last 35 years, I commend Paul Bray's book to you. Much has been achieved but there is still so much more to do. Our young people cannot wait whilst politicians prevaricate. They need this education now and those of us engaged with their lives owe it to them to provide the very best.

David S Stewart
OBE D.Litt.h.c. DL
Nottingham

Introduction

'Sexual health requires a positive and respectful approach to sexuality and sexual relationships, as well as the possibility of having pleasurable and safe sexual experiences, free of coercion, discrimination and violence.
For sexual health to be attained and maintained, the sexual rights of all persons must be respected, protected and fulfilled'

(World Health Organisation, 2006)

I was wondering how to produce a clear, visual and excepted example to help us understand *why* Relationships and Sex Education (RSE) is a vital part of all our learning and development.

As you will find out during your journey through this book; either as a read through or a dip into, there are many examples of convincing research and eloquent arguments that re-inforce the need for RSE for our special learners. However, I still found myself wanting that clear image to share with you; for me it is all about the *why*.

Maslow's hierarchy of needs is viewed as a little old fashioned by many; overused by some, overlooked then forgotten by lots of us as we look for the new and the next modern theory. Whatever your view, one cannot deny it comes close to explaining what makes us, as human beings, 'tick'.

Maslow's hierarchy of needs is a motivational theory in psychology comprising, initially, of a five-tier model of human needs, often depicted as hierarchical levels within a pyramid.

The theory offers us the presumption that the levels of the hierarchy must be satisfied from the base up before individuals can attend to needs higher up. From the foundation base of the hierarchy upwards, the needs are: physiological, safety, love and belonging, esteem and self-actualization. I believe there is a direct link from the hierarchy of needs to our learners' readiness for learning and becoming as independent as they can.

Why Maslow matters

Maslow's hierarchy appears in pretty much all talks on educational theory. Although usually presented as a hierarchy of needs many commentators describe it as a way to understand how learners reach their potential and what barriers might exist to them getting there. For me as an educator it's a great reminder that it's not just about what I do in the teaching session. The success of an educational intervention is deeply influenced by the learners' experiences, motivations, behaviours and psychology. We can do much to accommodate them to make learning better.

(Carley, 2015)

Over the years Maslow re-visited the model and his own understanding of us as individuals within society and he refined the theory over several decades, from the 1940's to the 1980's (Maslow, 1943). During this time, and subsequent years, the physiological baseline needs remained constant. However, depending on the interpretation of the baseline needs by those that would share Maslow's model, there has been one important element that has gone 'missing' from time to time.

I will not ask you to guess; this is a book about Relationships and Sex after all.

Maslow (1943) suggests that people are hard-wired to get their needs met and that some of our needs take precedence over others. At the Physiological level these needs can and do overlap.

I have read and heard many an argument for learners needing a 'state of being' to be able to learn; an emotional, safe state that reflects their wellbeing and mental health needs. I absolutely agree. What I would also like to be accepted within these discussions is that being 'ready to learn' requires us to be aware of *how* we can achieve the safe state we all want for our special

Figure 0.1 Maslow's hierarchy of needs five stage pyramid.

learners; an understanding on our part that we cannot pick and choose the particular needs of our learners we will support based on what we are comfortable to address.

Our most basic need is for physical **survival,** and this will be the first thing that motivates our behaviour. If we don't feel safe that will reflect in our behaviour, and all behaviour is communication. How many of our learners display distressed communication, because they cannot get their needs met, cannot communicate their choices appropriately or are in a state of hypervigilance and constantly feel unsafe?

These 'survival modes' are instinctive, deeply wired into us as human beings and absolutely natural. For some of us, we have developed our social skills and self-control to a point that we can self-regulate. For many of our special learners achieving self-regulation is a difficult process.

Physiological needs

These are biological requirements for human survival: air, food, drink, excretion, shelter, clothing, warmth, sleep and ... sex.

'If these needs are not satisfied the human body cannot function optimally' (McLeod, 2020). Maslow considered physiological needs the most important as all the other needs become secondary until these needs are met. One can choose to delete the words we do not like, reproduce Maslow's model and focus on a more contented route, or we can embrace the fact that we are all born as sexual beings and that sexuality is a major part of our baseline physiological needs.

Maslow (1943, cited by McLeod, 2020) thought our behaviour could be multi-motivated and that 'any behaviour tends to be determined by several or all of the basic needs simultaneously rather than by only one of them'. So we need to understand the range of potential triggers to our learners' communication. If we as educators choose to turn a blind eye to the needs of our special learners as sexual beings then should we be surprised if certain distressed communication and challenging behaviours are presented?

Deficiency needs vs growth needs

This five-stage model can be divided into deficiency needs and growth needs. The first four levels are often referred to as deficiency needs and the top level is known as growth (or being) needs.

Deficiency needs are driven by deprivation and motivate us to act when they are unmet. The motivation to meet such needs become stronger the longer the needs are denied. For example, the longer we go without drink, the thirstier we become.

Growth needs are not driven by a lack of something, but from a desire to develop as best we can. Once these growth needs have been, if not met, but reasonably satisfied, we may be able to reach the highest level called self-actualisation.

Safety needs

Once our physiological needs are addressed, our need for security and safety become the drive. We want to experience order, predictability and control in our lives. These needs can be fulfilled by our family, our school and the wider society.

This could be a drive to achieve emotional security, freedom from fear, health and wellbeing and stability in our lives.

Love and a sense of belonging needs

The third level of our human needs is social and involves gaining a feeling of belonging. The need for interpersonal relationships motivates our communication and therefore our behaviour.

This could include finding friendship, intimacy, trust, and acceptance. The receiving and giving of affection and love or being part of a group.

Obviously those of us who do not fit into a neurotypical group will have other drivers that perhaps do not reflect the social need level of Maslow's hierarchy, but we all rely on relationships at a certain level, even if it is only to get our most basic needs met.

Esteem needs are the fourth level in the hierarchy – which Maslow classified into two categories: esteem for oneself and the desire for reputation or respect from others. We know that all healthy relationships are built on solid self-esteem.

Self-actualisation needs are the highest level in Maslow's hierarchy. This refers to achieving our potential. Maslow (1943) describes this level as the desire to accomplish everything that we can, to become the most that we can be.

I hope I have found for you the clear example of why Relationships and Sex Education is vital for our special learners. It is because our sexuality and this basic physiological need are integral to us all. We cannot chose to ignore one aspect of the human needs and rights of our learners and expect them to flourish.

Throughout the book there will be reminders of the difficulties we face as RSE providers and the safeguarding implications of our decisions. I have no desire for this to be anything other than a positive read, but I do have to temper this with the reality of the world we and our special learners live in.

Ultimately, my 'drive', my 'need' is to play a small part in advocating for the unmet needs of the individuals we support. To help you to persuade others that we can make a real difference to the life outcomes of our special learners.

What we want for the learners in our schools and our homes is for them to fulfil their potential, to be the most they can, to be as independent as possible and to live a life that is full and fulfilled.

1 The importance of relevant RSE for special learners

Those of us who support children or adults with learning disabilities are often reminded by others that we have what must be 'a very challenging but rewarding job'.

I agree, we have. It is challenging on many levels and equally as rewarding. When we have the pleasure of witnessing real progress that will impact on our special learners for the rest of their lives, it gives us perspective and encouragement. That breakthrough with an independent living skill or beginning to show powers of self-regulation, seeing those initial steps of independent communication to get themselves 'heard' are magic moments that we hold dear. We are enabling our special learners to become as independent as possible as they journey through life. After all, that is our job. Is it not?

Some of us have been creative in choosing what we believe our learners need to become as independent as possible as part of their curriculum. We have allowed ourselves to focus on a relatively narrow range of knowledge and skills rather than understand that for our special learners to truly develop and grow they must be prepared and supported in their development and growth. Our 'job' should be far more than striving to hit academic targets and demonstrate progress through questionable curricula and flawed assessment. Our special learners should also be supported emotionally and physically as sexual beings.

I have yet to meet a parent or carer of a special learner who considered academic progress more significant in their child's life than developing independent living skills. I believe that the most rewarding part of our job is to advocate for and support our special learners to live as fulfilling a life as they can. What we should acknowledge is that Relationships and Sex Education is a vital element in that process.

The background of relationships and sex education for special learners

We are in a period of history where we are now seeing the start of a healthy national debate about what Relationships and Sex Education should mean for our learners. The fact that this political and social debate is focused on mainstream learners should come of no surprise to those of us in special education. There are an array of factors that make us as a society uncomfortable discussing Relationship and Sex Education within mainstream schools and significantly darker factors (Barker, 2010; Rohleder, 2010; Imray et al., 2012) that urge some to ignore the need for RSE at all in special schools.

As a society I believe we have become complicit in allowing ourselves to pick and choose which aspects of the UN Convention on the rights of the Child (1989) that we adhere ourselves to. If it was not the case, then surely every learner would have the education they need. Instead, for decades, we have chosen a potentially limiting curriculum that is imposed rather than agreed (Apple, 1993; Barker, 2010; Imray et al., 2012) with active side-stepping of acknowledging the need for relationships, sexuality and self-advocacy to be an integral part of our relevant curriculum.

The fact that curriculum content and the importance of what our learners should (or should not) learn remains in the hands of political parties is only open to abuse or some questionable dogma bias at the very least. Cajani sums it up when he writes about the influence on school curricula by political parties and observes that 'political bias is a constant threat' (Cajani et al., 2009).

Nearly 30 years ago, Michael Apple put the 'why' and 'what' of how we teach into perspective for me.

> Education is deeply implicated in the politics of culture. The curriculum is never simply a neutral assemblage of knowledge, somehow appearing in the texts and classrooms of a nation. It is always…someone's selection, some group's vision of legitimate knowledge.

> It is produced out of the cultural, political, and economic conflicts, tensions, and compromises that organize and disorganize a people…the decision to define some groups' knowledge as the most legitimate, as official knowledge, while other groups' knowledge hardly sees the light of day, says something extremely important about who has power in society.
>
> (Apple, 1993)

This 'truth' does not sit well with me but experience tells me it is where we are and I can only hope that eventually we will be able to offer a curriculum that each individual learner, with unique individual needs, deserves. A curriculum that assists our special learners to develop and fulfil their own wishes and potential. Reassuringly, history demonstrates that views will inevitably change and outcomes for those we support will improve. There are many examples of determined work by a range of individuals and organisations to promote RSE for those with additional needs and they have produced compelling arguments for a societal re-think (Stewart, 2009). We cannot allow any political party, influenced by a gambit of extreme ideologies, to determine what our special learners are taught. Without the determination of certain advocates, who have been clear in their persuasiveness, we can lose sight of the importance of RSE due to the pressure to focus on areas of learning that provide questionable evidence of academic progress.

For our special learners, I would argue for a curriculum that is functional skills based and develops self-esteem, independence, self-advocacy and social inclusion; in short, having a relationships focus. It is also healthy for our soul to understand why there has been, and remains, a reluctance to pursue this obvious route.

There are deep social construction theories (Rohleder, 2010) as to why we, as a society, see our special learners in the light we do and how this influences our understanding of disability and sexuality. Social construction theory takes into account how our formed knowledge and what we *know* to be 'true and trusted' about the world around us is formed through our shared language and conversations. The social model of disability draws on this perspective to argue that all types of disability are not located in the individual, but rather in society's constructions of the environment and what is considered to be 'normal' and what is 'abnormal' (Marks, 1999 cited by Rohleder, 2010).

> Using a psychosocial approach to consider how disability is thought about and experienced can help us understand the often emotional reaction to disability and perhaps help explain what may be thought of as resistance to providing sex education for people with disabilities.
>
> (Rohleder, 2010)

I would urge you to read Rohleder's paper to gain more food for thought, but ultimately is it just a lack of knowledge and understanding that we have been blighted by? Has our ignorance of disability and differences influenced our shared language and conversations?

> A lack of information and education on sexuality and disability was felt to be a major contributing factors towards the stigma attached to disability and sexuality…Societal attitudes and perceptions are driven by education and knowledge, if there is no exposure to sexuality and disability, it follows suit that society would have a narrow understanding of these issues… Further research should focus on how best to educate and inform all members of society.
>
> (Esmail et al., 2010)

Historically, our special learners were often seen as 'eternal children' (McCarthy, 1999) because they were considered 'innocent and asexual'. Our wider society assumed that education around sexuality and relationships was irrelevant because of the young people's cognitive levels and limited communication.

Society's construction of disability and sexuality was easier to accept with the shared language being; 'they would not develop sexual feelings' (Garbutt, 2008).

The extreme juxtaposed view of 'innocent and asexual' was the fear that people with learning disabilities were 'over sexualised' and unable to control their sexual urges. This fear also needed to be addressed in a way that satisfied society's alternative construction.

During the Eugenics movement, particularly in the late 19th and early 20th century, it was argued that the procreation of people with learning disabilities should be managed to prevent what was seen as their 'defective' genetic material being passed on and endangering our society (Blacker, 1950) and, as a consequence, many women with learning disabilities were sterilised. In 1913, the Mental Deficiency Act recommended the segregation in colonies or institutions of people deemed to be 'defective, idiots or imbeciles', and anyone certified as such by two doctors could be held against their will (SEAD project, 2015).

I implied earlier that history suggests that we will improve as a society, and I have confidence that this has to be the case, but this process has not yet had the dramatic shared change that we need. In 2013, A High Court judge decided it was in a man's 'best interest' to be sterilised (Doughty, 2013). He had a learning disability. In 2015, a judge ruled that a mother with a learning disability could be sterilised for health reasons and authorised medics to 'force entry' into the woman's home to restrain her (Press Association, 2015). Also in 2015, a wife was banned from having sex with her husband for over a year until her husband had received Relationships and Sex Education. He also had a learning disability. In 2017, that same man was awarded £10,000 in damages at the Court of Protection for a breach of his human rights. The council that gave the initial sex ban did not (or could not) provide the RSE required for over 15 months (Carson, 2017). Where were the advocates, where was the support and guidance that the couple, and obviously the authority, in 2017, needed?

The politics of RSE; where is the informed guidance to be found?

As previously mentioned our political and social divide and questionable political dogmas that are constantly bickering rather than listening to reason is of no help either.

Back in 2000, the then Labour Schools Minister Ed Balls promised that Personal, Social, and Health Education (PSHE) was to become a mandatory part of the British National Curriculum. This was also to make Relationships and Sex Education statutory in all schools and of all ages. RSE would help to support 'real lessons in life, dealing with certain situations, emotions, and decisions', not 'just a biology lesson' (Knight, 2008 cited by Moore, 2011).

> Nonetheless, the attempt to get it onto the curriculum shows up the fact that there are two stories to tell about British education policy concerning sex education.
>
> (Moore, 2011)

I see these two stories as the acceptable and unacceptable faces of Relationships and Sex Education. It appears that as a society we are comfortable with the biological, heterosexual 'sex education' within science but less so when delivered within a personal, social, health, sexuality and relationship context. That fact has always confused me; knowing that it is the act of 'sex' that many are concerned over whilst RSE offers such a wide range of important life and relationship experiences that have no need to focus on a narrow biological element.

In 2010 there was another attempt to make RSE statutory and was lost in the 'long grass' of a Labour government trying to implement other legislation before their time was up. Fast forward to 2015 and the Liberal Democrat Party announced that if they gained power they would make RSE, under PSHE, statutory for all state-funded schools, including free schools and academies (Garner, 2015). A promise that was also made by the Labour Party:

> Questioning the logic of Deputy Prime Minister and Liberal Democrat leader Nick Clegg in siding with the Tories against statutory SRE [RSE], Mr Miliband said: 'Making sex education in schools compulsory is the right thing to do, it's the right thing for our young people, it's the right thing for our country, and we should have the courage of our convictions.'
>
> (Miliband cited by Roberts, 2014)

However, the Prime Minister at the time, David Cameron, giving evidence to the Commons liaison committee earlier in the year, said he did not back calls for wider reform of sex education.

> Do I want to open up the whole of sex and relationship education, and have a mega-debate about every single aspect of it? I'm not sure. I think you then go into all the theocratic arguments between left and right, localist and centrist, abortion and all the rest... I would rather as a practical person, add some sensible bits and work with what we have... rather than open up the whole Pandora's Box.
>
> (Chapman et al., 2014)

That was, in my opinion, a bit of a cop-out with so many organisations rationally and articulately calling for a debate on the importance of PSHE and RSE (NSPCC, 2011; Sex Education Forum, 2008; PSHE Association, 2014). Maybe Cameron had the 'constructed shared conversations' of certain familiar members of our society in his ear. Those wanting to either erase RSE completely from the curriculum or to have it kept from becoming statutory (Wells, 2009; Catholic and Loving It, 2014).

> The increasing influence of conservative political, religious, and cultural forces around the world threatens to undermine progress made in Sexual health and [RSE] education since 1994, and arguably provides the best example of the detrimental intrusion of politics into public health.
>
> (Glasier et al., 2006)

With research shared, facts determined and hard to dispute arguments made, in 2018 we all celebrated the reassuring news that RSE will in fact become statutory from September 2019. Maybe after so many false dawns was there really a change of mood or at least the willingness to accept the weight of evidence within credible campaigns to make RSE and PSHE statutory subjects? Despite these previous promises, at the time of writing, RSE still remains non-statutory; a combination of timing and the reluctance to make it a statutory subject by the various governments that have had plenty of opportunities have kept RSE in its place.

We were then informed that RSE will not become statutory until September 2020.

The Department for Education wanted another round of consultation; but in the meantime we were offered some guidance, in the form of a draft, that one hoped would at least point us in an informed and helpful direction. Disappointingly for those of us working in Special Education there was very little guidance or direction, draft or otherwise.

The impact that Covid-19 had specifically on curriculum development was to impact again on the implementation of statutory RSE. The date was extended to 2021.

During the conversations and consultation process about the content of proposed statutory RSE the needs of our special learners was unsurprisingly lost. My question of the importance of either statutory or non-statutory RSE status is, why should it make a difference to those of us who support special learners? Surely we know that this is an area of knowledge and confidence that is vital for our young people to develop as individuals and, importantly, keep themselves safe. Statutory or not. Guidance or not.

The DfE's guidance states; 'Schools should be aware that some pupils are more vulnerable to exploitation…due to the nature of their SEND'.

This is a little loose with the truth; children with disabilities are three times more likely to suffer from abuse, and suffer from all types of abuse (NSPCC, 2011) and why it is therefore unforgiveable if we are not doing all we can to safeguard our learners by providing them with relevant Relationships and Sex Education.

The role of RSE in safeguarding

> Disabled children have an equal right to protection, yet barriers can exist at all stages of the child protection process.
>
> (National Working Group on Child Protection and Disability, 2003)

We are all terribly earnest, agreeing enthusiastically about the need for safeguarding to be at the forefront of all we do in schools, whilst not giving our learners the skills to safeguard themselves. I remain confused and frustrated with this conflicting truth.

The rights of our learners to protection from abuse are enshrined in the UN Convention on the Rights of the Child (2009) and all that we do to protect and safeguard our learners should be grounded in the Convention. Article 19 protects our learners from 'all forms of physical or mental violence, injury or abuse, neglect or negligent treatment, and maltreatment or exploitation, including sexual abuse'. Article 2 confirms the rights of all children, without discrimination of any kind, to all rights enshrined in the Convention, irrespective of the child's disability. Article 23 shines light on the right of our learners to enjoy a fulfilling life with support that ensures dignity, promotes self-reliance and facilitates our learner's full participation in their community.

The UN Convention on the Rights of Persons with Disabilities, ratified by the UK in 2009, states that all disabled people must enjoy all human rights and fundamental freedoms, and Article 7 informs us that all necessary measures should be taken to ensure the full enjoyment by our learners of all human rights and fundamental freedoms on an equal basis with others.

Article 16 clearly protects the right of all our learners to be free from exploitation, violence and abuse.

So, how have we been doing as a society with ensuring the human rights of our learners are upheld? Research studies consistently show that our special learners are three times more likely to be abused than their mainstream peers (Jones et al., 2012 cited by NSPCC, 2014).

Mencap's report in 2001 found that the number of incidents where people with disabilities have been sexually abused is four times higher than for those without disabilities and young people with learning disabilities were reported to be most at risk (Mencap, 2001). For our learners with more complex needs they are even more likely than their peers to experience abuse (Grieve et al., 2006 cited by Family Planning Victoria, 2015). Another study by Beadle-Brown in 2010 found that alerts about possible abuse of adults with learning disabilities made up 30% of all possible abuse reported to local authorities (SEAD project, 2015).

> …disabled children are three times more likely to experience abuse, more likely to be subjected to multiple abuses and endure multiple episodes of abuse. This risk is true for children of all disabilities and from all forms of abuse.
>
> (NSPCC, 2011)

With so few of our learners having the opportunity to take part in relevant RSE, that can develop self-esteem and self-advocacy, is it a surprise that, compared with the general population, our learners are approximately twice as likely to suffer sexual abuse and four times more likely to be victims of sexual crimes? (Swango-Wilson, 2011).

> …partly because they frequently have difficulty distinguishing between abusive and non-abusive behaviour and may lack the communication skills required to report any abuse they may experience.
>
> (Barnard-Brak et al., 2014 cited by Family Planning Victoria, 2015)

As a society and educators, our attitudes and assumptions about our special learners can disempower them and negatively impact upon their confidence, self-advocacy and self-esteem. This all has worryingly significant implications for safeguarding. Developing self-esteem, self-advocacy skills and relationship skills are vital ingredients for our learners' positive self-image and therefore supporting them to keep safe (Marchant and Page, 1992; Sobsey, 1994; Briggs, 1995; Blake et al., 2004 cited by FPV, 2015).

Time to address the obvious. For many of us in special schools it is difficult to think that our learners are in danger, let alone suffering any type of abuse. But, if all my learners are safe and all your learners are too, then where are the learners that all the research has consistently proven are suffering; the learners that are in danger? We need to be a little more realistic and a little less blinkered. There are special people of all ages that are suffering now. What are the chances that you know one of them, teach one of them, but do not know the full picture of their life?

> Providing sexual education to students with intellectual disabilities actively reduces their risk of abuse by increasing their capacity to protect themselves from abuse.
>
> (Grieve et al. 2006 cited by FPV, 2015)

Many of our special learners have not had the opportunity to learn about themselves, their changing bodies through puberty, how to keep themselves safe, about different relationships we develop as we grow older, the pleasure of consensual physical contact, the confusion over public and private or safe and unsafe touch.

For many of our learners, healthy relationships, body changes, naming body parts (including proper names for genitals) and keeping safe should be a learning priority. The issue of our learners having the ability to name private parts of their bodies and those of the opposite sex has been seen as a child protection issue for some time; failing to teach the correct names for the sexual parts of the body could be a safeguarding issue because it leaves children without the words to describe their bodies (Fyson, 2007; Emmerson, 2013). To promote the safety of our special learners, we need to support them to develop skills to communicate effectively; however, they are able to communicate. The NSPCC also encourages us that this can be achieved through relevant RSE that develops our special learners' conceptual understanding relating to personal safety, feelings, relationships, safe and unsafe behaviours and how to seek help (NSPCC, 2015).

Research studies (Briggs, 2006; Marchant et al., 2008; Stephenson et al., 2011 cited by NSPCC, 2014) into safeguarding practice have consistently raised the need for personal safety skills programmes, including Relationships and Sex Education, to be part of our safeguarding strategies. In Briggs' 2006 study, it was concluded that learners who had completed a RSE/personal safety/child protection programme were more likely (52%) than their peers (12%) to know that adults are not allowed to do 'sex things to kids' (Briggs, 2006 cited by NSPCC, 2014).

RSE can certainly support many of our learners to understand that they have a voice and an understanding of what they are happy with through self-advocacy or what is inappropriate behaviour. Whether that is their own or the behaviours of others. This understanding may help in identifying and stopping sexually based crimes (Swango-Wilson, 2011) so we should therefore be compelled to raise our learner's awareness of abuse and ability to seek help (Briggs, 2006; Marchant et al., 2008; Stephenson et al., 2011 cited by NSPCC, 2014). Having a voice and the understanding of self-esteem and self-advocacy will be the best safeguarding tool you can give to your learners; although I understand that for many this is a more complex issue than 'simply getting on with it'.

Despite the detailed evidence, why are we in SEN schools not providing RSE?

There are well-practiced and well-thumbed arguments about a lack of suitable resources for our learners and a lack of suitable training for our colleagues. There are many culturally excusable barriers that we can hold close to excuse our decision not to take the difficult path of providing RSE. Ultimately, it appears we can use these handed-down batons of denial to ensure our creative choice about what is important to teach our special learners is socially acceptable.

Can the decision not to acknowledge the obvious needs of our learners be attributed to our attitudes and the lack of will to accept and address the human rights of our special learners as sexual beings?

> Professionals might like to honour the 'right to sexuality' of people with learning disabilities, but many do not know how to do this in practice…
>
> (Garbutt, 2008)

…or wish to address their own moral dilemma about providing RSE. The repeated conclusion is that RSE has been 'poorly provided for' (NSPCC, 2011) or simply 'not good enough' (Ofsted, 2013). How does this sit comfortably with the rights of the child and young person to equality and not to be discriminated against due to any disability? Can this really fit in with the SEN Code of Practice (2014), The Equality Act (2010) and the United Nations Convention on the Rights of the Child (1989)?

We know from the pockets of great RSE provision across the country that through a well-planned, long-term, whole school RSE programme a lasting impact on confidence and knowledge for our learners does happen. For those schools that already provide good quality RSE the progress made by their learners continually reflect that statement.

What we are missing is a coordinated, country-wide support network for all special schools to improve their RSE provision.

Ruth Garbutt, in her paper 'Sex and Relationships for People with Learning Disabilities: A Challenge for Parents and Professionals' (2008) paints a clear picture about the support that was around at that time and understandably concludes rather downbeat:

> There seems to be no coordinated, consistent support for people with learning disabilities in [the area of RSE] or for the frontline staff who are dealing with the issues. Parents and professionals are responsible for providing the training and education individuals need regarding relationships and sexual expression, yet, in general, within our research we have found that neither feels prepared.
>
> (Garbutt, 2008)

Twelve years on from Garbutt's enlightening paper, it feels that we have not moved on that much at all. Whether the proposed statutory status of RSE will encourage the DfE to look at providing the support schools need time will tell; there is certainly no mention of this within the DfE's RSE guidance.

The role of RSE within a relevant curriculum

> Education is the mechanism to promote the decision-making abilities and empower the individual. Education will not only contribute to reducing vulnerability but also contribute to the reduction of inappropriate sexual expression.
>
> (Swango-Wilson, 2009)

With the reigns being relaxed to enable us in special schools to start designing our own curricula and not having to be restricted to the irrelevant National Curriculum, one would think that empowering and safeguarding our special learners would be shining through these polished new 'learning areas'.

Thirteen years ago Simon Blake, the then head of Brook, wrote a piece that still should be taken as relevant right now and act as a warning to all of us that theoretically have our special learners' best interest as our paramount concern.

> The recent politics, policy and practice of sex education continue to prevent all children from receiving... quality [RSE] education. These include our failure as a nation to truly acknowledge the rights of children and young people set out in the UN Convention on the Rights of the Child. There are inconsistency and inequity of provision, with a concurrent lack of targeting to meet local and individual needs. We have a culture which does not generally respect young people's sexuality, and despite the best efforts of individuals, there is still limited capacity for developing robust partnerships that maximise the skills of different professionals.
>
> (Blake, 2007)

There are different professional colleagues that not only have developed inspirational RSE provision but are more than willing to cascade their knowledge through partnerships. We need to be able to find a way to share the great Relationships and Sex Education work special schools and organisations across the country are providing, driving best practice and developing knowledge and understanding for all. Again, it is perhaps my childlike enthusiasm that encourages me to believe, but there *has* to be a national SEN/RSE advisory body set up before too long.

Unfortunately, we will still need to convince some of our school leaders that they *should* be heeding this advice. Much of the research undertaken over many years has concluded, that for a significant number of us in special schools, RSE is an area of learning that we have lost in our periphery whilst the focus has been on a more comfortable and well-practiced route.

This is not meant as a criticism of my teaching colleagues; I was also blindly following that same path. The pressure we feel in schools to 'toe the line' and focus on demonstrating progress within questionable academic subject areas can be disorientating. Without the encouragement from school leaders to question our practice and our pedagogy it is difficult to navigate a rewarding professional development route. Having the emphasis on the requirements of inspections has allowed Relationships and Sex Education to stay in the shadows of our otherwise new bright curricula. We also have a plethora of those pre-made socially constructed views to hide behind to condone our decisions.

This all combines to appear to those that are striving to advocate for our special learners that some of our colleagues have generally wished the sexual essence of our shared humanity to be ignored; if they do not look, their moral conflicts will magically 'disappear'.

This has been a familiar picture for many years, a lack of knowledge and reluctance to accept what type of learning opportunities our special learners truly need. When you combine this with a short-sighted, rarely challenged curriculum that many of us willingly adopted for our special learners, then it is unsurprising that acknowledging and even understanding the human rights of our learners, and creative thought required to address those rights, were suppressed for so long.

> *...the national curriculum excluded many learners in special education and was written with mainstream learners in mind. This lack of inclusion, and a neglect in terms of provision for a large number of learners resulted in many schools making the changes in isolation, developing a diverse range of responses to the national curriculum...*
>
> *The [National Curriculum] has brought with it greater accountability through Ofsted, reporting data and monitoring of outcomes. This level of dictate often meant that [SEN] educators became inflexible in their approaches, driven by the perceived need to deliver... and teach to the test. In addition, the high levels of central government prescription through the national curriculum and the national strategies have de-skilled many in the current [SEN] workforce.*
>
> (Barker, 2010)

In the truly enlightening and inspirational 'Not fit for purpose: a call for separate and distinct pedagogies as part of a national framework for those with severe and profound learning difficulties' (2012), Imray and Hinchcliffe argue convincingly that it is long overdue that we think again about what and how we teach those with SEN. They quote Ware and Healy (1994) who describe schools being forced to follow the mainstream linear curriculum as providing at best 'a façade of competence'. They go on to point out that Barber and Goldbart (1998) described the acceptance and teaching of National Curriculum subjects in Special Schools as being adopted only to satisfy the demands of Ofsted and had no relation to good SLD [Severe Learning Difficulties] practice (Imray et al., 2012).

> The threat of failing an Ofsted inspection was a powerful and motivating factor that worked to ensure the rhetoric of the National Curriculum could be seen to be implemented in full by the majority of SLD schools.
>
> (Aird, 2001, cited by Imray et al., 2012)

During the research project carried out by CHANGE, in partnership with the Centre for Disability Studies at Leeds University, a national organisation that fights for the rights of people with a learning disability, they found many of the teachers interviewed said that the National Curriculum was restrictive in special schools because it did not take into account the needs of young people with learning disabilities. They also stated that the National Curriculum was not appropriate for young people with complex needs. A number of teachers said that life skills, sex education, survival and happiness were more important subjects than reading and writing for some of our special learners. Due to the demands of the National Curriculum, teachers could not respond to the individual needs of their pupils in relation to their own personal development and independence. The suggestion was that RSE needed to be higher on the agenda in special schools.

> They said that there was a need for a national recognition by the Government of the particular issues around sex and education faced by teachers working in special schools.
>
> (CHANGE, 2010)

In one of my previous roles I was Head of Post 16 and also Behaviour Lead of a multi-need special school. Subconsciously I too kept RSE in the shadows until an individual's inappropriate behaviour insisted we shed some light. All too often we would have to react to certain challenging sexualised behaviours rather than being pro-active and planning ahead to prepare the learners and their families for the foreseeable. Puberty.

The realisation that we were letting individuals and families down by shying away from providing relevant RSE, then reacting too late to behaviours, made me question, try to understand then endeavour to change our practice.

Even if we were all determined and willing to provide RSE, it is still perceived as a difficult area to teach; there is very little training and support during initial teacher training courses, limited guidance and a scarcity of relevant resources that you can pick off the shelf. Teacher confidence in delivering Relationships and Sex Education has historically been very low, with 80% of teachers feeling not suitably trained or confident to deliver RSE (NCPTA, NAHT and NGA, 2010). Some of those working with special learners have been reluctant to become involved in Relationships and Sex Education due to their moral beliefs, their attitudes towards RSE or a lack of confidence in their abilities to provide adequate RSE due to an apparent lack of available education materials (Murray and Minnes, 1994; Howard-Barr et al., 2005; Garbutt, 2008 cited by NSPCC, 2014).

In Rohleder's study of those working with special learners he found that staff taking part, although providing Relationships and Sex Education, struggled with their anxiety of opening up a 'Pandora's box' due to the potential sexual behaviours of people with learning disabilities arguably being encouraged by providing RSE. His study shows that the anxiety levels of staff are high and that, in turn, causes a dilemma about providing Relationships and Sex Education. Although there is recognition of the need to provide RSE to those with a learning disability, there is a real fear that RSE will lead to 'problematic sexual behaviours'. In some cases where we are not prepared or lack certain knowledge, RSE can be perceived as having the potential to cause more 'harm' (Rohleder, 2010).

UNESCO's 2009 guidance reassures us all that it is 'illogical and fallacious' to assume that teaching children and young people about their inevitable sexual maturity at puberty leads to any encouragement of sexual activity. In fact evidence demonstrates that well-planned, relevant and accurate RSE helps delay sexual activity, promote responsible behaviours and prevent harm (UNESCO, 2009).

What are the consequences of not trying to empower our learners; what happens when they grow up, when they are no longer at school being 'looked after'? It is important that we understand our duties and our 'duty of care' to listen to our learners and listen to the lessons that others with learning disabilities are trying to tell us. The Relationships and Sex research project undertaken by CHANGE has given a wider range and a louder voice to many so they can share their views, and I for one appreciate it. CHANGE found that many people with learning disabilities said that they were *never* told about sex and relationships when they were younger. Never. Those questioned said that if they had had better RSE (or any sex education) they might have made different choices as adults (CHANGE, 2010).

Earlier this year, I met with a group of adults called CHAMPs (Cornwall Health and Making Partnerships). They are a team of ten people with learning disabilities who help to make sure that other people with a learning disability get equal access to health services. They very kindly agreed to help me with my research around RSE provision for special learners and were willing to discuss with me their own experiences around their sexuality and support they received as they grew up. We had some difficult, emotional conversations. There was one young man who could remember 'something happening at college'. All he could remember from that one RSE session was that it was '*rushed and scary*'. No-one else had received any kind of RSE support from school, college or residential care homes.

One man told me his story of growing up and realising he was attracted to a young lady. They both lived in a residential school, the attraction was mutual. The 'support' this man received when he was caught kissing the young lady was to be hit by a member of staff. He was unable to talk to anyone about his confusion. He was not offered anything other than fear and the fact that his feelings were 'obviously' wrong. Whist living in a care home, after leaving school, this man started another relationship. Scared, he didn't feel able to seek advice or support about his sexual feelings. He 'knew' that relationships were not for people like him. He and his partner started a sexual relationship that produced a baby. In hindsight he would have liked to have known about contraception. However, they were happy and wanted to be together.

This likeable, friendly man has never seen his baby boy. The baby was taken into care straight after birth. The relationship ended. 'Paul, I have thought about my boy everyday'.

Asking the group what they would have wanted to learn when at school, if they had RSE, it was clear that the 'rules' of relationships would have been welcomed. 'We can feel that because we like someone then they are boyfriends or girlfriends'. 'We need help to know that is not how relationships work'.

For learners that I have worked with the consequence of not understanding the 'rules of relationships' is that they could have been deemed as sexual offenders when in truth they were just ill-educated in the things that matter; Personal, Social, Health, Relationships and Sex education. As a society, we choose not to consider RSE as important for those with learning disabilities because they are seen to be different to us (Rohleder, 2010). However, when it comes to their inappropriate behaviour they are then punished the same as us and this leads to the 'labelling of some acts as sexually abusive, which plainly were not, and to the labelling of some people as sexual abusers, who plainly were not' (Fairbairn, 2010).

UK studies have noted the overrepresentation of young people with learning disabilities when researching the factors behind those young people who sexually abuse others.

> A study...found that 44% of referrals to a clinic for young people who sexually abuse others had some degree of learning disability, with half of these having attended a special school.
> (Fyson, 2007)

A special school just like ours?

Relationships and Sex Education should be a fundamental area of learning for special schools to provide. Our special learners have not got the option of cancelling puberty and sexual maturity, it will happen. They will grow into adults and hopefully find a safe role in their community and develop respectful relationships. Are we are willing to provide the RSE that they require?

We *can* change the quality of our RSE provision but it is not without a few heartfelt conversations and a determined attitude. I hope that within this book I will have shown that taking routes towards staff training to enhance confidence, parental workshops to encourage a collaborative focus, tailored planning and resources suitable for your learners; then you and your colleagues can make a real difference.

One just has to *want* to improve the Relationships and Sex Education provision for our special learners. That is the true battle and one that helps reconcile the challenging views; we have to ignore the conflicting messages and the spectre of discrimination and do what we believe in.

> Schools should be aware of short-comings and act to create their own rounded programme of sex and relationships education.
>
> (Emery, 2013)

We all agree that our special learners require a curriculum that will enable them to be as independent as possible and to be able to lead fulfilling lives both as children and when they eventually leave school and become adults. I would argue that a 'broad and balanced' (DfE, 2013) holistic curriculum needs to include a rounded programme of RSE for our learners.

Significant change is required to adapt our view on the importance we bestow on areas of learning for our special learners. They deserve to be afforded their given human right to receive and obtain benefit from quality RSE. Within this we should also equip our learners with skills, knowledge and strategies that enable them to take responsibility for their sexual expressions. It is important that our RSE provision should also 'actively challenge the hetero-normative perspective' (Löfgren-Mårtenson, 2011).

> The content needs to move from focussing on the biological aspects of sexuality to a curriculum that focusses on developing a healthy sexual identity, respectful relationships, safer sexual practices, informed decision-making, protective behaviours and sex in the context of intimacy, desire and pleasure.
>
> (Löfgren-Mårtenson, 2011; Blanchett et al., 2002; Katz and Lazcano-Ponce, 2008 cited by Family Planning Victoria, 2015)

And, if you do need to convince a reluctant SLT member or governor, point out that schools that provide RSE and PSHE encourage learners to take responsibility for their physical and emotional health and 'in doing so raise levels of achievement and drive up academic standards' (Weyman, 2004).

After years of eloquent campaigning by individuals and organisations, all schools will eventually be expected to provide RSE through the new statutory status that has been bestowed; whenever the eventual start date. That said, I do not believe that statutory status will ensure that the RSE provision is tailored and relevant for all our special learners.

That is going to be down to you.

I hope through the pages of this book we will get to where we all want to be; supporting each other to be able to provide outstanding Relationships and Sex Education for our special learners that has assessment, reflection and on-going development entwined.

We do have extremely challenging and equally rewarding jobs. The challenge of providing quality Relationships and Sex Education for your special learners will be one that will reward you like no other, because you will be giving them the opportunity to be who they want to be.

2 Whole school RSE self-evaluation, assessment and development planning

In this chapter, we will do the seemingly hard background work. First we will explore whole setting Relationships and Sex Education (RSE) self-evaluation tools and then the cycle of evaluation and development, which can be adapted for your establishments' particular needs. We will also look into how your organisation can use adaptable assessment tools to baseline knowledge and understanding of the individual learners to inform personalised RSE planning and then go on to use the tools to demonstrate learner progress. This is not for any other reason than to gauge and celebrate learning.

We will then compare some planning examples for a variety of learners. Furthermore, we have the opportunity to explore the newly released Roadmap to RSE designed in collaboration by Sex Education Forum and Personal, Social and Health Education (PSHE) Association.

If you are in the position to commit to improving your RSE provision, then we need to have some concrete idea of your starting point. In short, how good is your current provision, how do you know and how can we get a baseline judgement to work from? I will offer a model self-evaluation tool that you can use, so you can gain a better understanding of the content and quality of your current RSE provision. It will also offer ideas for a logical step by step process to plan for whole-setting RSE improvement and development with key standards based on best practice and up to date guidance.

I want this to be a positive process and will try to make the self-evaluation and assessment tools as accessible as possible by encouraging you to see that the suggested content can be adapted for use not only in schools, but all establishments. There will be plenty here for various organisations to use and adapt to suit your particular requirements.

As we know, those supporting our special learners can, and do, make a difference to their outcomes, and ultimately their prospects of a fulfilling future. This perhaps obvious fact that we can have both a positive and also a negative influence on learner outcomes has encouraged the development of school improvement research and practice. There are a variety of interpretations about the definition, but as far as we are concerned, we'll use John MacBeath's definition of self-evaluation:

> Self-evaluation is a process of reflection on practice, made systematic and transparent, with the aim of improving pupil, professional and organisational learning.
>
> (MacBeath, 2005)

The self-evaluation process should be seen as a positive journey for helping your school to improve RSE provision. This should be shaped by yourselves, involving all stakeholders in a collaborative practice of sharing views that will ultimately reflect on the impact of your school's actions on your learners understanding and self-advocacy skills.

> It makes sense that schools should regularly ask themselves questions about how they are doing and what could be done better.
>
> (Chapman et al., 2008)

As Chapman also points out, we need all stakeholders involved in self-evaluation and development. However, from experience I would offer one piece of sage advice for you to make this process a success; become a Headteacher, a Senior Leader or the boss of your organisation. If that is going to be a journey you have no wish to take, then get your boss on-board and get them to own this journey with you. There is a real threat to your intention of improving RSE provision if you do not carry leadership influence with you. Securing leadership support at Headteacher or Head of Setting level, prior to engaging colleagues' commitment, is vital to ensure a successful programme of whole school improvement (Potter et al., 2002).

Although I am at pains to stress to you the importance of getting leadership support in your pursuit of outstanding RSE provision, your self-evaluation and any consequential development plan will only truly work with a whole setting approach, involving all stakeholders; including parents and carers. The research completed on successful school improvement programmes demonstrates that a bottom-up rather than a top-down approach to change, increases the chances of success. It makes perfect sense to put learners and teachers at the core of improvement efforts, although for the sometimes contentious nature of RSE, we also need a multilevel approach and the commitment of senior leaders.

Some of your colleagues will face some challenging situations and conversations during the process of promoting RSE. Having full confidence in the knowledge that you are all in it together, with agreed goals, will make those challenges seem more like opportunities to share.

We know that there are many reasons and excuses left lying around for people to pick up and convince themselves there is no reason to commit to this difficult route of developing RSE provision. If we can, we should take these opportunities to convince our colleagues and parents or carers to see the excuses not to support our learners in their personal development as sexual beings, as just that - an excuse.

Individuals are almost always the catalyst for change, but believe me, if you don't gain some wider understanding and support, you will be carrying far too heavy a load by yourself. So, some positive, encouraging and understanding partnership work will be required.

If you have a committed team working together, all the foreseeable challenges of explicitly developing your RSE provision can be addressed. Sounds easy right? Like you, I know it can be quite the opposite.

Potter, Reynolds and Chapman ask schools to understand that:

- every school can improve
- every individual in the school has a contribution to make the improvement
- schools should help themselves and guard against creating dependency
- everyone in the school should be learning from others

(Potter et al., 2002)

MacBeath (2005) points out that for many countries school inspection has traditionally been the external barometer and judge of quality assurance. Putting evaluation under the control of schools themselves is now viewed as being 'more economical and growth promoting'. For some schools there are always the temptation to choose the ease of following a model self-inspection approach as opposed to a more organic wide ranging and more purposeful self-evaluation. Try to avoid that temptation.

Essentially, teachers and school leaders are the key agents of change (Hopkins et al., 1994; MacBeath, 1999) but to ultimately have a successful RSE programme, we need the input of all stakeholders. None of us have all the answers and as David Stewart was at pains to point out during his keynote speech at the inaugural RSE for Special Educational Needs (SEN) 'getting it right' conference (Jan 2018, London) 'there are no experts' when it comes to designing RSE for the learners you know best. You can have the support of the expertise of others in this field, but ultimately the journey of providing quality, relevant RSE for the needs of your particular learners are yours and your community's journey. Just make sure you plan well to ensure you arrive at a successful destination.

This is a guide, an example, and should not be seen as a tool to constrict what you wish to achieve. Do not be restricted in your views or your aspirations for the content of your provision. Your knowledge of your learners and what content they need in their RSE curriculum will inform your imagination and, with collaborative working, you will be able to design the quality RSE provision your leaners deserve and are entitled to. Do make this *your* evaluation and development plan, to focus on what you know to be important for your learners, and not allow yourself to simply follow loose and, arguably, unchallenging DfE RSE guidance (DfE, 2018, 2019).

> *…school improvement is about raising student achievement through focusing on the teaching and learning processes and the conditions that support it. It is about strategies for improving the school's capacity for providing quality education in times of change, rather than blindly accepting the edicts of centralised policies and striving to implement these directives uncritically.*
>
> (Hopkins et al., 1994)

The much anticipated DfE RSE draft guidance, which was released in July 2018, followed by the equally anticipated final guidance (2019) gave all of us working with special learners the square route of no guidance at all, so I wouldn't worry about blindly accepting the edicts from the DfE. In fact, we would all be better off if we concentrated on improving our own capacity and RSE provision as a SEN sector, sharing best practice and driving the quality of provision ever forward, together.

Here are the SEN specific guidance points from DfE guidance to improve your RSE provision;

Pupils with special educational needs and disabilities (SEND)
Relationships Education, RSE and Health Education must be accessible for all pupils. This is particularly important when planning teaching for pupils with special educational needs and disabilities as they represent a large minority of pupils. High quality teaching that is differentiated and personalised will be the starting point to ensure accessibility. Schools should also be mindful of the preparing for adulthood outcomes, (10) as set out in the SEND code of practice, when preparing these subjects for those with SEND.
'Preparing for adulthood' outcomes are set out at section 7.38 of the SEND code of practice: 0 to 25 years.
Schools should be aware that some pupils are more vulnerable to exploitation, bullying and other issues due to the nature of their SEND. Relationships Education can also be a particular priority for some pupils, for example some with Social, Emotional and Mental Health needs or learning disabilities. Such factors should be taken into consideration in designing and teaching these subjects.
In special schools and for some SEND pupils in mainstream schools there may be a need to tailor content and teaching to meet the specific needs of children at different developmental stages.

Relationships Education, Relationships and Sex Education (RSE) and Health Education, Guidance for governing bodies, proprietors, head teachers, principals, senior leadership teams and teachers (DFE, 2018)

At least within this draft guidance document it makes it clear that *all* schools will be required to provide RSE

> *Unless otherwise specified, 'school' means all schools, whether maintained, non-maintained or independent schools, including academies and free schools, non-maintained special schools, maintained special schools and alternative provision, including pupil referral units.*

Special schools do not get any real guidance from the document apart from the suggestion of 'you know what you're doing, get on with it'. Well, as we know, many SEN schools do not know and need some supportive guidance or at least sign-posting to access advice and training. Where is the realisation that when we instruct schools to provide this potentially difficult area of learning shouldn't we also provide training and support?

The guidance talks about SEN schools needing to provide; *'High quality teaching that is differentiated and personalised…to ensure accessibility'.*

I would like to think that the writers of the draft understand that teachers in special schools make the most difficult of concepts accessible to our learners. Delivering differentiated, personalised learning experiences is what they do all day, every day.

The guidance goes on to state; *"Schools should be aware that some pupils are more vulnerable to exploitation…due to the nature of their SEND".*

We have demonstrated the importance of the relationship between Safeguarding and RSE in the previous chapter, but I will continue to make the links. I wish to make it clear that RSE is not only a given human right but vital in safeguarding our special learners. If I can convince you of the same, I will be content.

> *Relationships Education can also be a particular priority for some pupils, for example some with Social, Emotional and Mental Health needs or learning disabilities. Such factors should be taken into consideration in designing and teaching these subjects.*

Again, these 'factors' are considered every day in special schools; what is needed is some actual guidance that supports our special schools to improve their provision, not continue with what they are doing.

> *In special schools and for some SEND pupils in mainstream schools there may be a need to tailor content and teaching to meet the specific needs of children at different developmental stages.*

As you can see, despite the statutory status RSE will eventually be awarded we may have to wait for some actual RSE SEND guidance. Would the better route be to improve our RSE provision ourselves and use our self-evaluation tool and subsequent development plan to do so? Would we then share our findings and successful practice with our wider community?

> *It is an index of a nation's educational health when its school communities have a high level of intelligence and know how to use the tools of self-evaluation and self-improvement. In healthy systems there is a sharing and networking of good practice within and among schools ... It is an unhealthy system which relies on the constant routine attentions of an external body to police its schools ...*
>
> (MacBeath, 1999)

We have the opportunity in schools to adapt our provision, and our curriculum, to suit the needs of our learners. Why are we waiting for 'external permission' to remove barriers to life-long learning that can make a real difference to the outcomes of our learners? It has been argued that our special learners face barriers to education and support that ultimately affect their sexual health and potentially mental health (Curfs et al., 2013). Generations of special learners have consistently said the RSE they have received was not good enough (SEF, 2008; CHANGE, 2010). Ofsted have discovered a familiar pattern during inspections and found RSE provision 'still not good enough' in far too many schools (Ofsted, 2002, 2010, 2013).

There have been some RSE programmes developed by professionals working in the world of special education over the years that have aimed to overcome these barriers and we need to thank these trail blazers for acknowledging the problem and trying to do something about it. The individuals and schools that constantly evaluate and improve their provision do so because they want the best outcomes for their learners.

There have been many other programmes that have perhaps started with good intentions but have not been built on solid foundations. Curfs and colleagues undertook a study in 2013 to explore the development and success of these programmes. The results were unfortunately disappointing:

> *All programmes lack specific outcomes, do not have a theoretical basis, did not involve members of relevant groups in the development process and lack systematic evaluation. Conclusions: Based on our findings and the literature, we conclude that these programmes are unlikely to be effective. Future programmes should be developed using a more systematic and theory and evidence-based approach.*
>
> (Curfs et al., 2013)

If we can, as a team, be clear about the process and build on the trusting relationships that we have to carry out our school self-evaluation, this could be a positive process where teachers and learners feel at the centre and have control and ownership of the outcomes. Self-evaluation can be a positive activity to engage in and this will be a process where all members of the school community, especially the learners and teachers, are engaged in promoting their own learning through the systematic and evidence-based approach encouraged by Curfs and many others.

There will be certain explored ideas during your self-evaluation that some may feel uncomfortable with; that is more than okay, it is to be expected. What we all need is to be able to share our concerns in an environment where all views are welcome. When this clarity of openness and direction has been understood and accepted the self-evaluation process will be more able to fulfil its aims of promoting learner and professional learning.

> *...most teams will only vent their feelings, discuss their problems and seek help when they feel secure...reduce any potential threats [and follow] the teams' agenda. This [will help] develop a sense of safety and openness.*
>
> (Kember et al., 2006)

A framework for self-evaluation

The extensive work in the area of school-self-evaluation and frameworks of best practice has been and pulled together by Chapman et al. (2013) and I have used the key areas that were collated to offer a set of questions that can be used in the reflective planning stages of the self-evaluation process.

1. **Why are we doing this**? I will expand on the importance of why, later in the chapter, but a discussion among all stakeholders to come to a shared understanding of the aims of the self-evaluation process is a healthy start.
2. **Who is this for?** Are you doing this for Ofsted or are you doing this for your learners? Is the focus one of accountability rather than improvement? If the school as a whole is the beneficiary then we may have teaching and learning at the centre of our self-evaluation which directly impacts on learners outcomes.
3. **What is the best structure?** As educationalists, we are natural evaluators (and self-critics) with self-evaluation occurring naturally within our classroom or even department. To have whole school influence and impact, a framework for self-evaluation needs to be developed to formalise the process.
4. **How are we to judge?** Performance data in the form of test or exam results as indicators of improvement will not help you within RSE. However, we will have individual assessment baselines and 'improvement' data that will be produced over time through learner evaluation, or by conversations with external agencies acting as critical friends. In this way the ownership of the self-evaluation process lies with you and your establishment. In this way the improvements can be on-going and only restricted by your own ambition.
5. **What do we do?** Self-evaluation can be seen as a standalone moment in time rather than a process where all stakeholders contribute to each 'standard' over a period of time. When self-evaluation is embedded, as an ongoing process in the life of the wider school it can be evidenced through individual learner assessment and progress diaries, examples of work, shared teaching and learning experiences and notes from stakeholders meetings or workshops. The self-evaluation process can become part of our own individual Continuing Professional Development as stakeholders. What was my RSE knowledge baseline? What were/are my personal views on RSE for our learners? Have my attitudes changed? Has my confidence improved?
6. **What are the tools for the job?** Simple evaluative tools have a tendency to be used more effectively. For example, in evaluating learners' understanding, stick to the augmentative communication tools that we are used to. This will give us all more confidence in evaluating whether learners have understood what they are trying to learn and may be as effective as a more complex tool.
7. **What does the final product look like?** You may want the self-evaluation process to be written up in reports for various audiences, and that is a solid way to keep an overview as to where you are in your journey. As self-evaluation is essentially a formative, on-going process, it is unlikely that a final concluding stage or end-point will be identified.

(MacBeath 2005, Cited by Chapman et al., 2013)

Successful self-evaluation should be guided by a framework that communicates desired outcomes along the path to consistently improving RSE provision and is clear in its aims for developing practice. From previous experiences of self-evaluation and writing school improvement plans, I also need to understand the 'why'.

Within the self-evaluation model I have attempted to make the 'why' as clear as possible. It may also help with conversations you will have as you move forward.

> *...A framework [needs to] be underpinned by a rationale for why these particular outcomes and developmental aims are important.*

(Chapman et al., 2008)

> *It is all too easy to identify a weakness and include that area for development without diagnosing exactly what needs to be done and why. An intelligent self-evaluation will identify the precise issue that needs tackling and what to do about it.*

(DfES, 2004)

The RSE self-evaluation example

The evaluation tool takes you through a suggestion of what your set of Key Foci should be; then these are broken down to your 'minimum key standards' under each. These categories will enable your setting to focus attention on the areas that are important to you, with the Key Foci providing the standards most settings would hope to achieve in time.

Because of the varied nature of the settings our special learners attend; both the wide variety of special schools and mainstream schools, supporting a wide range of need and abilities, we cannot come up with every key standard that will meet all the needs of all our learners. There are those standards that are obvious to include, those that have been assumed will come from future DfE RSE guidance and those that I consider *should* be in new guidance. As we all know, our colleagues in special education are the most creative of educators and the task of adapting a standard or two for the particular needs of your learners is not to be shied away from. See Figure 2.1.

Figure 2.1 The cycle of self-evaluation and development.

Evaluation

As a team decides on the make-up of your self-evaluation, you may want to design your own, adapt this model or others like it, but be familiar with it and own it. The self-evaluation should be coordinated by the RSE lead (who, ideally, will also be part of the leadership team). This should be shared as widely as possible and as often as possible, with all stakeholders providing observations and evidence.

Develop

I would consider setting up a steering group at this point; members of which could and should include; senior leadership team (SLT), RSE lead, teacher, teaching assistant (TA), parent, governor, school nurse, respite staff, social worker. The completed self-evaluation document is then analysed and a subsequent development plan designed and shared with all. There will be understandable variants but your setting should be looking to be able to cover as many key standards as possible.

Deliver

When the development plan has been agreed and key standard areas of need addressed, the plan will roll out for delivery. Support around planning and resourcing will be needed. It may be an idea to explore schemes of work and training for your staff to access. It will be important that everyone is as confident as possible before you start providing RSE for your learners. It is common in schools to re-evaluate our plans each year, but I feel with the nature of this work we may need to react a little quicker.

On-going assessment and adaptation

Most models of self-evaluation present it as a cycle, like a review or audit, taking place at a given time, with planning, data collection, analysis, presentation of findings and agreeing next steps in a set time frame throughout the school year. I am not convinced that this model allows for speedy sharing of good practice as you develop your provision. Whilst we would probably accept the fact that things can change unexpectedly and very quickly in special education, we should also acknowledge that if an unexpected learning breakthrough or a creative teaching technique has success then we should be flexible enough to add this to our RSE development plan and share with teaching staff so they can adapt delivery at that point rather than waiting until the evaluation stage of the cycle.

Whole school self-evaluation audit tool

5. Excellent/Exceeds Standards

4. Satisfactory/Meets Standards

3. Some Progress Made/Approaching Standards

2. Must Address and Improve/Standards Not Met

1. Standards not applicable to our learners

Figure 2.2 Whole school self-evaluation audit tool.

KEY FOCUS 1 – LEADERSHIP AND MANAGEMENT
See Appendix for photocopiable table. The headings will be;

Table 2.1

Target standards	Why are these standards important?	Evaluation					Observations and actions required. Who? What?
		1	2	3	4	5	Reason for standard not being applicable

Table 2.2

Target standards	Why are these standards important?
1(a) There is an identified RSE lead, with appropriate status (ideally SLT member) time, Continuing Professional Development (CPD) training and senior leadership support.	1(a) An identified RSE Lead will be able to coordinate the self-evaluation and action plan. With confidence and SLT support they will be able to lead by example.
1(b) A RSE policy is in place which mirrors best practice and meets (and ideally exceeds) DfE guidance.	1(b) The policy will commit the school and stakeholders to improving RSE provision, following best practice.
1(c) The RSE policy reflects a process of consultation with all stakeholders.	1(c) With all stakeholders involved there will be a sense of shared ownership.
1(d) The entitlement of all learners to RSE is guaranteed through policy and planned provision for RSE across the whole age range and various cohorts.	1(d) The policy and RSE provision should involve all learners, irrelevant of individual needs or age. All learners are entitled to quality RSE.
1(e) RSE is taught following best practice through the suitable curriculum area. (PSHE, My Body, Independent Living Skills etc.)	1(e) If RSE is to work in reality then it needs to be evident throughout the curriculum and throughout the school culture of positive relationships.

KEY FOCUS 2 – THE RSE PROVISION TEAM

Table 2.3

Target standards	Why are these standards important?
2(a) Quality CPD relating to RSE in a SEN setting is completed by all staff who contribute to learners' progress in RSE; including teachers and all teaching assistants.	2(a) We know that confidence in providing RSE is low across the teaching profession. Without the relevant training and support confidence levels will remain low, as will the quality of RSE provision.

(Continued)

Table 2.3 (Continued)

Target standards	Why are these standards important?
2(b) Support and RSE workshops are available for **parents and carers** so they can gain a better understanding and contribute to the RSE programme.	2(b) Training and/or workshops for parents is as important as staff training. With the parents' understanding and backing of the type of provision you want to develop you have every chance of real success.
2(c) Good internal and home/school communications ensure teachers are aware of personal issues that may affect the issues addressed in sessions or pupils' responses to them. Appropriate referral pathways for pupils are established if necessary.	2(c) If you have a working partnership with parents in providing RSE then you will gain a better understanding of any issues that some learners may have. By developing a close working relationship with external partners the relevant support will be available.
2(d) Teachers of RSE are willing and committed to the teaching of this subject, and are supported as they gain knowledge and experience.	2(d) Training and support can have a limited influence on some staff who oppose RSE for special learners due to fear or moral beliefs. These need to be addressed.
2(e) Teachers of RSE have the necessary confidence, subject knowledge and skills to provide RSE, understanding the sensitive and personal nature of RSE.	2(e) Through a programme of training and support teachers will develop the confidence to adapt sessions or groupings to reflect any difficulty an individual may have. As above, the partnership with parents will certainly help overcome any problem.
2(f) All teaching staff have the confidence, knowledge and skills to deal with sensitive matters concerning puberty, emotional changes and inappropriate behaviour. Additional support for those learners identifying as transgender, homosexual or bisexual is accepted and sought.	2(f) Preparing our learners for puberty and the physical and emotional changes that will take place is vital. An understanding and acceptance that certain behaviours need to be treated with sensitivity will better support our learners. If we accept the fact that we humans do not conform to gender and sexual 'stereotypical' norms then we need to have an awareness of potential support needs for learners and staff.
2(g) School nurses, LD nurses and/or Health Promotion Service contribute to the RSE programme. *This links with 2.f*	2(g) Having the resources and knowledge of your various health teams to support your provision is important for the confidence in learners and the health teams as the learners transition from school. *(2.f)*
2(h) There is whole school awareness of the RSE policy and programme in order that all staff (including governors) may respond appropriately to questions or issues raised by outside agencies or individuals.	2(h) Demonstrating a shared understanding and commitment of the RSE provision (and process) to those who may not be part of the stakeholder group will generate greater confidence of your wider community.
2(i) Whole setting knowledge and understanding in place that all stakeholders have a safeguarding responsibility to all learners.	2(i) With our learners being 3 times as likely to suffer from all types of abuse; understanding the signs and having a safeguarding awareness of child protection shared by all stakeholders is paramount.
2(j) The teaching of RSE is effectively monitored and supported, and all members of the team share in self-evaluation and development of the RSE provision.	2(j) There need to be a culture of learning from each other. No one has all the answers. Through shared self-evaluation and shared input into development plans RSE provision will continually improve.

KEY FOCUS 3 – LEARNING AND TEACHING

Table 2.4

Target standards	Why are these standards important?
3(a) The structure of RSE provision is planned to ensure progress over time (long term, whole school planning). The assessment of individual learner's progress informs future planning and the re-visit of certain elements of RSE.	3(a) Where possible we need to ensure that our learners have the access to a wide ranging RSE curriculum, covering all areas. If we agree the content at different stages of a long term plan then required coverage will be secured.
3(b) All RSE learning groups agree 'ground rules'. Staff creates a safe and positive learning environment for RSE sessions.	3(b) RSE group agreements are important to ensure that both learners and staff are clear on expectations, the process and content of the sessions.

(Continued)

Table 2.4 (Continued)

Target standards	Why are these standards important?
3(c) Appropriate RSE resources are sourced with regard to the learners' age, cognitive levels and background. Resources reflect the diversity of the settings community. Where appropriate, single sex groups are formed.	3(c) As with all learning experiences we plan, relevant RSE resources suitable for the needs of your learners is important. Your Health Promotion Team will be a good source of sexual health resources.
3(d) Where possible the single sex groups share knowledge with each other, demonstrating the importance of understanding the differences between the sexes as we grow and change. Within either group understanding that individuals can be homosexual or identify as transgender.	3(d) If you choose to have separate single sex groups for particular sessions, having the opportunity for the groups to share their learning is a good way of extending learning of the opposite sex, and of Homosexuality and those who identify as transgender.
3(e) RSE sessions are wide ranging and address all agreed areas of learning; (e.g. This is Me, My Changing Body, Gender, My Emotions, Being Healthy, Staying Safe, Public and Private, Relationships, Consent and Sexual Expression).	3(e) As for 3(a), the areas of RSE learning need to be accessed by all learners throughout their time at your setting. Some areas may seem difficult to address; but as with a jigsaw, learners will not see the bigger picture if we only select comfortable areas of learning to focus on.
3(f) Strategies are in place to ensure the learning programme is responsive to the real needs of learners, including issues raised by families and the school nurse.	3.(f) The individual assessments and parental questionnaires will give you an idea on individual RSE 'learning gaps'. If you can be responsive to changing needs it may have a lasting positive effect.
3(g) RSE lessons support learners to develop confidence when exploring sensitive issues and to appreciate a range of views people may hold about them.	3(g) We are all different; we are all unique. Strong relationships start with strong self-esteem; therefore we need to encourage learners to reflect on what makes them great.

KEY FOCUS 4 – THE WIDER LEARNING COMMUNITY

Table 2.5

Target standards	Why are these standards important?
4(a) All staff are trained and know the safeguarding/child protection procedures and what to do in the event of a disclosure or behaviour that raises concerns.	4(a) With our learners being three times more likely to suffer from all forms of abuse than their mainstream peers it is vital that safeguarding procedures are understood. Your RSE sessions will bring a better understanding of inappropriate behaviours and therefore the chance of disclosures.
4(b) Learners are involved in all stages of the planning, evaluation and development of their RSE provision wherever possible.	4(b) Having all stakeholders; including learners, involved in the whole process will give them ownership. It may also offer some surprising topic areas for you to plan for.
4(c) Parents and carers are informed, and listened to, in the consultation process through information drop-ins and are invited to RSE workshops to support them in continuing the learning with their children at home.	4(c) Getting parents and carers on board is an obvious standard to reach for. This may not be as straight forward as one would like, but it is worth the time spent on encouraging parental involvement form the start of the process.
4(d) External partners (Social Care, LD Health teams and Family Support teams) are invited to join with consultation process and add their on-going support to individuals and their families.	4(d) If we are to see the outcomes quality RSE can provide for our learners then we need to be working in partnership with all interested parties. This will have positive long-term implications for our learners.
4(e) A working partnership is established with similar schools and colleges, which serves to promote cross-phase continuity and progression in children's experience of RSE (particularly during transition if applicable).	4(e) A partner school could support you in the self-evaluation process and act as your quality assurance as you support them. As for learners who will be transitioning to colleges it is important that colleges are able to build on your work and develop the knowledge and confidence built by the learners.

KEY FOCUS 5 – RSE PROVISION CONTENT

Table 2.6

Target standards	Why are these standards important?
5(a) What makes us all unique. Things learners enjoy and are good at. Sharing qualities and likes with peers. Peers identify qualities in others.	5(a) Strong relationships are built on strong self-esteem. It is important that our learners identify what makes them who they are and build confidence.
5(b) Relationships. How our relationships with family and friends can change as we get older. What makes a good friend? (see 'Relationship target game')	5(b) Understanding that our relationships are different (family, friends, school staff, peers, loved ones) and that these relationships can change is significant learning. Identifying the traits of a good friend will support choice making and keeping safe for our learners as they get older.
5(c) Demonstrate the link between positive self-esteem and being able to develop healthy friendships and relationships.	5(c) Strong relationships are built on strong self-esteem. It is important that our learners identify what makes them who they are and build confidence.
5(d) Knowing the proper names for the main parts of the body, including both male and female genital names and internal sexual/ reproductive anatomy where appropriate.	5(d) Vital learning. Without the ability to use proper names for genitals our learners become more vulnerable and have been classed as unreliable witnesses in abuse cases.
5(e) How boys' and girls' bodies, feelings and emotions change as they approach and move through puberty. What to expect and how to manage periods. What to expect and how to manage wet dreams.	5(e) Vital learning. The least we can do for our learners is to prepare them for the inevitability of puberty; both the physical and the emotional changes they will encounter.
5(f) Public/Private. What is a public place? What does it mean to be in a private, safe place? What can we do in private that we cannot do in public?	5(f) Not as straight forward as one would initially think. The interchanging, contradictory definitions are difficult enough for us. Our special learners will benefit greatly if this area of RSE gets the attentions it needs.
5(g) Public/Private. What parts of our bodies are private to us?	5(g) Vital learning. With some complications and contradictions for some of our learners who rely on personal and intimate care.
5(h) The importance of personal hygiene and understanding how to keep ourselves clean and healthy.	5(h) For our learners be as independent as possible in personal care routines should be a shared aspiration.
5(i) Good and bad touch. Consent. Learners are given opportunities to advocate for themselves; learners practice asking for permission and respecting others' decisions.	5(i) Vital learning. Having knowledge about what constitutes good or bad touch, and our individual preferences, supports our learners to keep safe; as is consent and respecting others views.
5(j) The ways in which the media and peer group may influence individuals' behaviour and choices.	5(j) Giving our learners the tools to identify and reject unwanted pressure to behave in ways that may be harmful.
5(k) Keeping Safe. Who do we talk to if we are concerned about a situation or behaviour?	5(k) If our learners feel unsafe or worried, the fact they know who they can approach can give them confidence.
5(l) How to identity and access sources of help, support and information (including online, if appropriate) independently whilst keeping themselves safe.	5(l) Knowing how to ask for help, and the different ways to access support, will develop confidence and self-help skills.
5(m) The influences that lead to early sexual activity, and the issues, including physical and emotional risks, associated with this	5(m) With many of our learners being trustful, and keen to please others, they need to recognise the risks of the decisions they make.
5(n) Where appropriate, an understanding of the law in relation to consensual sexual activity and mental capacity.	5(n) A number of our learners will go on to develop sexual relationships. If appropriate, they need to know the facts about their rights as sexual beings.
5(o) Conception and reproduction in humans. Sex for pleasure.	5(o) Building on learning done through statutory science, expanding on the 'biology' of reproduction - and looking at why people have sex (sex for pleasure) will give our learners a better understanding.
5(p) Contraception. The personal and social implications of teenage pregnancy. The realities of parenthood.	5(p) Keeping safe and making decisions around safe sex and contraception will be an important part of RSE for your older learners. Understanding the realities of parenthood can support learners to make appropriate decisions.

External support; a critical friend...or two

If the impact of statutory Relationships and Sex Education is to have real influence on the outcomes and life chances of our learners then inspections will need proportional focus on RSE. Unfortunately, I doubt that this will be particularly high on many Ofsted inspectors' hit list initially.

For many, school self-evaluation is associated with external inspection; almost all of the interviewees in Hall et al. (2009) research referred to Ofsted when asked 'why we self-evaluate'. In 'collaborative' school groups, there was a sense of equipping 'our people' with what they needed to know when faced with 'people coming in from the outside'. Hopefully, your self-evaluation will be completed for the right reasons; with your learners' best interests and their human rights as paramount concern. If, however, the imposing shadow of inspectors and the statutory status of RSE is going to be the reason you focus on RSE then, I guess, so be it. I would rather you address the obvious need, whatever the true motivation.

Whatever the reason, you may consider calling a friend. It may be a school you are linked to that are going through a similar process, it may be a consultant or an RSE advisor form your local authority. Peer evaluation could be a positive part of this process; whoever you choose, a friend (critical or otherwise) may be a valuable ally.

The success of self-evaluation and the impact of external support from a critical friend on that success is down to good timing as anything else. For example, do you need support from a school that has implemented RSE into their curriculum already? Do your members of staff need some training on delivery or external support to make gains in their self-confidence, before the delivery stage?

What can a critical friend do to support self-evaluation?

> *Where self-evaluation is entered into voluntarily with the singular purpose of self-improvement, the latitude for the critical friend is wide and potentially highly creative.*
>
> (Swaffield et al., 2005)

Your initial steps into your self-evaluation will determine the agreed nature of any external support you may require. You can determine the extent and nature of support the critical friend can offer you; you just need to find the right friend at the right moment.

> *The other key determinants are time and the stage of development of the school on its self-evaluation journey.*
>
> (Swaffield et al., 2005)

The role of critical friend needs to be carried out with sensitivity. While it will be important to raise questions, this needs to be done in a constructive way. The role has been described in the following terms:

In carrying out this role, the critical friend will be able to listen, observe and learn about the school's ethos and targets. In partnership they will help to identify issues and make creative suggestions and offer alternative evidence and expertise. This expertise may be from other schools or from unexpected sources within the school. Most importantly if you can find a critical friend who is honest, accessible, flexible, discrete, friendly, patient, communicative and accountable, then the process will succeed.

What you should be aware of is the critical friend who wants to assume a directive role and simply offer solutions or provide quick fixes whilst imposing agendas of their own. There have been some consultants, that take on the role of critical friend, that believe that to get respect, they need to appear to know the school better than those in the school. This causes not only confusion but conclusions and recommendations that have little bearing on the needs of the school or its learners (MacBeath, 2005).

Individual assessments and progress indicators

The curriculum should include an assessment of students' current sexual knowledge in addition to observable and measurable outcomes.

(Blanchett et al., 2002)

There are some good examples of Individual assessment tools that can be used to gauge your learners' current knowledge. I have successfully used and adapted an assessment tool published by 'Me and Us' called *'Sexual Knowledge and Behaviour Assessment Tool'*. It is worth exploring the content and imagery of the tool and see how the language of the questions suit your learners. Creating your own individual assessment tool does give you the option to direct questions; although be aware that you may subconsciously leave out areas of knowledge you feel uncomfortable with.

As the learning needs of individual students differ greatly, it is vital that the curriculum be tailored to the unique needs of each student, taking into account factors such as their maturity levels, life experience and preferred method of learning.

(Löfgren-Mårtenson, 2011)

The assessment tool you design (or one you use form the shelf) needs to be visually accessible, with clear unambiguous language. It will need to start at the correct level for the needs of your learners. *'Sexual Knowledge and Assessment Tool'* uses line drawings throughout and your learners may interact more easily with photographs of real people. However, as the assessment tool questions evolve and move towards more explicit imagery this may not be either practical or comfortable for assessor or assessed at this early stage of proceedings. Certainly for the initial steps of RSE assessment photos can be more 'concrete' and real for many. As part of the assessment and early planning stages I would ask my learners to bring in photos of themselves as babies and toddlers. I would also ask for photos of their family members.

As there are many variants of 'a family' all need to be acknowledged and celebrated.

The first questions within the *'Sexual Knowledge and Assessment Tool'* relate to a 'nuclear family' that could be described as stereotypical; man, woman, boy and girl. This works well as an image to tease out our learners' knowledge around gender, identifying all four characters and deciding which one they feel similar to, but perhaps a little conformist as a 'typical family'.

The assessment tool goes on to provide imagery and questions around friendships, romantic relationships, body parts of both sexes before and after puberty, periods, wet-dreams, masturbation, sexual intercourse, pregnancy and contraception.

I would suggest that it may be useful to add imagery and questions relating to 'private and public places', 'public and private body parts' and 'good or bad touch and necessary touch'.

The assessment section of Alex Kelly's and Emily Dennis' *'Talkabout Sex & Relationships 2'* is also well worth a view. It is designed for older learners and adults. This again can be adapted to the needs of your more cognitively able learners as can many of the activities within this helpful addition to their first book.

Ultimately, what we want to produce is an assessment tool that is relevant to our learners. For those learners with Profound and Multiple Learning Disabilities your 'RSE assessment tool' may look very like your Personal and Social Development Programme outline. We will explore in more detail the particular challenges for us when assessing and planning RSE for Profound and Multiple Learning Difficulties (PMLD) learners later in the book.

Individual learner assessment

Figure 2.3 Individual learner assessment
See Appendix for photocopiable table. The headings will be;

Table 2.7

Name:	Evaluation			
RSE individual assessment areas	**NO**	**WITH HELP**	**YES**	Observations

RSE individual assessment areas

Table 2.8

Can identify own gender*
* A learner may not identify their own gender due to genuine confusion. We humans do not necessarily assimilate to the gender, sexuality or role that we were 'assigned'. Obviously this is as true for our special learners as anyone else, so we should stay creative and open in our interpretations of answers to RSE related questions as we would with any other area of learning.

Can identify similar peers (gender and age) from a range of ages and genders

Can identify differences between male and female bodies (clothed and naked)

Can identify differences between adult and child bodies, both male and female

Understands that these changes (at puberty) happens to all of us - and will happen to them

Can identify and name body parts, including proper names for sexual body parts

Can identify their own body parts that are private to them*
*contradictions may apply to those learners that rely on intimate care – understand that permission should be sought and received before intimate care routines take place

Can identify the body parts of others that are private (male and female)

Can offer examples of personal care routines and why it is important that we keep our bodies clean

Can identify public and private places from a range of examples

Can identify certain activities that are private and those that are not

Can identify the difference between good and bad touch and offer examples

Understands that we should all ask permission (consent) before physical contact (relate to peer massage)

Understands that friends can make you feel that you should do things for them (peer pressure) but it is okay to say no

Can explain that even if they may like to hug or kiss someone, it is wrong unless the other person wants a hug or kiss

Can identify who or where to go for help if feeling unsure of the behaviour of someone else

Can offer examples of different types of relationships people have; family, friends, romantic and sexual

Can identify different type of romantic relationships (e.g. heterosexual, homosexual)

Understands what periods are and that it is females that have periods

Can give examples of how to manage periods ('I change pad' routine)

Understands what 'wet dreams'* are and that this happens to some males when asleep
*certainly for ASD learners this needs to be expressed clearly. '"Wet dreams" are not necessarily wet or dreams.

Understands what masturbation is and where this should happen (link to 'private places' and 'keeping clean')

Can offer a reason why people enjoy masturbation (an understanding of arousal and orgasm)

Understands that when two people want to be close and then hold each other, then there are changes to our bodies that make us feel aroused (e.g. penises becoming erect, vaginas becoming lubricated and there is increased heart rate)

Understands that sex does not have to penetrative and there are different ways that people can enjoy each other safely

Understands that sex should be pleasurable for both, and that people have sex for pleasure as well as (heterosexual sex) for pregnancy

Can give a description of pregnancy and how pregnancy occurs

Can give examples of how pregnancy can be avoided (methods of contraception)

Can give examples of how mothers and fathers take care of babies and some examples of the care needs of a baby

Understands that people can get sexually transmitted infections (STIs) from having unprotected sex

Can give examples of how to keep safe and healthy when two people are planning/wanting to have sex

When you get to a point where the learner cannot answer or make an informed choice then stop the assessment process. You will have an idea where you need to start, what you need to reinforce and what you need to plan your next session around.

Again, use this as an example of what you can create yourselves; an individual assessment tool that can be adapted for cohorts of learners and also for those individuals that have particular support needs around growing and changing, relationships, public and private, amongst others areas of RSE. For many of you the language used in the above individual assessment tool may not be relevant for the learners you support, but it will give you a structure, with natural progression, that you can hopefully adapt.

The starting point of understanding, who we are and identifying our gender is a helpful place to begin for many, but I will add an obvious word of caution.

There may be a need to be flexible when interpreting the outcomes of initial assessments. On the surface it may be all too easy to conclude that a learner cannot distinguish their own gender due to the answers or images they have chosen in response to a particular question. However, be aware that there may be more depth to their answers.

We humans do not necessarily assimilate the gender, sexuality or role that we were "assigned". Obviously this is as true for our special learners as anyone else, so we should stay creative and open in our interpretations of answers to RSE related questions as we would with any other area of learning. It also highlights the importance of working collaboratively with parents and external partners to ensure the correct advice and support is available when there is some ambiguity in our assessments.

Planning examples

Figure 2.4 Planning examples

Table 2.9

RSE lesson ideas: Develop an awareness of different families and the nature of adult relationships

KS3, KS4, Post 16

Session/title	Learning outcomes	Activities	Resources
Session 1	To develop and understand the different nature and make up of families	Circle time – introduce ourselves, shake hands and greet everyone Introduce Learning Outcomes to class and explain what we are going to do. Activity 1: Family guided Q and A • Who is in a family? • Are families big/small • Do families always live together? Activity 2: Look at photos of different families Put photos on whiteboard and feedback if possible Closing thoughts: A family is……	Camera Family photos
Session 2	To develop and understand the different nature and make up of families	Circle time – introduce ourselves, shake hands and greet everyone Introduce Learning Outcomes to class and explain what we are going to do. Activity 1: View last lesson: What is a family? Read a book about a family (Todd Parr?) Activity 2: Drawing a family – labelling the members of the family Closing thoughts: Look at all the different families – if possible ask for volunteers to talk about the family they have drawn.	Camera Family book Large sheets paper Pencils

(Continued)

Table 2.9 (Continued)

RSE lesson ideas: Develop an awareness of different families and the nature of adult relationships

KS3, KS4, Post 16

Session/title	Learning outcomes	Activities	Resources
Session 3	To explore how we grow and change	Circle time – introduce ourselves, shake hands and greet everyone Introduce Learning Outcomes to class and explain what we are going to do. Activity 1: Look at pictures of different generations in a family Q and A: What ages are the people in the family? Activity 2: Order family into age, lifecycle – at what part does a new life get made (by adults) What can a baby do, a child etc. Closing thoughts: Use picture of child and that of a young adult to explore what changes when we become adults?	Camera Family pictures
Session 4	To consider some physical and emotional changes that happen as we change from children to young adults	Circle time – introduce ourselves, shake hands and greet everyone Introduce Learning Outcomes to class and explain what we are going to do. Activity 1: Review changes that happen from child to young adult (physical and emotional) Activity 2: Do our relationships change? Ask class what grown-ups in a relationships do that children do not? May need some guidance: touch, intimacy etc.	Camera Photo prompts DVD

Table 2.10

RSE lesson ideas: Developing an awareness of my body

PMLD KS2 (7–11years)

Session/title	Learning outcomes	Activities	Resources
Session 1: Our heads and faces	To explore through drama and social interaction our own and others faces	Sound for start of lesson In small circle – from a bag choose/ given a choice of object and encourage to put on As above and chose someone else to wear object Take photos Song to finish	Sunglasses Masks Hats Makaton signs Camera
Session 2: Heads and faces	To explore and look at our faces.	Sound for start of lesson Put on an object from last lesson – can we look in the mirror? Exploring faces – squirt cream on mirror Song to finish	Sunglasses Masks Hats Makaton signs Camera
Session 3: Our hands and feet	To develop an awareness of our own feet and hands. To feel and explore different textures on hands and feet	Sound for start of lesson Textures on hands – choose Shoes and socks off – different textures on feet – choose Song to finish	Textured objects – silk, cotton wool, play dough, sand paper Makaton Signs Camera

(Continued)

Table 2.10 (Continued)

RSE lesson ideas: Developing an awareness of my body

PMLD KS2 (7–11years)

Session/title	Learning outcomes	Activities	Resources
Session 4: Massage	To explore and develop an awareness of our bodies through massage	Sound for start of lesson and scented candle Jungle Massage (1) **Snake** Snake song from Jungle Book Smooth slippery green fabric to handle Massage on arms up and round forearms keeping contact all the time Make hissing sounds **Jungle ants** Music Bumble Bee Small beans in cloth bag to handle Fingertips walking light and fast from one hand, up an arm, across the back of the shoulders or over the head then down the other arm and hand Song to finish	Candle Snake song (Jungle Book) Bumble Bee song
Session 4: Massage	To explore and develop an awareness of our bodies through massage	Sound for start of lesson and scented candle Jungle massage(2) **Gorilla** Monkey song from Jungle Book Fur to handle Massage soles of the feet and stamp them on the ground **Butterflies** Children to be moved together Staff to wave different coloured cloths above them and brushing their faces	Candle Fur Monkey Song (Jungle book) Silks – different colours
Session 6: Photos	To be able to recognise pictures of ourselves.	Sound for start of lesson Printed up photos from prior lessons. Teacher, TAs to support with choosing one (their own one) decorates it – pointing out relevant parts of the body. Song to finish	Photos Glue Glitter Decorations

Table 2.11

RSE lesson ideas: Developing an understanding of public and private, good and bad touch, differences between boys and girls

KS4+ (14–19 year olds)

Session/title	Learning outcomes	Activities	Resources
Session 1	To identify different types of touch people like and do not like To talk about ways of identifying and dealing with unwanted touch	Calm music to start with and include touch (massager) Pass objects around one by one and ask children to show (thumbs up/sound/ observation) which they like to touch and which they dislike. If possible find out why they like/dislike the feel and reinforce that different people like different things 'RSE' song to finish	Music Touch massager Bag of textured objects

(Continued)

Table 2.11 (Continued)

RSE lesson ideas: Developing an understanding of public and private, good and bad touch, differences between boys and girls

KS4+ (14–19 year olds)

Session/title	Learning outcomes	Activities	Resources
Session 2	To identify different types of touch people like and do not like	Calm music to start with and include touch (massager) Discuss/recap on previous session and ask for different ways people touch each other. Think of as many different types of touch as possible (push, hug, scratch and kiss) use puppets to reinforce Ask children which types of touch they like/dislike and if it makes a difference who is doing the touching. 'RSE' song to finish	Music Touch massager Puppets Makaton signs Prompts Thumbs up, thumbs down yes, no signs and actions
Session 3	To name male and female body parts using agreed words	Calm music to start with and include touch (massager) Repeat circle activity in session 3 Encourage children to identify to 'private' body. Explore definition of body parts that are private. Makaton signs for penis, breasts and vagina, male/female 'RSE' song to finish	
Session 4	To explore the concept of public and private (1)	Calm music to start with and include touch (massager) Introduce session Create a private space (behind a screen/ white-goods cardboard box) Show photos of public and private places Take in turns to select an item of clothing and decide if would try it on in public or private. Who may wear this and where on the body? What parts of our bodies do swimming wear cover? Reflect on last session. 'RSE' song to finish	Music Touch massager Makaton pictures and signs for private and public Wash basket full of clothes – hats, scarves, wigs, shoes, underwear, swimming wear etc.
Session 5	To explore the concept of public and private (2)	Calm music to start with and include touch (massager) Create a private and public space – which is private/public, what if we open the door? Look at clothes. Can we put them in the space we would try them on? Children can try on if they want. Is 'private' is when door is shut? 'RSE' song to finish	Music Touch massager Makaton pictures and signs for private and public Wash basket full of clothes – hats, scarves, wigs, shoes, underwear, swimming wear etc.

Table 2.12

RSE - lesson ideas: Developing a sense of self and awareness of each other

EYFS and KS1

Session/title	Learning outcomes	Activities	Resources
1. Myself	To develop an understanding of who we are	Sound for moving into circle Looking in mirrors (close, far away) Maybe use funny noses, head boppers, silly hats…to encourage looking at themselves? It may take two sessions – looking at themselves can be a real challenge for some learners. Hands on mirrors – use coloured water, slime …. squirty cream (VI pupils and those that eat everything!) Taking photos of each other (including the adults) Song to finish	Musical instrument Thunder drum Mirrors Liquid Digital camera Head, shoulders, knees, toes
2. Myself (2)	To consider who we are and what we look like	Sound for moving into circle Use photos to make badges Mix up badges – students to find own ones (maybe put in a magic bag to pull out – choice of two) Choose own badge and clip onto clothing Song (same as last week)	Musical instrument Printed up photos form last lesson. Yellow card, tape, safety pin Head, shoulders, knees, toes
3. Myself and my body	To recognise principal external parts of our body	Sound for moving into circle Look at badges Point to eyes, mouth etc. Look in mirrors. As previous session – great sensory fun. (Use full-length mirrors if possible) Touching body parts game – teacher claps hands (2 hands, 4 feet etc.) Song to finish	Musical instrument Badges form last lesson – visual cue cards photo of eye, nose, ear etc? Full length mirrors?
4. Boys and girls (1)	To begin to understand the differences between boys and girls	Sound for moving into circle Look at badges – who are girls and who are boys? Move pictures into correct circle – Make into a timed game or musical game. Games with puppets, to reinforce boy and girl Song to finish	Musical instrument Badges from last lesson PE Hoops Boy and Girl signs – possibly photo support here for younger pupils Puppet dolls
5. Boys and girls (2)	To be able to recognise the primary sexual characteristics of a boy and a girl	Sound for moving into circle Repeat boy girl exercise from previous lesson Using male and female dolls talk openly about body parts and name correctly Show class pictures of naked babies – sort into boys and girls Song to finish	Musical instrument Badges PE Hoops Boy and Girl signs Dolls Baby pictures Head, shoulders, knees and toes
6. Others	To consider the others around us	Sound for moving into circle Look at badges on desk Can we find (a name from class) again? Can learners find the peer whose badge they pulled out from the bag? Guess who? Make A4 jigsaw photo. Guess who? Why do some pictures fit together? (These could go home as activities to reinforce learning) Hand Massage, puppets to help us – use this with calming music, massage bag prompt. Song to finish	Musical instrument Badges from previous lessons Heads, shoulders, knees and toes

Table 2.13

RSE lesson ideas: Develop an understanding of our bodies in relation to private (public) and touch

KS3 11–14 year olds

Session/title	Learning outcomes	Activities	Resources
Session 1	To name the main external parts of our body including the primary sexual characteristics	Circle time – introduce ourselves, shake hands and greet everyone Introduce Learning Outcomes to class and explain what we are going to do. Activity 1: Warm up – wave our hands, wiggle our toes, clap our hands, bend to the side, roll our shoulders Activity 2: Use body board to point to and identify parts of body. Make this body a boy and now a girl. Provide students with choice of vagina, penis, and breasts. (Teachers to facilitate but try not to guide) Activity 3: Looking at photos of naked babies – which one is a boy? Which one is a girl?	Camera Body board Whiteboard resources Naked baby photos
Session 2	To explore the use of a 'private space' so we do not show our 'private' body parts	Circle time – introduce ourselves, shake hands and greet everyone Introduce Learning Outcomes to class and explain what we are going to do. Activity 1: Interactive whiteboard body parts activity. Look at baby photos on board – is it a boy (male) of girl (female) and why? Activity 2: Private parts – we cover them because they are private... Where do we put on our pads, pants, vests, bras etc.? Introduce P.A.N.T.S – (NSPCC) Activity 3: Wash basket	Camera Whiteboard resources Naked baby photos Clothes Wash basket P.A.N.T.S.
Session 3	To explore the use of a 'private space' so we do not show our private parts To develop an understanding that touching our 'private parts' also happens in private.	Circle time – introduce ourselves, shake hands and greet everyone Introduce Learning Outcomes to class and explain what we are going to do. Activity 1: Look at wash basket clothes. Create a private space in classroom. Where would we put on these clothes? Who would wear them (boy, girl, anyone)? Activity 2: Private parts are private –P.A.N.T.S. Closing thoughts: Complete the sentence – "I would put on … in …"	Camera Clothes Wash Basket P.A.N.T.S.
Session 4	To explore the difference between boys (males) and girls (females) and how they change to become young adults	Circle time – introduce ourselves, shake hands and greet everyone Introduce Learning Outcomes to class and explain what we are going to do. Activity 1: Look at pictures of children and adults – can we identify them, are they different? Activity 2: Using naked outlines of boys/girls and men and women. Circle the differences. Emphasise that the changes happen as we grow up, are natural etc. Closing thoughts: What is different about a child and an adult – encourage key changes and if possible some emotions	Camera Pictures of children and adults Naked outlines of children and adults

(Continued)

Table 2.13 (Continued)

RSE lesson ideas: Develop an understanding of our bodies in relation to private (public) and touch

KS3 11–14 year olds

Session/title	Learning outcomes	Activities	Resources
Session 5	To focus on changes that happen to boys To explore how we manage these changes	Circle time – introduce ourselves, shake hands and greet everyone Introduce Learning Outcomes to class and explain what we are going to do. Activity 1: Review changes; focus on boys – larger penis, pubic hair, facial hair, sperm etc. Activity 2: Managing change 　Play Kim's game – 　Who can you talk to? Closing thoughts: One thing I have learned. . .	Camera Naked outlines and body board for review Products for Kim's Game: Deodorant, shower gel, soap, comb, razor, shaving foam
	To focus on changes that happen to girls To explore how we manage these changes		

Policy

What should be covered in a RSE policy?

The guidance below has been adapted from an excerpt from Sex Education Forum's RSE Policy Guidance (2013) and presented here with permission.

- Define RSE
- Describe how RSE is provided and who is responsible for providing it
- Say how RSE is monitored and evaluated
- Include information about parents' right to withdrawal; and
- Be reviewed regularly

It is good practice for the RSE policy to be part of the PSHE education policy. In addition, the Sex Education Forum recommends that the RSE policy includes:

- The aims of RSE in the school and how they are consistent with the values and ethos of the school
- Who teaches SRE and how they are supported through training
- How teachers, including support staff, are consulted and advised about the policy
- How RSE is timetabled
- How RSE is linked to other areas of the curriculum
- Information about how RSE is assessed
- Choice of resources including any external visitors contributing to the RSE programme
- Terminology/language used in RSE, e.g. that the correct medical vocabulary for parts of the body will be used throughout
- Details of how learners and parents have been consulted about the school's RSE provision
- (Where relevant) how faith groups and diocesan boards of education have been consulted, advised and involved in developing the policy
- Information about how the needs of particular learners will be met
- How RSE provision is inclusive of all learners and consistent with the equalities duties
- How to deal with disclosures; links to other relevant school policies including the confidentiality policy
- How progression is ensured from early years/foundation to secondary and post 16
- The name of the governor(s) with responsibility for RSE

Ofsted state that:

> Lack of high-quality, age-appropriate sex and relationships education in more than a third of schools is a concern as it may leave children and young people vulnerable to inappropriate sexual behaviours and sexual exploitation. This is because they have not been taught the appropriate language or developed the confidence to describe unwanted behaviours or know where to go to for help.
>
> (Ofsted, 2013)

Getting started on updating the policy

A good RSE policy will be the outcome of the process of reviewing your RSE provision in consultation and discussion with parents, carers, learners, staff and governors.

The RSE working group set up to oversee the self-evaluation process is the obvious group to take responsibility for updating the school's SRE policy. As mentioned before membership could include the RSE and PSHE education coordinator, a parent/carer, the school nurse, a governor, a member of the senior leadership team, a teacher, a teaching assistant and, of course, the learners. This group will draw up a timetable for the development of a policy, identifying the working party's meetings, key tasks (with deadlines), and the proposed date of formal presentation and adoption by the governing body.

The step by step process could follow this pattern:

1. Form a small working group
2. Draw up timetable for updating the policy
3. Consider relevant national and local guidance (DfE, Ofsted, Public Health)
4. Consider any changes in school population or learners needs (learner needs assessment)
5. Audit current provision and policy and consider the results
6. Draft changes to the policy
7. Consult on draft (for example, discussion of a draft at parents/carers, staff, governors and school council meetings)
8. Finalise the draft
9. Present to governors to ratify and set review date
10. Present to parent/carers and put on school website
11. Policy implemented
12. Monitor policy against specific success criteria
13. Review policy every 12 months

SEF/PSHE RSE route planner

Developed in partnership, the PSHE Association and Sex Education Forum produced a helpful self-evaluation roadmap (Figure 2.5). The original design is an aesthetically pleasing, free-flowing and colourful graph with helpful hyperlinks. It is reproduced and reimagined here with kind permission.

These 10 steps provide a guide to support school leaders in preparing to provide high quality RSE as an identifiable part of PSHE education. These steps are based on established good practice and evidence.

Lucy Emmerson, Director of the Sex Education Forum, said:

> *The vital ingredient in effective RSE are the people who teach it. The guidance on what the statutory curriculum will cover is well underway, but what training and support will be available to schools remains to be seen.*
>
> *We have a relatively short time to prepare for statutory RSE. Some schools will need to adjust their timetable and staffing to accommodate statutory status. We hope that the roadmap will help school leaders to start taking steps now. We urge the Government to commit money to training in this area so that all staff teaching RSE feel confident and knowledgeable to do so.*
>
> (Emmerson et al., 2014)

Be clear about the facts: Relationships and Sex Education will be required in all schools. Do you know what the new legislation means for your school?

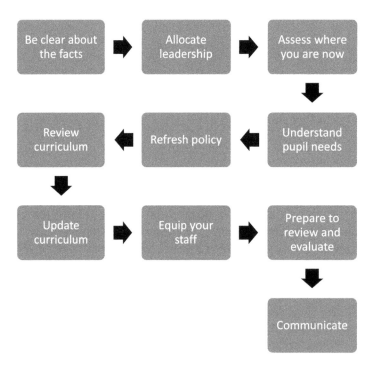

Figure 2.5 SEF/PSHE RSE route planner.

Allocate leadership: Effective change will involve the Senior Leadership Team together with RSE and PSHE lead staff and a linked governor. Who is going to oversee this change?

Assess where you are now: There is a clear evidence base for high quality RSE and it requires regular timetabled lessons within PSHE education. How would you describe your current provision?

Understand pupil needs: Using local data and consultation activities will ensure you can tailor provision to meet the needs of all pupils. Have you conducted a pupil needs assessment?

Refresh policy: An RSE policy will be required in all schools – it should set out your whole school approach and make links with school ethos, safeguarding policies and The Equalities Duty. Does your policy reflect your aims for RSE and schools values?

Review curriculum: An effective RSE and PSHE education curriculum will be comprehensive, spiral and responsive to pupil needs. Does your curriculum take this approach? Where are the gaps?

Update curriculum: Regular updates will ensure your programme is inclusive, has engaging lesson plans that reflect real-life issues (including the digital world) with a balance of skills, knowledge and personal attribute development. Is your curriculum now updated and inclusive?

Equip your staff: All staff will have a role to play and some will need specialist training. What are you staff CPD needs? How can these needs be met?

Prepare to review and evaluate: As with all subjects, effective monitoring and evaluation will tell you if planned outcomes are being met and what needs to change. Do you have systems for monitoring and evaluating RSE within PSHE education?

Communicate: Bring the whole school community with you, through continuous dialogue with parents, staff, governors and pupils. Are there mechanisms for ongoing information sharing about RSE and have you shared your plans?

Next steps

I hope that some of what we have explored here can be of use. I have great confidence in my colleagues who choose to support our special learners; you are highly skilled, reassuringly creative and determined to find ways to make a real difference to the life chances of others.

What you may need help with is developing the self-confidence of some of your colleagues when it comes to RSE delivery. We will explore that task in more detail in Chapter 3.

3 Developing staff confidence in the provision of RSE

Research from a range of countries, across a wide time frame, suggests confidence levels and attitudes of staff towards providing Relationships and Sex Education has a huge impact on the success (or failure) of an establishments' RSE programme. In this chapter, we will look at how we can influence these areas of doubt and have a direct impact on the confidence levels of our colleagues.

We will also consider how to get all stakeholders involved with RSE improvement and how vital their engagement is. We need to understand the areas of concern that colleagues may have when it comes to their views on the type of RSE their learners require. We may have different views on what is important and what should (and should not) be taught. How do we find compromise and ensure what we provide is in our learners' best interests?

We should accept the fact that there will be a need to work in a supportive way with all stakeholders. A robust attitude on our part may not always be the best tactic (although understandable). There will be teaching and support staff that feel uncomfortable, for a range of reasons, with the prospect of delivering RSE to their learners and we need to convince them of the clear reasons why they should address their feelings.

In July 2019, the National Education Union (NEU) and the National Society for the Prevention of Cruelty to Children (NSPCC) published their findings of a fairly wide-ranging survey of 2,175 mainstream school leaders and teachers on attitudes towards the delivery of RSE. It is a helpful overview of our shared level of confidence. The glaring lack of insight and views from SEND schools was unforgiveable, although unfortunately not surprising. Perhaps yet another reason for us to take it on ourselves in advocating for our special learners.

The survey highlighted the constant, repetitive message about our schools' poor state of readiness for the roll-out of statutory RSE.

It found:

- 47% expressed a lack of confidence in their ability to deliver the RSE/relationships education. 15% were very confident in their ability;
- 52% expressed uncertainty that their school would be ready to deliver the subjects in September 2020;
- 61% of secondary teachers said they do not feel confident about teaching the impact of pornography;
- 54% of secondary teachers were not confident about teaching lessons on female genital mutilation.

Face-to-face training and support was identified by 78% of respondents as the format that would give them the confidence and skills to deliver high-quality RSE.

This has been the number one concern for many years. Teachers have cited a lack of training, resources and guidance as reasons for not providing RSE (CHANGE, 2010; Ofsted, 2013). Even more concerning was that those teachers that did receive support state that their RSE training was inadequate (Howard-Barr et al., 2005). Others have shared their concerns that they fear getting it wrong would be worse than trying.

In some schools, and for a variety of reasons, there is no RSE provision at all (Rohleder, 2010).

To confuse things a little more, we as teachers may view our learners in terms of their cognitive rather than chronological age and can be prone to using subjective judgement instead of objective assessment to determine our learners' RSE and learning needs (Barnard-Brak et al., 2014). As teachers, our own experience of relationships and sex education (and relationships and sex themselves) means that some of us can talk about RSE with a 'matter of fact' confidence, whilst others feel inhibited and scared about saying the wrong thing. This inconsistency in RSE training, support and our teaching has serious repercussions; many young people do not and will not get access to the quality RSE provision that they both want and deserve (DO RSE, 2018).

There has been a constant failing on the part of education authorities, trusts and government to address the obvious need for support and training around both Special Educational Needs

(SEN) and RSE for longer than we would care to imagine. Historically, people with learning disabilities were often *'constructed as either being child-like and asexual, or as over-sexed or sexually inappropriate'* (Craft, 1987). This view still resonates within our society, and within many of our schools. As a result RSE for our special learners is often seen as unnecessary, as they are considered to be asexual, or even dangerous, in that it encourages sexual expression.

> *In order for adequate sexuality education for students with intellectual disabilities to become a reality, it is vital that these barriers be addressed.*
>
> (FPV, 2015)

RSE can be a challenging subject to teach, but it can also be very rewarding for us – and equally rewarding for our learners

RSE requires a particular style of pedagogy not often embraced in other curriculum areas. Relationships and Sex are huge topics, surrounded by controversy, stigma and diverse beliefs. It is very easy to 'drop' certain themes from our RSE sessions due to the difficulty they present. However, this perceived difficulty should never stand in the way of providing our special learners the opportunity to receive the many benefits that relevant RSE offers (DO RSE, 2018).

Even when we feel the 'argument has been won' with looming statutory status achieved, remember that convincing someone of the facts and logic of your argument does not address their 'wired' deep-set fears. *'When the importance of providing sex education is recognised, the thought or practice of providing sex education may increase the anxiety of the persons tasked to do so'* (FPV, 2015).

For example, Parritt et al. (2000) found that the professionals they observed expressed greater anxiety raising issues of sexuality with disabled clients than with non-disabled clients. This will be true throughout your observations and conversations also.

> *Educators may feel that providing sex education may have adverse reactions from students with learning disabilities.*
>
> (Brantlinger, 1992)

This has been the finding of many research projects, over many years, into the provision of RSE for those with additional needs. (NSPCC, 2014; Howard-Barr et al., 2005; Rohleder, 2010) The belief that RSE would lead to inappropriate sexual behaviour that would be difficult to manage, is a real fear for many.

> *Barriers to the provision of sexuality education for students with intellectual disabilities stem in part from educators themselves, who frequently report feeling unprepared to teach sexuality education to these students and experience high levels of discomfort with this subject matter.*
>
> (Howard-Barr et al., 2005)

There are social, economic and personal benefits of improving outcomes for our special learners at school and in further education and employment through quality RSE provision. Family planning educators in Victoria, Australia, have experienced first-hand the benefits of providing RSE to special learners. These benefits included measurable increases in capacity to protect themselves from sexual abuse, demonstrable reduction in the rates of Sexually Transmitted Infections (STIs) and unplanned pregnancy along with increased contraception use and significant reductions in sexualised behaviours of concern (Family Planning Victoria, 2015).

As a safeguarding tool, providing RSE may also support the understanding and reporting of sexual abuse. As we have explored already the fact is our special learners are three times more likely to be subjected to abuse than their mainstream peers. The assessment of cases of sexual assault of people with learning disabilities includes assessment of the individual's capacity to consent, which includes knowledge about healthy relationships and sexuality (Dickman et al., 2005).

We may have moved so far forward as a society and as educators over that last few decades in terms of our understanding of learning disabilities and our drive to be inclusive; but that shudders to a halt when we start being asked to advocate for our special learners as sexual beings.

> *Your own personal attitudes to sex cannot take precedence over your professional duty.*
>
> (Down's Syndrome Association, 2013)

We will explore staff workshop tips, RSE training courses and team planning ideas to enable you to help develop staff confidence and reduce anxiety levels. The workshops and courses can also be adapted and made available to governors and your external partners from Social Care and Health.

Special schools cater for a vast range of complex learning difficulties and, certainly in the case of RSE, one 'size' certainly does not 'fit all'. Ideally, we would ensure consistency yet have a flexibility of provision to be able to provide RSE for all of our learner population; our autistic learners with a diagnosis of Autistic Spectrum Disorder (ASD) and Profound and Multiple Learning Difficulties (PMLD) especially. Coupled with this is the need to ensure that issues and questions of appropriateness in terms of content are constantly addressed.

Exploring the correlation between confidence levels in teaching RSE and the range of individuals that are being taught will help focus the support required by your staff team. For example, are teachers less confident if they are expected to teach RSE to those who have PMLD or to those autistic learners (ASD)? The accepted 'truth' in most schools is that those with Moderate Learning Difficulties (MLD) are the easiest to teach, with that cohort typically being our higher achievers with a better cognitive understanding of new concepts.

If you take time to find out about not only the overall confidence rating of your staff, but the perhaps less obvious reasons behind those ratings, you can plan your support and potential staff training in a more tailored way. The outcomes may be different in all schools (for example some of my teaching colleagues who teach PMLD learners are some of the best RSE providers I have come across) but the answers you receive from your questioning will enhance any improvement plan and therefore focus on developing staff confidence across your establishment in delivering RSE.

A photocopiable Staff Questionnaire can be found in the Appendix.

Demonstrate the 'steps' rather than the whole journey

When confronted by the prospect of delivering RSE some of my colleagues over the years have struggled with the task. As we have previously explored, this may have been due to their own personal attitudes and experiences of RSE, seeing it as irrelevant for their learners. Perhaps they were concerned that they did not have the knowledge and strategies to deliver RSE and worried that they would get it wrong. It may also have been simple embarrassment.

For some I wonder if it was because they saw a vast, spiralling RSE 'beast' with all of its tentacles disappearing into dark scary corners of inappropriate sexualised behaviour, safe and unsafe relationships, consensual sexual intercourse, reproduction, STIs, contraception, mental capacity, sexual abuse and so on.

That is not the whole truth of RSE. Although these areas will be part of what we will have to address for some of our learners; what we initially deliver is in reality something far less scary.

Make it clear to staff that they are providing RSE all day, every day. How they interact with each other, modelling good peer to peer respectful interaction (hopefully) irrelevant of hierarchy, race, gender or sexuality. They will constantly be providing RSE in how they interact with their learners; demonstrating and encouraging (hopefully) mutual respect, good self-esteem and a drive for equality.

That is RSE at its essence, not the scary beast some would have you believe it is.

Tips on how to plan for your RSE staff training

1. **Know your colleagues needs.** If this is In Service Training Day (INSET) or twilight training, use your previous staff questionnaires to inform your content.
   - What are your colleagues' roles?
   - Do all colleagues already know each other?
   - What previous RSE training have they done and how long ago?
   - What are their expectations of this training?
   - What is the purpose of this RSE training?
   - Do you know what your colleagues want to achieve?

   This will help to tailor the training to their specific needs and improve confidence levels. Improved confidence levels will be your ultimate objective. Make sure your wider learning objectives come out of your previous research; that all objectives are clearly identified at the start of the training and returned to at the end of the session to assess whether they have all been achieved.

2. **Ensure you focus on a group agreement at the start of the day/training session.**
    - Confidentiality is vital. The importance of being able to share feelings and concerns during these sessions is paramount. Learn together, in an environment that is supportive, not judgemental.
    - Be open about the content that will be covered, acknowledge that it can be a sensitive and challenging area of work for some of your colleagues.
    - Understand that how your colleagues work together during the training can model the principles of mutual respect and tolerance that will be highlighted in the training session and hopefully throughout your establishment.
    - A good group agreement will mean that your colleagues feel safe and able to take a full part in the sessions. Everyone should know what the ground rules of the group are and have some input into the creation of them. To create a group agreement, ask your colleagues what topics they think they want to include. Rules that are worded positively so the group knows what to do, rather than what not to do feel warmer and more acceptable. For example, if someone suggests a rule of 'no shouting out', suggest 'Give yourself and each other space to think' as a way of re-phrasing this.

The group agreement should be written up briefly on flip chart paper so that everyone can see it. If it makes life easier edit it into a PowerPoint presentation and/or get it typed and printed off so that it can be referred to each session or given to colleagues for inclusion in folders, if you are using/collecting CPD evidence.

Try to ensure that all the following ideas are included in the group agreement, no matter what words you use.

Confidentiality

Explain that personal information which people share in the group must stay in the group and must never be discussed anywhere else. Tell your colleagues that it is good for them to share the new factual information and strategies learned, and that they can share what they have learned about themselves.

Under safeguarding procedures make sure that your colleagues understand that you cannot keep confidentiality if someone says that a child or other person at risk has been harmed or is at risk of harm. Explain to you colleagues that if you need to break confidentiality you will let them know first wherever possible.

Only share what you want to share

Explain that it is okay to discuss the situations that relate to helping our learners understand about sex and sexuality. Your colleagues should only share as much or as little as they feel comfortable sharing. It is important to remind them that they should consider what information they want to share with others before talking. I have seen and heard colleagues start a 'confessional' about their own relationships that are quickly regretted. If anyone starts to feel uncomfortable whilst they are talking then they can confidently state; 'I want to stop there' even if they were in the middle of saying something.

Own your opinions

Explain to colleagues that they should try to use 'I' as much as possible when they are sharing a point, so that everyone knows that they are stating their own opinion. For example, saying, 'Learners don't need to understand about same-sex relationships until KS3' gives the impression that everyone thinks this. It is better to say, 'I think that learners don't need to understand about same-sex relationships until they are 12'. Your colleague can then prepare to be challenged.

Accept and respect

Your colleagues will all have different viewpoints and will have a wide range of experiences and opinions. As a group you may find that there are colleagues whose lifestyle is different to many others in the group (for example, people in same sex relationships or people with a strong religious viewpoint). Our colleagues need to be able to accept and respect a person, even when they do not agree with their opinion. Explain to your colleagues that it is normal to feel uncomfortable sometimes when discussing topics concerning relationships, sex and sexuality.

It's okay to disagree

All your colleagues will be different. There are going to be disagreements. Explain to your colleagues that it is okay to say that they have a different opinion. Colleagues should be persuaded to use an agreed 'script'; 'I disagree with what you have just said because…' rather than 'You're wrong'.

Listen to each other
Encourage all your colleagues to take turns to talk one at a time (from previous experience of school training days that may be a tough one!).
There is no such thing as a silly question
Remind your colleagues that we all have different levels of knowledge and experience and that we can learn from each other.
Possible Group Agreement
- Confidentiality, caveat for Safeguarding Children/Vulnerable Adults
- Please refer to 'someone I know/knew/teach/care for...', avoid using names
- Respect others opinions, experiences and values
- Have fun!
- Keep to time
- Be supportive
- Listen to each other – try not to interrupt or talk over others
- Give yourself and each other space to think
- It's ok to leave the room if you need to
- Only share what you want to share
- Own your opinions – 'I' think...
- It's ok to disagree/challenge respectfully
- Try to join in all activities, but step away if you feel uncomfortable – that's ok!
- There is no such thing as a silly question...!

3. **Try to be realistic** and honest with your colleagues (and head of your establishment) about what can be achieved in the session or sessions you have available.
   - Developing particular factual RSE knowledge can be achieved during a certain session but improving skills and confidence can take any amount of time and understanding of individual needs – and the needs of the learners.
   - Exploring and reflecting on the attitudes and beliefs of your colleagues is difficult; yet this is what will be needed to enable your team to reflect and be able to deliver the Relationships and Sex Education your special learners deserve.
   - One RSE training session will not result in you creating a team of enlightened, confident, knowledgeable RSE practitioners; but it will be the start of a shared journey towards where you want to be.

Whilst supporting others in how to provide Relationships and Sex Education for our special learners it often becomes apparent that your colleagues may not have had a great previous education on these matters themselves. Have time to reflect on how your colleagues learned about Relationships and Sex. Would they have changed how this was provided; and by whom?

One way to achieve this is to ask where they got their 'RSE knowledge' from.

You could use something close to the questions I use at the beginning of staff training below;
- How happy were you with the Relationships and Sex Education you got when you were growing up?
- What information did you get: From your parents?
- From school lessons?
- From your friends?
- From magazines, internet or elsewhere?
- What did you think about the information; then and now?

As a colleague, trainer and facilitator, you cannot assume a certain shared level of knowledge and understanding about RSE in any group of adults. We all have a variety of experiences and knowledge due to a range of factors. For some of us the consequences, throughout life, of having poor RSE education in childhood means that we will need more support in reducing the anxiety around talking about and providing RSE.

I would stress that there will be significant differences in where we have gained our relationship and sex knowledge. From many a RSE training session delivered, in many schools, in many parts of the country, I can confidently conclude that the majority of us received our RSE knowledge predominantly from our friends.

Now, I don't know about you, but my friends were a little 'loose with the truth' and I subsequently spent most of my adolescence feeling completely inadequate (but that is too much to share here, I know!).

The question to be asked of your colleagues, the one to have them reflect on over a break possibly is this; If the majority of our special learners don't get their RSE information from family, from media or from school, then where do they get their knowledge? Is it from their friends, as we did?

Sadly our learners do not have the access to their peer network like neurotypical children; even if they are able to access clubs and activities of an evening or weekend, they will have some type of 'support'. Supervised fun.

We, the professionals, the 'educationalists', need to be the ones having discussions with our learners' support network, to ensure we attend to the knowledge and skills that our special learners need. Not want, but need, to keep themselves safe and to have as fulfilling a life as possible both now and in their future adult lives.

4. **Make it clear to staff that they are providing RSE all day, every day.**

    It can be reassuring for our colleagues to know that when they do work around self-esteem, mutual respect, body image, managing conflict and communication skills they are also doing valuable RSE work. By demonstrating how some aspects of this learning are already well within the comfort zones of most of us, it can help build confidence to provide RSE knowing what they are already doing.

5. **Include some 'quick wins'**

    … of resources, websites and activities that can be easily replicated in practice. Giving your colleagues the opportunity to directly experience activities will give them added confidence to use them in one-to-one or group work with their learners (RSE Hub, 2015).

6. **Guidelines for colleagues providing RSE sessions**

    The climate we create in the classroom when providing RSE should always be positive with the core values of respect and responsibility modelled and expected in return.

    - Acknowledge the fact that talking about relationships, growing up, puberty and sexuality can feel awkward and embarrassing. This acknowledgement should reassure our learners their school is a place where important and sometimes sensitive issues can be discussed safely.
    - Set agreed rules and boundaries in relation to the language that is used and respecting others with different life experiences from our own.
    - Use correct terminology. Some colleagues may feel uneasy about this, but that should be balanced with how important it is for our learners to be clear about what is being discussed. These words are just that and should be 'normalised'.
    - Boundaries of discussion topics; 'personal experience' – ensure learners are aware of the boundaries of confidentiality and our child protection duties.
    - Consider the layout of the physical environment where possible. Arranging chairs in a circle without any tables works well to create an informal atmosphere.
    - Ensure you and your colleagues sit within the circle, with your learners, so to be part of the group.
    - Ensure other colleagues or learners do not interrupt the sessions so that the right to privacy is respected.
    - Start and build up a folder for each learner to keep their work in.
    - It is good practice to begin each session with a recap on the previous sessions' learning.
    - Diversity should exist in the group, even implicitly with on-going discussions of the range of diversity with our communities. Awareness of cultural differences in relation to relationships and sexuality will also need addressing.
    - Myths or stereotypes in relation to our special learners as sexual beings will need exploring.
    - In order to reinforce the message of appropriate touch, ensure learners have the opportunity to practice appropriate greetings at the beginning of each session.
    - Parents and carers of your learners need to be informed of session content according to the school's policy and procedures.
    - Your first session should involve developing agreed group rules to follow throughout the course. A gentle reminder of these rules on subsequent sessions will be helpful as will agree adaptations.

If we break down the elements of a well-rounded, long term, RSE programme what do we expect to see?

It is essential for our learners' development and well-being that they experience a programme of RSE at a level which is appropriate for their age and physical development as well as being mindful of cognitive ability to understand new concepts (Dixon, 2006).

Your colleagues may need support to find the most effective teaching methods and resources to use in their classroom. RSE knowledge becomes deeper if our learners work in a supportive group where they feel safe. Keep activities interactive where possible and use strategies which encourage plenty of practice of useful skills. As with everything we do in special schools, constant repetition and reinforcement is key.

When providing RSE to special learners, our work in class will need to be explicit and terminology correct, in concrete terms. We need to ensure the use of correct words for body parts and functions, from everyone in the school. While we can accept words and slang used by learners, the shared, clear message must be that 'we use the correct words here so we can all understand what we mean'. There have been cases where our learners have been classed as 'unreliable witnesses' in investigations of sexual assault due to their inability to use correct names of body parts. It is not our children's or our learners' embarrassment of these words that dissuade us to use the correct names for body parts – but our embarrassment. And that is shameful.

Visual material must be clear and unmistakable, as must anatomically correct, three dimensional models (Dixon, 2006).

Attitudes, skills and knowledge that may be covered in RSE (in no particular order)

- Developing a positive attitude towards self and others including developing self-concept and self-esteem
- Developing effective communication skills including elements of non-verbal communication such as personal space and body language
- Vocabulary (and use of augmentative communication) to discuss feelings and ones' body (including the correct names for genitals)
- How to look after our bodies; personal hygiene and health screening
- How we change as we grow up; we all need to be prepared for puberty
- Differences between males and females
- Differences in family construction; what makes a family?
- Public and private behaviour, modesty and privacy
- Appropriate and inappropriate touch of self and others
- The importance of consent to touch another person's body or have someone touch us
- How to keep ourselves safe and be assertive
- Relationships; family, friends, school staff, future work colleagues and potential sexual partners
- Developing a positive attitude to self and others
- Sexuality and gender
- Identifying as transgender or non-binary
- Who to talk to and ask for help or support
- Bullying; why it can happen and how to get help
- Reproduction and how to prevent pregnancy
- Sexually transmitted infections and how they can be prevented

Pupils who use alternative methods of communication

Some learners will have physical, visual or hearing impairments or are unable to use speech and may use signing, symbols and/or communication switches and aids. Our colleagues should adapt their RSE provision to ensure that all learners have equal access. (For example 'Writing with Symbols' software includes 'private' body parts, with a range of clear images of body parts and functions. 'Proloquo' has a RSE page and body part images available).

Our special learners with PMLD will not be excluded from your school's RSE journey

Using the skills and knowledge of appropriate strategies and activities, our learners with PMLD can experience the vital RSE elements: self-awareness, gender awareness, body recognition, privacy and self-advocacy.

Autistic learners may require individual teaching strategies to meet their specific needs. RSE can be part of a TEACHH programme and Picture Exchange Communication System (PECS) is suitable for many RSE areas of work. Again, explicit clear teaching and use of correct words, pictures and visual aids are essential to avoid confusion (Dixon, 2006).

It is obviously important to find the right balance between supporting our learners to understand and experience different kinds of relationships, and empowering them with the knowledge and skills they need to safeguard themselves from every type of abuse. The protection of our vulnerable learners is crucial and their welfare must be considered at all times, whilst not restricting their learning to a life without relationships and mistakes.

I am sure we have all made a mistake or two in a relationship, or in our choice of relationships. Our learners need to know that they too may make mistakes, but by giving them the understanding and skills to self-advocate in terms of relationships and choices we enable them to share their voice.

Let us be honest with ourselves, our learners and their parents

Be clear and honest to your colleagues that talking about relationships and sex can feel awkward. Also encourage you colleagues to share this acknowledgement with parents, carers and their learners. Hopefully it will reassure learners and their parents that their school is a place where important and potentially embarrassing issues will be discussed and shared with sensitivity. The learners know that their school, college, care home, respite or hostel are places where they know they can talk, be listened to and have support and factual information.

As we have seen with the protests organised by some religious and parental groups across the country; it is one thing to convince our colleagues of the importance of Relationships and Sex Education, it can be far more challenging to get the parents and carers on board.

4   Getting parents and carers on-board

'I found the statistics on disability and sexual abuse alarming. After reading these I knew I needed to do what I could to protect my child. I researched and started doing teaching with my child from an early age' (A Parent's view; Department for Children, Schools and Families, 2009).

We should not rely on scare mongering tactics to influence parental participation, although they deserve to know the facts, but we do need to rely on developing relationships.

'To maximise generalisation of knowledge, it is also useful for the curriculum to include strategies that foster collaboration between educators and caregivers' (Blanchett et al., 2002, cited by FPV, 2015).

This chapter will seek to demonstrate how vital it is to get the parents and carers involved with RSE provision. It will explore how we can develop our partnerships and our understanding of concerns and fears that parents and carers hold when it comes to Relationships and Sex Education (RSE). Honestly, if we are to provide successful SRE that will impact positively on the long-term outcomes for our special learners then we need to develop mutually beneficial partnerships between parents, carers and schools.

RSE is often a confidence thing. We can gain the trust and therefore the confidence of parents and carers if they are invited to play a part. They need to be consulted about the role and content of RSE within the school and given the tools and knowledge to do their bit. OFSTED's (2002) report into RSE acknowledged that young people would like to be able to talk to their parents about sex, and vice-versa, but the feeling of embarrassment frequently prevents any open discussion from taking place (Garbutt 2008). For many parents, the topic of sex was not discussed within their family when they were growing up, so when it comes to their role in Relationship and Sex Education it seems the parental talk about 'the birds and the bees' simply does not happen. A 2009 report by The Department for Children, Schools and Families confirmed the majority of parents and carers side-step starting conversations around RSE. In the report a number of parents stated that while they provide life advice for their children, they actively avoided talking to their children about sex as they felt embarrassed. (Parent; Department for Children, Schools and Families, 2009)

For others, talking about relationships and sex was a case of 'when they're old enough to ask, they're old enough to know'. That is to say, this sample of the parents' approach to sex education was reactive rather than proactive – they waited for questions to be raised (and hopefully answered) rather than develop a plan looking ahead for the right time and place for the appropriate conversations. They saw themselves as simply there to fill in the information gaps, if they could.

For our special learners, we all have to think ahead. Always. We cannot rely on hindsight, cannot rely on a reactive strategy. Their parents need to be encouraged to see that for themselves and be offered advice about how to plan ahead.

There is also a genuine fear that talking about sexuality, sex, relationships and reproduction will encourage an over developed curiosity in their children. As we have previously mentioned, the fact is people with developmental disabilities whose parents and caregivers discuss all aspects of sexuality with them, are better prepared to protect themselves from abuse and make informed decisions about how they will express their own sexuality (NSPCC, 2014). These are the facts that need to be shared with the parents you will be working with.

Some parents are not sure what their children, whether they be teenagers or adults, need to know. A common historical myth is that children and teens with developmental disabilities do not need to learn anything about sexuality because they will not develop into sexually mature adults. I have worked with some parents that *wanted* the myth to be the truth; then time and nature did their thing and both parents and their children were ill-prepared for the inevitable process of both puberty and adolescence. The truth is that all children are sexual beings from the beginning of their lives and will continue to develop socially and sexually throughout their lives.

If we really want to provide a successful RSE programme that offers our learners the content and learning opportunities they need, we have to work collaboratively with their parents and carers. We need to talk, to share, also to learn. We will need to be sensitive to parents' experiences and concerns about their children's level of vulnerability whilst offering comforting reassurance. Despite what we as professionals may think, parents play a key role in all aspects of their children's education. We may have different views on what is important and what should (and should not) be taught so how do we find compromise and ensure what we do provide is in their child's best interests?

Parents of our special learners will provide invaluable insight into the most appropriate approach to working with their child. Their unique and insightful knowledge on how their children best communicate and understand information should provide us with a core platform. This sharing of knowledge, however, needs to be a two-way street. We also need to share our expertise and demonstrate what we are planning to teach; and *why*.

We have a duty to inform parents about all educational opportunities that we are providing. This duty is particularly important for sensitive issues such as RSE, so that parents are fully informed of what their children are being taught, can be involved and can be encouraged to engage their children in partnership with us. Thankfully there are parents who hold positive views that RSE is a way to offer their children the knowledge and skills required to understand various types of relationships, how to keep safe and understand their changing bodies. However, similarly to our colleagues' range of views, there will be parents that will think differently than us on the importance of RSE. There could be a variety of reasons for this reluctance and we should be ready to have honest conversations whilst keeping aware of our priorities.

My belief is that the overwhelming majority of parents want to provide the guidance and knowledge their children need to become safe and happy adults. Some parents may not have the knowledge, skills or tools to do this without our support; it does not mean they do not want the best for their children. Most parents take their responsibility for keeping their children safe from physical and emotional harm very seriously but, like some of us 'professionals', at times they are afraid of talking about the realities of growing up with their children and therefore choose not to.

Some of the parents will feel uncomfortable that their children may not be ready to learn about relationships and sex, that they are 'too young for all that'. The government has secured the power for parents to withdraw their children from RSE, under the 2019 RSE DfE guidance, and many of them will take comfort in this right. We need to reassure them that the RSE content that we provide is what their children need, when they need it, as they grow into adults. It is reassuring to note from the Department for Children, Schools and Families (2009) research, that once parents are informed about the content of the RSE curriculum the majority of them do not believe parents should exercise their right to withdraw their child from RSE. They felt that to do so would potentially disadvantage their child for life and rob them of fundamental life skills.

This study shows over 90% of parents support school based RSE when they understand content and ethos, however over half of parents in an Ofsted survey said they believe we, as teachers, provide too little information about Relationships and Sex Education (Ofsted, 2002).

From the 2009 report, by far the biggest criticism of RSE in schools was the perceived lack of standardisation. Some schools were seen as excellent; communicative, involving and active, whilst others were seen as more 'vague' in their approach.

Parents who had children in these vague-like schools said they had to rely on getting information from their children about what they have been taught. They wanted greater levels of understanding of the RSE structure and content being provided within their children's schools. What should give us confidence is the fact that when parents had the opportunity to explore the content of the sessions they were surprised and reassured at how age appropriate the RSE sessions seemed and the style of approach.

It appears that most parents would like schools to share with them what they are doing in RSE, so that they can feel reassured and informed and, if they choose, reflect on and reinforce the important messages at home.

> *I think schools need to let parents know more details about what's being taught. If there was a newsletter sent out each term which explains what your child is going to be learning, if I'd have known what they were teaching in sex education, I could have reinforced what they were learning.*
> (A Dad's view; Department for Children, Schools and Families, 2009)

Why can it be so difficult to engage with parents around relationships and sex education?

When RSE was at last welcomed as part of the National Curriculum for all ages; it was caricatured by the media as 'SEX ED SHOCK Parents' fury as kids as young as SIX get compulsory sex education lessons... (Locket, 2019) and 'Children as young as SIX are to be given compulsory self-touching lessons that critics say are sexualising youngsters' (Manning et al., 2019). Complete misrepresentations of the truth. This typical hysterical headline grabbing narrative creates an atmosphere where one is encouraged to question the importance of RSE and understandably it can lead to a certain level of doubt on the part of some schools and some parents in implementing RSE fully.

RSE is frequently portrayed in our media in the most extreme terms, with schools cast as moral battlegrounds for the hearts and minds of our learners, and of their parents. With the media doing their well-practiced scaremongering and politicians not always defending the well-rounded and convincing argument for statutory RSE, it remains a contentious issue and therefore parents and carers can be no clearer if not properly informed.

Some of you would perhaps understand a parent that objected to RSE on religious or moral grounds, but the overwhelming sentiment among most parents that engage with RSE is that all children, regardless of religion, race, background and cognitive ability, have a fundamental right to RSE. To deny it would be to disadvantage them for life, and to disregard their given Human Rights. In the 2009 report most parents felt RSE was as essential as literacy and numeracy.

We can't talk about parental involvement in RSE provision without acknowledging the determination of a significant minority of religious and parental organisations to undermine and threaten statutory RSE provision, based on misinformation and questionable dogma.

'Protests against Lesbian, Gay, Bisexual and Transgender (LGBT) lessons in Birmingham schools have been hijacked by those with a 'religious, extremist agenda' who are holding schools 'under siege', MPs have said, as the number of schools being targeted has grown' (Parveen, 2019).

Also in 2019 protests appeared outside a Nottingham primary school against RSE and LGBT lessons. The demonstrators were opposed to relationship and sex education lessons being taught to children; but not necessarily their own children. The Nottingham City Council leader at the time described the protest as 'worrying and alarming' and urged parents to not listen to the 'misinformation' from the protest group.

One protester, who did not even have a child at the school, stated; 'These lessons are indoctrinating children that LGBT relationships are normal'.

A different view of a parent of two children that actually attended the school, said: *'I think the protest is outrageous, it's nothing to do with the curriculum … Their videos spoke about teaching kids sexual acts, which is not true, it's a non-argument'.*

> *No-one is promoting anything in the lessons and no one is being forced to choose their sexuality. The lessons are a positive way for kids to understand the world around them. Just as my kids who aren't religious learn about religion.*

(Gant, 2019)

It is not for me to speculate on the true agenda of these protest groups; but it is for me to say that intimidation, threats and bullying outside of our school gates is no way to share opinions. I am of the opinion that we should be striving to become a welcoming, tolerant, open society. If all we do is advocate for those who share the same class, religion, colour, sexuality, gender, ability or opinions, we will ultimately fail as an inclusive society. Placing recent party politics aside which has, by design or 'happy' accident, empowered those with intolerant views, we need to focus on what lies within the truth behind these ill-informed protests.

The reality is that our special learners need RSE to nurture self-identity and self-esteem; to keep themselves safe and to become part of society. Our inclusive society. For *all* of our special learners to develop a real sense of belonging as part of the wider community and as sexual human beings.

Disability does not recognise religion, race and colour, so why should we?

I am extremely wary of any form of labelling, but reluctantly accept that on occasion it is required for context. For those of you reading this out of context you will think me to be a huge hypocrite with all the acronyms used to describe the neurodiversity and primary diagnosis of our special learners. That said, it is clear from the little research completed to date that minority ethnic disabled children and their families are susceptible to higher levels of need, risk and safeguarding. To reiterate my point, we should be acutely aware that there are differences within and between minority (and majority) ethnic groups, and this fact should be recognised when considering all findings. Context.

A research study based on interviews with 600 minority ethnic parents and carers (Chamba et al., 1999) found that families from minority ethnic groups experienced even greater disadvantage and difficulties in caring for a disabled child than their white counterparts. Additional barriers to secure safeguarding were highlighted in the study; barriers that we as professionals need to address. Our lack of cultural awareness, inappropriate assumptions, poor augmentative communication skills and limited knowledge of child protection procedures were identified as reasons for the imbalance. All these areas need to be considered when working with our special learners and their families.

> *Absence of support services for minority ethnic disabled children and their families is likely to increase levels of stress and isolation and have implications for trust and seeking help if there are concerns for the child's safety and wellbeing... It is essential that professionals develop cultural competence if they are to protect minority ethnic disabled children.*
>
> (NSPCC, 2014)

Hussain et al. (2002) found minority ethnic disabled young people and their families experienced more difficulties in finding services and support from professionals than non-disabled peers or white families. They felt their worries were not always listened to or taken seriously and this brought a lack of trust between families and professionals. The study concluded that a lack of understanding of the culture of many minority ethnic groups created barriers and problems for those families in need of welfare support. This was not true of families of disabled young people in general.

Mitchell and Sloper (2003) stress the importance of cultural sensitivity towards families of disabled children from minority ethnic groups. They describe how the parents of disabled children from ethnic minorities felt that services did not listen to their child or respect their culture. I understand there needs to be a balance in everything; understanding the context of what we are presented with. However the weight of research is consistently telling us clearly that we as professionals are letting down families in our communities, due in large part to the differences in our ethnicity. Surely this needs to be acknowledged and addressed?

> *These findings highlight the importance of teaching disabled children sex and relationships education and wider personal safety skills training to equip them with the knowledge, vocabulary and confidence to make informed choices, to recognise abuse and to seek help when they have concerns.*
>
> (Kovic et al., 2009)

> *When a young person is disabled, their mothers sometimes smother them too much, they need to let them go, they need to learn for themselves and experience the real world.*
>
> (NSPCC ambassador, 2014)

What we have are parents and carers that are confused and concerned by the lack of clear, honest information shared by the government, the media and the often muddled information shared by schools. It has to be good practice to encourage staff to spend time with the learner's parents and carers in order to develop trust and confidence. Proactive liaison with parents will mean we can really listen and respond to their concerns. In time parents can reinforce RSE concepts and knowledge at home through everyday family situations that complement their beliefs and culture. If we are not proactive there will remain parents that feel confused, marginalised and pressured by others into thinking they need to withdraw their children from our RSE sessions.

> *If the child's not getting it [RSE] at school and the family aren't providing it either, you are going to get problems.*
>
> (A Dad's view; Department for Children, Schools and Families, 2009)

Should a parent be considering such a step, there are guidelines to follow. We should encourage parents to talk it through with their child and then with either the head teacher or the teacher with responsibility for RSE at our school. If the parent or carer still decides that step is necessary, then the school should provide information about the sessions being missed and ideas for other sources of support for them.

We need to be clear during these conversations; RSE is not teaching the mechanics of sex, promoting any ideology, sexuality or lifestyle but encompasses broader, interpersonal and life skills. A small part of this broad range is for our special learners to recognise inappropriate and unwanted sexual behaviour and therefore be able to challenge that behaviour.

> *Sometimes because parents don't let them experience the real world, they don't know what abuse is.*
>
> (NSPCC ambassador, 2014)

Now, we can all read between the lines of what is being said and maybe not said, within conversations around the withdrawal of a vulnerable child from RSE, but I want to make this clear, offering some context. Safeguarding. Best Interests of the Child. Relationships and Sex Education.

If a parent or carer refuses to allow their child to take part in RSE, especially after considered conversations with staff, then I would be concerned. As a former designated safeguarding lead and now as an Ofqual regulated safeguarding trainer, I would want to know why. When the syllabus and reasons behind the content of our RSE provision is shared I would expect the vast majority of parents and carers to be enthusiastic in supporting the learning. If they do not want their vulnerable child to be given the knowledge and skills to identify and understand abusive behaviour and types of abusive relationships, then I would have to question the rationale behind their decision.

Ultimately, our special learners have a human right to express emotions and sexuality, and develop relationships as an important part of a full and equal life based on a right to independence, control and life choices.

Let us not forget that our special learners have given human rights:

- To fulfilling personal and sexual relationships
- To marry or cohabit
- To make an informed choice about whether or not to have children
- To take risks and make mistakes in personal relationships
- To privacy and to be free from exploitation
- To receive sex education, including counselling on personal relationships, sex and sexuality, contraceptive advice and sexual health support services

It is obviously important that our special learners, our vulnerable children, young people and adults are fully protected, but this should not be at the cost of respecting their human need and right to love and to be loved, to have friends and to express their sexuality in ways that suit them and which are safe.

Lord Laming said in the Victoria Climbié Inquiry report (2003) that 'Safeguarding is everybody's responsibility', and we have a given Duty of Care towards the special learners we support. They are our safeguarding priority.

Working in partnership with parents and carers can promote and uphold the wellbeing of our special learners and help to safeguard them and it is absolutely to be encouraged. We also need to be self-critical when it comes to recognising our shared culture of reluctance to challenge parents and carers, and our colleagues, during times of concern.

Serious care reviews have often identified an overly parent-focused approach and a reluctance to challenge parents' and carers' explanations to concerns for the wellbeing of a child. This leads to a lack of direct interaction with the child as their point of view is diminished. There becomes an over-reliance on the parent or carer's account of a child's behaviours and needs. This risk of this happening for our special learners is much greater than their neurotypical peers. We may feel the parent or carer is doing their best and we obviously want to continue to find ways of working together. When we make those choices, do we compromise our child protection standards? Are we failing to advocate for the child's best interests?

> *Professional relationships can also act as a barrier to questioning and challenging the judgement and behaviour of colleagues, as can personal values, attitudes and assumptions about disabled children.*
>
> (NSPCC, 2014)

I will not go through a list of examples; you can correctly assume there are many. In 2011, Ofsted offered their view on the challenge of promoting partnerships with parents and carers whilst advocating for our special learners. One case illustrated the need for us all, as professionals, to challenge parents when the concerns arise. *'The Children with Disabilities Team saw their role as family support workers to the exclusion of identification of child protection risks'* (Ofsted, 2011). The child suffered a serious incident of domestic abuse.

The serious case review found that the need of the professionals to be seen as supportive and respecting the privacy of parents had led to an *'inadequate focus on the child'*. All effort and attention had been toward forming a trusting relationship with the parents at the expense of considering the welfare of the child and what was in that child's best interests (Ofsted, 2011).

> *I'd have workshops for young people telling them what's safe – what they can do, where to turn to. And giving the same to parents, to professionals, to teachers. They need to be aware of the young person's needs.*
>
> (NSPCC ambassador, NSPCC 2014)

Parents and carers need to know that the school's RSE programme will complement their role and support them as the main RSE educator of their child. They will be, whether they are aware of the significant role they adopt by default, or not.

Plan to be pro-active and accept that there will be misgivings shared by some parents. Plan for your governing body and school leadership to consult with parents and carers when developing the school's RSE policy and content. Make sure there is a timeline of opportunities for parents and carers to engage in that goes back to the start of your journey. You should also demonstrate the parents' views are heard and, where possible and practicable, what is taught in RSE is also culturally appropriate and inclusive of all learners. You cannot win them all, but you can do something to negate the inevitable.

Conversation starters for you with parents

What is relationships and sex education?

RSE is lifelong learning about physical, moral and emotional development. It is about understanding the importance of healthy relationships, in their various guises, sexuality and sexual health. It is not about the promotion of sexual orientation or sexual activity.

Sexuality is not just sexual intercourse or sexual activity. Sexuality has to do with being female or male, and how females and males are alike and different in the way they look and act. Sexuality is how we view our bodies and our relationships with each other. Sexuality is an important part of being human and healthy sexuality is an important part of a person's overall health and well-being (Calgary Health Region, 2009).

Why does relationship and sex education matter?

As parents, you are already teaching your children many things about relationships and sexuality and have been since the day they were born. You are and have been the main RSE educator for your child. They learn from the way they are touched by you and others, the way their bodies feel to them and what your family believes is okay and not okay to do. They will learn from the words that you as a family use (and do not use) to refer to parts of the body and, of course, from watching the relationships around them.

Your children are also picking up a great deal from a variety of sources that may not be of your choosing; whenever they watch television, listen to music, talk with their friends and interact with the world around them.

Our children learn about relationships and sex from a very early age, even if we don't talk with them. Some of the things they may learn are incorrect, confusing and possibly frightening. In a world where sex is used to sell almost anything and even our mildest T.V. programmes come with the possibility of discussing and clarifying issues, giving our children the correct information becomes ever more necessary. For our special learners, and your children, RSE becomes the area of learning that is arguably the most important they will engage in; either at school or at home.

As well as the specific reasons that RSE is vital for our special learners; there are some other factors that could be shared (where appropriate).

In the UK, we have one the highest rates of teenage pregnancy in Western Europe. We also have high rates of sexually transmitted infections (STIs). The range of research concluded with eloquence by UNESCO's International Technical Guidance on school-based education for puberty and sexuality, states that effective RSE does not encourage early sexual experimentation, but actually helps in delaying experimentation (Goldman, 2012).

Quality RSE provision enables our special learners to mature, to build up their confidence and self-esteem and understand healthy relationships.

Parents' role in reinforcing relationship and sex education

What children learn at school is just part of the puzzle, your children can and do continue to learn from you at home.

For some parents and carers, it can feel like a natural progression to discuss relationships, puberty and sexual intercourse with their children as they grow; while for others it can seem stomach churning and almost impossible. Let us accept that talking to our children, whatever their age, about sex is daunting. If your child has a learning disability, there may be many reasons why you are worried about answering questions or bringing up sex in conversation. You may be concerned that although they may be young adults and need to be treated as such, they may be vulnerable and need careful support. You may be unsure about how much they will understand about sex, or you may be worried that your openness will encourage them to follow their curiosity, or even engage in sex.

Your child's physical, social and emotional needs will be the same as most children and teenagers as they grow up, and they may have a lot of questions for you; however the questions are formed.

Whatever your starting point on the RSE confidence scale, it is important to keep these key points in mind:

- We all want children to feel safe and to be happy and healthy
- We need to be mindful of their needs
- We need to make talking about relationships, our changing bodies, puberty and human reproduction as normal as possible; it is normal after all!
- We may need to challenge our own thinking; why we think the way we do? How were we spoken to as we grew up, how did we learn what we now know?
- We have choices; we can avoid all conversations or we can communicate openly and honestly with our children. Where do you want your child to get their information from? You, your family and their school – or friends, TV shows and on-line?

Here are some tips for talking to your child:

- Enjoy it. Laugh with each other. Laugh as a family. Share *your* embarrassments so they do not have to share theirs in the future.
- Always respond. If you do not, they may think it is wrong to talk to you about relationships, their changing bodies or reproduction. As a result you may find further conversations either strained or even impossible to start.
- Listen rather than judge.
- Always answer questions and do not be afraid to say; 'Wow, I really do not know. Shall we work it out or look it up together?' Have a handy phrase in mind for potential awkward moments, such as; 'That is a good question, let me have a think and we will talk about it about it later'. Give yourself processing time by asking something like, 'What do you think that means?' or 'Why do you ask?'
- To gain yourself some 'distance' use opportunities to talk about people in books, films or your child's favourite T.V. programmes (the soaps are awash with conversation starters!).
- Remember that children are naturally curious and just want to try to understand the world around them. Do not let your mind wander into dark places and possible horrors that an innocent question could be about. It may be that your child just needs a very simple answer to a natural concern about growing up, *'Am I going to have hair there too!?'* Your answer needs to be at your child's level, not at yours. Hopefully this will be the start of an on-going conversation that will develop as your child does, encouraging you to talk openly and enabling them to ask further questions if and when needed.

- Please, please use correct terminology. This is vital for safeguarding. We do not want our children confused by hints, euphemisms and innuendo; use correct scientific terminology whenever you can, especially for body parts.
- Listen to what your child says they need. Research consistently demonstrates that RSE provision that is age, and stage appropriate, that reinforces healthy relationships and recognises emotions, has a measurable impact on the knowledge and life-skills of our children. Effective RSE delays sexual activity, ensures children are safer and empowers them to make their own healthy choices about relationships (Jigsaw, 2018; PSHE Association, 2014).

We may feel that they know too much, when actually ignorance is the enemy of innocence.
(Department for Children, Schools and Families, 2009)

- Work in partnership with the school. As parents and carers you want your children to be healthy and happy; so do their schools.

When parents have worked in tandem with schools they see how the two combine for the benefit of their child's on-going development. The RSE provision at school going hand-in-hand with their own role as positive influencers (Department for Children, Schools and Families, 2009). How can we ensure that type of relationship is developed?

There will be a need to provide RSE support and workshops for parents and carers

In a perfect world, we would be starting RSE provision and engaging with the parents of early years learners, so our journey becomes a natural one; with parents and teachers aware of child development and prepared. In reality, we will obviously partner with the parents of our youngest learners, as with the parents of all our special learners; but the honest truth is we will also have limited time to engage with the parents of our older learners before the onset of puberty and the specific challenges that unexpected puberty can bring. Getting the parents and carers involved with our RSE provision *before* there are worrying issues and possible inappropriate behaviours to address is in everybody's best interests.

When I first started to introduce adapted RSE provision into SEN schools, I always had the plan of involving parents and carers from the outset. What I struggled with, but ultimately needed, was a variety of ideas and strategies to engage with them in the process.

How do you get parents and carers into school when you need mutual commitment?

I press-ganged the county's Speakeasy coordinator; the wonderful Many Lancaster, into helping me. We designed a SEN specific RSE parents' course that was based on the Family Planning Association's Speakeasy course. We gained permission from the FPA to adapt the course structure and content. We kept the accreditation option available for the parents and carers that wanted the route to certification. Our first attempts at parental engagement were less than perfect, but when the workshops eventually became popular the sessions helped parents and carers become more confident in talking to each other and their children about relationships, sex and growing up (Bray, 2015). The workshops gave parents and carers the opportunity to learn together, building on what they already knew and sharing experiences, as well as gaining ideas for how to communicate sometimes sensitive and sometimes difficult concepts to their children.

Some parents didn't know if they should talk about sex to their sons and daughters. [They] didn't always feel ready for their child becoming a teenager. Many parents and most young people think they should have the right to sex education. No parents had been given information about sex and relationships without asking for it. They "had to fight for it.
(CHANGE, 2010)

When you are planning for your parent and carer RSE workshops, it may be useful to have a structure to follow, or at least adapt.

A parent relationship and sex education course in brief

The main aims of the course are

- to encourage parents and carers to provide positive Relationships and Sex Education in the home in partnership with the school;
- to encourage parents and carers to take on the role of their child's key relationships and sex educator.

Course objectives would be

- identify parents' and carers' needs, fears, concerns and hopes
- provide a safe and comfortable environment for learning
- help parents and carers access relevant information and support in their role as RSE educators
- develop parents' and carers' confidence, sensitivity and skills in relation to their children's relationships and sex education.

By the end of the course parents and carers will have

- an understanding of the physical and emotional changes taking place at puberty.

We need to provide information about how our bodies grow and change – before their children start puberty. *'Puberty and sexual health is an area of their child's development that should be thought about, discussed and planned for. It is best if this is done in advance and support should continue throughout their adult life'* (Down's Syndrome Association, 2013).

- an awareness of what Relationships and Sex Education means in the context of their family life
- confidence and skills in identifying and responding to the particular needs of their own children
- an understanding of social and cultural attitudes towards sex and sexuality as it relates to all children
- information and knowledge on child protection strategies
- knowledge of the different kinds of contraception that are available
- information on Relationships and Sex Education taking place in their child's schools

(FPA, 2007)

Obviously you do not have to go down the 'Speakeasy' route for the structure of your parents and carers workshops. Assess the particular requirements for your school and plan to provide and develop the type of workshops you feel the parents and carers of your special learners need. However, it may be prudent to heed lessons learnt from those who have tried, and often failed, before.

Ideas for encouraging parents and carers to join your RSE information workshops

- A one-to-one personal invitation is often the warmest method of getting parents and carers on board, certainly if you feel that particular participation is needed.
- A course outline presentation for your school colleagues based on what you plan to provide. This will support your colleagues in the engagement of interested parents and carers and possibly their involvement in the delivery of the workshops.

- In areas where 'Speakeasy like' workshops are already being delivered, it may be possible to enlist the help of an enthusiastic parent or carer from a previous course to promote your workshops.
- Where possible get a parent or carer to help deliver the workshops. (This may take time, but I promise you, after your first workshop you will get the support you need).
- Publicity. Get the news of your workshops and details about the course included in school emails, newsletters and local mail-outs if possible.
- Deliver a taster session to generate interest.

Delivering a RSE parent and carer workshop taster session

- A taster session for parents and carers is a great idea to generate some interest in your proposed RSE workshops.

The outcomes of your taster sessions will hopefully be to

- let parents and carers know what the workshops are about
- let them know how the workshops relate to the RSE learning their children will be engaged with in school
- let parents and carers know about the practical arrangements for the upcoming workshops. For example, proposed days and course times, refreshments (teas and coffees are an essential) and if you can provide any child care support for younger siblings (FPA, 2007).

How long is a taster session supposed to be?

Taster sessions may vary in length and also take different forms. Depending on your assessment of need and your school's normal parental involvement the workshops can follow a formal format or have an inviting informal feel. However you couch the feel of your session try to ensure you convey as much workshop content as possible. The session could be in an informal setting; outside of the school environment is often more appealing; maybe a local church, café or even a pub. If easier the sessions can be hosted at school, with a more formal approach and take the form of a session similar in format to a Speakeasy group session or a proposed introductory session you have planned.

However and whatever you choose, ensure you allow the parents and carers to get a feel for the course content, and a feel for you. You are doing this for the right reasons; celebrate that.

When should I deliver my taster session?

Taster sessions can be delivered up to a month in advance of the start of your planned workshops. A Speakeasy type course could last up to eight weeks if you wanted to embrace all sessions (at two hours per week). The delivery of a taster session the week prior to the course may feel too much for some parents or carers. Ultimately, depending on the format you and our school chose to adopt and adapt, you will be able to gauge the timings by trial and error.

Nothing can be certain and nothing can be promised; however, well you have planned your taster session. Just to give you some perspective; the first taster session we offered, after lots of promotion, had one parent turn up. One, it could not have been worse, because the one parent that did turn up was my sister-in-law!

After plenty of humble pie was consumed and deep perseverance found, we continued and learnt; by the end of our first year of delivering these sessions we could not cope with the amount of requests from parents and carers for a spot on the RSE workshops. Stay with it; keep to your shared goal.

Possible content of your parental workshops

The feeling that you need to adapt to every individual need feels even more apparent when trying to run a course designed for parents and carers with children who have a range of learning and physical disabilities. Please accept the fact that you cannot deliver the content that everyone feels that they need in the short space of time you may have available.

What you can do is deliver the sessions planned, facilitate conversations, offer a safe, welcoming place for shared experiences and propose suggestions and sign-post parents and carers to specific resources and support within your extended network that offer specific support.

The ultimate goal of your workshops is to secure parent and carer support for your Relationship and Sex Education provision and extend the reinforcement of learning at home. These workshops can help forge a solid route for families and schools to work together for the benefit of their children, our special learners. The content of the workshops you provide will develop to your particular needs, but I will offer a suggestion or two as we continue.

> *Sexual health is a state of physical, mental and social well-being in relation to sexuality. It requires a positive and respectful approach to sexuality and sexual relationships, as well as the possibility of having pleasurable and safe sexual experiences, free of coercion, discrimination and violence.*

(World Health Organisation, 2002)

Does your child actually know what you believe? Have you shared your values about sexuality as a family?

As a parent or carer, you will hope that your child will always make good choices that are based on the values that your family shares. An important part of discussing Relationships and Sex Education with your child is sharing with them what you think. What do you as a family believe?

What does it mean to be male or female? How are males and females different? How are we all alike? Is there a particular way we should act? Is that dependent on our gender; perceived, felt or given? Is there a double standard for males and females? Should there be?

What is attractive? Do people have to be young to be attractive? What messages do we give in the way we dress or act? How could the messages we give impact on our relationships with other people?

What makes a good relationship? How are the various relationships we have in our lives different? How should we show our affection in the different relationships we have? Can we accept there will be disagreements in our relationships, but find a way of securing these important relationships with mutual understanding?

What makes a family? What agreements do we have as a family have about privacy? What responsibilities does each family member have?

How do we talk about sexuality as a family? Do we use sexual slang or use euphemisms for body parts or bodily functions? How do we demonstrate comfortable, appropriate physical affection? Why do some people sometimes laugh and make jokes about the gender and sexuality of others?

What do we think about sexual behaviour? Do we have a view on people choosing to have an abortion? Do we know about the variety of contraception? Do we believe contraception is okay? How do we feel about people being homosexual? Some people will have problems with who they are supposed to be; what do we think about those who have confusion over their given gender? The people we know, or will meet, have made a range of choices in their lives in relation to their lifestyle. They may be single, be married or in civil partnerships, they may be a parent or have chosen not to be. Do their choices determine how we think of them? (Calgary Health Region, 2009)

Your child's development

Whether your child has a learning or physical disability, neither or both, their developmental stages will follow the similar pattern for us all. We all progress through the stages of social and sexual development to reach adulthood. Their particular development may be at a slower or faster rate, until your child passes through puberty and adolescence to become a sexually mature adult, but the pattern and changes will happen.

It is a good, healthy thing for you and your family to accept the inevitability of puberty and adolescence and start to talk about it. The discussions you start with your young child around becoming an adult should be able to continue with your young adult children. Discussions about the values that encompass our sexuality throughout our lifespan: self-esteem, caring and respect, intimacy.

Social and sexual development occurs together through interaction with your family and others. Learning about acceptable ways to behave socially is also learning to behave in sexually appropriate ways. The love and warmth a baby feels helps them to develop trust and the ability to give and receive tenderness and affection in later life. During this early time, healthy human sexual development is nurtured through the sense of touch, during comforting, feeding and being held.

Often parents and carers are embarrassed by their children's curiosity with their own genitals, but many health professionals and child development experts urge parents and carers to avoid knee-jerk reactions. Toddlers are naturally, and understandably, curious about their own bodies and many self-explore through masturbation. This is normal.

Children can learn at an early age that there are private times to self-explore such as their bedroom. It cannot be a 'no' from us, maybe just a 'not here'.

By being clear when self-exploration is not healthy or safe; when in public places or when others are around, while providing other times to be alone, teaches children early on about the concepts of 'private' and 'public'. Maybe use terms easier to understand such as 'being alone' and 'being with others'. A definition of 'public and private' is hard enough for us as adults to grasp.

During the early childhood years, children begin to learn about how people interact with each other by watching what happens between the people closest to them. Later on, their behaviours may reflect what has been modelled for them; by you.

Within some homes, families choose to behave more formally with each other, while in others affection is freely shown with plenty of hugs and kisses. Obviously, these interactions are lessons your children are learning about how adults behave in close and personal relationships. There is no wrong or right in the lessons you are providing, but your children are learning.

In the pre-school and early school years, children generally begin to ask more questions and become more interested in the body differences of playmates of the opposite sex. The curiosity about their own bodies and the body differences of others is normal. Children begin to understand what it means to be male or female and start to develop ideas about gender roles. Through the early school years children favour a social interest in either the same gender or in the opposite gender. Both are quite normal.

When having your chats use books and pictures that your children will understand. There are 'social stories' you can get help from the school to produce specifically for your child and the *'Beyond Words'* books may help also. Demonstrate to your children the differences between personal boundaries with family, close friends, acquaintances and strangers. You are modelling these differences all the time, just be explicit and explain these differences. It is important for them to understand at a young age that their body belongs to them, and that they have the right to tell others not to touch them.

At this stage, activities and games with friends or siblings will help your children to develop in their social world. Again, depending on the ability of your child, both cognitively and physically, give your children tasks at home that they are responsible for, and involve them in activities outside of the home to help build their self-esteem.

During the time of puberty they experience a great deal of change physically, emotionally and sexually. There is rapid bone growth, increased sexual drive and emotional ups and downs due in part to the uncertainty about what is happening to them.

Before the physical changes begin, talk to your children about what they can expect to happen. There are books and DVDs available to help you share this information in a way your children can understand. Knowing ahead of time what will happen can lessen fears and confusion, and help your child to build confidence and a healthy self-image. Help your children to recognise their strengths, focus on them and develop them together.

Following the rapid changes of puberty, adolescence begins. This time can be filled with confusion and a possible lack of the usual open communication between children and their parents or carers. Listen to and observe your children closely and allow them to express themselves and their feelings in a way that is safe and secure.

There could be a time of apparent conflict between you and your child; again this is a result of the normal adolescent need for more independence from their family, especially their parents. As your child sexually matures, there may be an increase in self-exploration and in self-pleasuring behaviour.

Health professionals and many religious groups, recognise masturbation as normal and harmless. Masturbation only becomes a problem if it is not safe. For example if self-exploration is done in public places or in front of others. Masturbation can also cause issues if we are made to feel guilty or fearful about this natural behaviour.

As parents you will need to make difficult decisions at this time about how much independence to allow your children. This will be based on your family beliefs and values and also your children's ability. When they are still children you will need to decide what you are comfortable letting them choose for themselves. These decisions may include choice of clothing, hairstyles, friends and some activities that they do alone. As your children get older, their given human rights should allow them to make mistakes, to make 'wrong' choices. This may not sit comfortably with you now, but your influence on their choices will inevitably have to reduce as they grow into adulthood.

The choices you allow your children to have at his time are all opportunities for your children to express themselves as individuals, to gain a little independence from you. The concepts of public and private and keeping safe by behaving appropriately should continue to be reinforced. Healthy sexuality means knowing the difference between being healthy, or unhealthy, keeping safe or being unsafe and taking responsibility for our own decision-making (Alberta Health Services, 2009).

Puberty

I know, we have mentioned this before, but I will mention preparing for puberty again. I have seen the consequences of choosing not to prepare our special learners for the inevitable arrival of puberty, and it does not have to be such a scary, confusing time for them that they start to self-harm due to a deep lack of understanding driving their fear.

Most children will start to experience signs of puberty between the ages of 9 and 13; some a little earlier, some later. Children with learning or physical disabilities may develop at their own individual pace due to their particular disability or associated medical condition, but develop they will. As a parent you will want to be ready to support and prepare your child for the changes that will happen to their bodies and to help them to develop the skills and knowledge to cope with these inevitable changes, before they happen.

Girls need to know about

For girls puberty usually starts between the ages of 9–15. Some of the body changes that occur are

- Growth spurts, which includes lengthening of arms and legs
- Weight gain
- Hands and feet grow bigger
- Hair grows under arms and on legs
- Hair on arms and legs may become darker
- Breasts grow and nipples become larger and fuller and they may become darker in colour
- Face shape changes and becomes less childlike
- Voice becomes slightly deeper, although not as noticeable as with boys
- Body shape changes as hips widen
- Pubic hair grows on vulva
- Vagina discharges a clear or slightly milky discharge – this is normal and helps to keep the vagina healthy
- Ovaries release an egg which, if not fertilised by sperm, is broken down and shed with the lining of the womb. (This is known as menstruation or a period.)
- Hormonal changes can lead to mood swings including irritability, tearfulness, overwhelming happiness and confusion

- They may feel intense emotions of love, low self-esteem, frustration and apathy
- They may become argumentative and bad tempered, and challenge authority
- They may be physically attracted to others (male or female)
- They will begin to want more independence from parents

(FPA, 2007)

It is so important that we discuss about **menstruation** with our daughters before their periods start. Start early; if as a mother, you have sanitary products in the house then explain what they are for. Stress the point that periods are a normal process of growing and changing and there is nothing wrong. Explain that the bleeding will last for a few days and the bleeding will continue to happen as part of her menstruation cycle. Use a calendar or diary to keep track of your daughter's menstruation cycle. This will help you, as a family, to plan for the next period. This does not need to be a role for mothers only!

When a girl first starts menstruation she may have a period and then not have another one for a few months. A more regular cycle of around 28 days usually settles down after a year; although there is not a concrete timescale. Maybe have some pads ready to show her what they are for. Perhaps mothers or sisters could demonstrate and explain the routines they follow. There is a great resource called 'I Change My Pad' by Bodysense/Me and Us. It is a portable little booklet that has great imagery and explanation of what a period is and how to follow routines. There is also a pictorial sequence to follow when changing a pad to support you and your daughter. The school should be able to source this for you.

Together you can organise a bag with clean underwear, pads and wipes. Keep it in an accessible place when at home, out and about or at school to help with unexpected periods. The importance of hygiene and cleanliness should also be discussed openly.

One of the early signs of puberty is usually **breast development**. Your daughter's breasts may be uncomfortable as the breast tissue can cause unfamiliar sensations. Wearing a bra, especially during physical activity can help. It is normal for one breast to develop and become bigger than the other.

A difficult subject to discuss is **masturbation**, especially when the discussion is with your child. The touching and rubbing of genitals for pleasure is a normal, natural behaviour. How and when you allow your daughter time to explore and touch her body will be based on your beliefs as a family, but do find a way of discussing your thoughts. Reinforce the message of being safe and that touching oneself is a private activity that is done in private; preferably in her bedroom or in the bathroom when alone. Sometimes physicality, or the need to wear pads or the reliance on medical support equipment can prevent your child from exploring their body; is there creative ways of allowing this to happen?

There have been families and residential care settings that have fixed a mirror to the ceiling of the bathroom or changing area so that those individuals who require a high level of support, with intimate and personal care needs, can see themselves without clothes or pads. The opportunity is then taken to show respect and privacy and allow the individuals time alone. As you can imagine, there can be some differences of opinion when it comes to navigating this moral maze.

For my part; we all have a human right to be treated equally. We are all sexual beings with the human right to sexual expression (The Equality Act, 2010).

It can be hard to imagine that our children becoming sexually active, and when our children are teenagers with learning disabilities the thought process could be twice as hard. The conversation about the use of contraceptives for birth control and protecting ourselves from STIs could be as necessary for you as it is for any family with teenage children.

If your daughter has the ability to access a level of independence, even with some additional support, like a personal assistant, it is advisable to be aware of the friends your daughter is socialising with and whether or not she is involved with someone special. I understand that I am stating the bindingly obvious, but do we ask about relationships, do we encourage relationships? Within your on-going conversations, continue to share your family's beliefs about safe, healthy relationships and mutually appropriate behaviour. Reinforce the concept of self-advocacy and about saying and hearing 'no'; and that no means no.

If you feel that it is appropriate, explore as a family the different types of birth control that may be the right option for your daughter. Plan a conversation with your family doctor or sexual and reproductive health clinic. Different medications can affect different forms of birth control, make sure your health care provider is aware of the medication your daughter is on and any medical conditions your daughter may have. Your daughter may need help remembering to take or use her birth control especially if the choice has been to use the contraceptive pill (Alberta Health Services, 2009).

Your daughter should know that it is possible to get Sexually Transmitted Infections through unprotected sexual contact. Talk to your daughter about using condoms every time they have intercourse as a contraceptive and for protection.

Boys need to know about:

For most boys puberty usually starts between the ages of 10–16. Some of the body changes that occur are:

- Growth spurts, including arms, legs and feet
- Testicles grow larger and fuller
- Penis grows longer and wider
- Pubic hair grows around the base of the penis
- Testicles start to produce sperm which mixes with fluid to make semen which boys ejaculate
- Spontaneous erections and wet dreams may begin
- Scrotum sac becomes darker in colour
- More hair grows on the body which may become darker on the arms and legs
- Body shape changes as boys develop broader shoulders and chest, and become more muscular
- Face shape changes and becomes less childlike
- Voice box grows which makes the Adam's apple look bigger, and the voice breaks and becomes deeper
- Hair and skin become oily, which may lead to spots and acne
- Body sweats more
- Growth of facial hair
- Hormonal changes can lead to mood swings including irritability, tearfulness, overwhelming happiness and confusion
- They may become argumentative and bad tempered, and challenge authority
- They may be physically attracted to others (male or female)
- They begin to want more independence from parents
- They may feel intense emotions of love, low self-esteem, frustration and apathy

(FPA, 2007)

There are an array of topics to discuss with your son before and during puberty. Discussing **wet dreams** before they happen can reduce a great deal of anxiety and confusion. Wet dreams happen when semen is ejaculated from the penis while asleep or possibly dreaming. We discussed the importance of using proper names when talking about relationships, sex and growing and changing with your children, and the term 'wet dreams' will not necessarily help when talking with your child who can be literal in their interpretations. Wet dreams are not always 'wet' and not always due to a 'dream'. However you choose to discuss wet dreams, make it clear that it is perfectly normal and that it will happen to some boys but not others. If it does not happen, this is also perfectly normal. You can help your son, and ease their potential embarrassment, by showing him how to change clothing and bedding independently, if at all possible.

The touching and rubbing of genitals for pleasure is a normal, natural behaviour but **masturbation** is a private activity and should be done in private; preferably in his bedroom or in the bathroom when alone. I will reiterate the messages from earlier; reinforce the message of being safe and that touching oneself is a private activity that should never be done in public. Sometimes physicality; the need to wear pads or medical support equipment can prevent your child from exploring their body; is there ways of allowing this to happen?

There have been families and residential care settings that have fixed a mirror to the ceiling of the bathroom or changing room so that those individuals who require a high level of support with intimate and personal care can see themselves without clothes or pads. The opportunity is then taken to show respect and privacy and allow them time alone. As mentioned earlier, there can be some differences of opinion when it comes to navigating this moral maze.

For my part; we all have a human right to be treated equally. We are all sexual beings with the human right to sexual expression (The Equality Act, 2010).

The conversation about birth control and STIs is as necessary for your family as it is for any family with teenagers.

If your son has the ability to be allowed a level of independence, even with some support such as a personal assistant, it is helpful to be aware of the friends your son is socialising with and whether or not he is involved with someone special. I understand that I am stating the bindingly obvious, but do we ask about relationships, do we encourage relationships? Within your on-going conversations, continue to share your family's beliefs about safe, healthy relationships and mutually appropriate behaviour. Reinforce the concept of self-advocacy and about saying and hearing 'no'; and that no means no.

Your son should also know that it is possible to get Sexually Transmitted Infections through unprotected sexual contact. Talk to your son about using condoms every time they have intercourse as a contraceptive and as protection (Alberta Health Services, 2009).

We cannot discuss the various conversations that we should be having with our children without talking about **sexual orientation.** Understanding sexual orientation, or why we feel attracted to people of the opposite sex, same sex or both sexes can be especially confusing when we are teenagers. This doubt can stay with us until our early adult life.

We should therefore equip our learners with skills, knowledge and strategies that enable them to take responsibility for their sexual expressions. It is important that our RSE provision should also *'actively challenge the hetero-normative perspective'* (Löfgren-Mårtenson, 2011).

There is a strong consensus that sexual orientation is set at birth whilst running along a continuum throughout our life. Therefore our sexual identity may ebb and flow until we are ready to recognise and accept our orientation. There are many of us that need time to come to terms with our orientation and we may not naturally identify as gay, lesbian or bisexual until we are confident and secure.

Our sexual behaviour may follow along another continuum as our identity and sexual orientation merge. For some, this may mean a period of exploration of our sexuality, be this through a crush or two or having fantasies. For us to enable our children to develop a strong identity and healthy sexuality, it is important that we remain open to the variety of possibilities for our children's sexual orientation and self-identity that their life will bring. Gaining an awareness and understanding of the issues they may face will be more than helpful.

> *It is hard to have a disability and be lesbian. I talked to my mom about it and she was really supportive in helping me talk to my doctor and a local support group which was very helpful.*
> (Alberta Health Services, 2009)

Transgender, gender confusion and our special learners

I do not have the knowledge or experience to write with authority about the complex issues surrounding transgender, although I am not going to shy away from opening the discussion here to encourage a better awareness and understanding from us all.

As the term transgender means different things to different people my ability to reach a definition remains out of touch. Those who identify as transgender sometimes choose to call themselves 'trans' as this term is preferred because it avoids ambiguity and still recognises the original distinct forms of identity and expression. This has become an umbrella term that can include transgender people, people who cross-dress and a range of other distinct forms of identity and expression.

Words used to identify gender confusion and transgender such as; 'Gender Dysphoria' are filled with nuance and need to be better understood. We also have the words; gender fluid, gender creative, gender diverse and gender non-conforming. It is always best to ask the young person or the family of the learner what term they prefer. However, some of our learners will not want any term used; they are a boy or a girl, even if that gender is not the one they were assigned at birth.

There is also lack of agreement within the trans community as to which terms they prefer. Therefore, the safest and most respectful practice is always to ask someone which way they would prefer to be identified (Lancashire County Council, 2013).

Brill et al. (2008) suggest that there are three main periods when people acknowledge their gender diversity: childhood, early adolescence or adulthood. There was a U.S. study in 2011 that found that the mean age for when participants became aware of being trans or gender diverse was 5.4 years (Beemyn et al., 2011). For children who acknowledge, and then disclose, that they are trans or gender diverse, the likelihood of having their gender affirmed by others is shaped by societal understandings of, and our attitudes towards gender diversity. It is clear, we have a way to go as a society in developing our understanding (Bartholomaeusa, 2017).

Obviously both home and schools constitute key contexts in which children may disclose that they are trans or gender diverse. This highlights the importance of schools in providing affirming and informed responses (Bartholomaeusa, 2017). We have a duty of care to all our learners, and this means that we also have a role to play in making our school cultures more aware and inclusive of gender diversity.

> *Being transgender is when you know there is a difference between your physical sex and your inner sense of being.*
>
> (CMG et al., 2020)

For those of us working with special learners 'Transgender: an easy read guide', developed by Care Management Group, CHANGE and Choice Support is a blessing. It can be used for developing our own understanding and also with our special learners and their families as a structure for conversations.

Whilst I will always advocate for every person's right to choose their own sexuality and identity, I have to temper my determination and find a balanced approach when our special learners identify with gender confusion. I would urge you to find your own balanced view for the day you may need to support a learner and their family with finding the right way forward for them.

We will explore this topic in a little more detail in a later chapter, but a brief explanation about the importance of finding a balanced view;

- In a study of young women who regret their transition, 94% said they did not receive adequate counselling before starting a path of medical transition so underlying problems were not resolved
- Around 35% of young people referred to the Tavistock clinic (a gender transition clinic) present with moderate to severe autistic traits
- Childhood gender dysphoria naturally resolves during adolescence in around 80% of cases
  (Transgender Trend, 2018)

For a well-rounded, well written transgender guidance paper, download the Brighton and Hove City Council Trans Inclusion Schools Toolkit (2018). This is the one authority paper that contains specific SEND advice.

> *I found the statistics on disability and sexual abuse alarming. After reading these I knew I needed to do what I could to protect my child. I researched and started doing teaching with my child from an early age.*
>
> (Parent's View Department for Children, Schools and Families, 2009)

Some statistics about sexual assault, abuse and developmental disability...

- The risk of being physically or sexually assaulted for adults with developmental disabilities are likely 4 to 10 times as high as it is for other adults (Sobsey, 1994).
- Children with any kind of disability are more than three as likely to be sexually abused (NSPCC, 2014).
- Regardless of age, race, ethnicity, sexual orientation or class, women with disabilities are assaulted, raped and abused at a rate more than two times greater than non-disabled women (Cusitar, 1994; Sobsey, 1994).
- Women with developmental disabilities are more likely to be re-victimised by the same person, and more than half never seek assistance with legal or treatment services.
- Although about 80% of women and 60% of men with developmental disabilities will be sexually molested by age 18, only 3% of their attackers go to jail (Hingsburger, 2002, cited by Alberta Health Services, 2009).

Children with learning disabilities are more at risk for sexual abuse and assault because,

- They often need assistance with personal care and hygiene;
- They may find it difficult to report abuse because of communication difficulties;
- They are often taught to comply with authority which may make it harder for them to recognise abuse;
- They may be targeted because of their lower cognitive functioning;
- They may not be believed when they report abuse.
  (Alberta Health Services, 2009)

What you can do as a parent or a carer to develop an awareness of self-advocacy and safeguarding

David Hingsburger, an author and educator who has works with people with developmental disabilities who have been sexual victims or have victimised others, suggests parents can support their children in a number of ways.

Giving your children the vocabulary and correct information about growing and changing and sexuality, and teaching them to use correct language for their own body parts is vital. Be certain your children understand and are aware of the concept of privacy. Teach about personal boundaries and when it is okay to say 'no'. Often our special learners are taught to do as they are told but more importantly they need to know they have the right to ignore certain requests and instructions when the boundaries are crossed. Teach about good touch versus bad touch. Ensure their children understand their personal rights and their choices for healthy sexuality. Hingsburger calls this the 'ring of safety' (Calgary Health Region, 2009).

Good touch, bad touch and necessary touch

Introduce the topic of touching by talking about different kinds of touches and when they happen; at home, at school, with friends. It may also be helpful to introduce the feelings that we experience when we receive different types of touch. Remember that for some of our special learners the feelings that touch brings will be unique to them and difficult for us to empathise with. For some soft touch would feel painful and deep touch reassuring, for others any touch would cause anxiety.

Some touches are important to get, that make us feel loved and cared about. The hugs, cuddles and kisses we receive from our family; handshakes a pat on the back and high fives from our friends.

There are hurtful touches that might leave a bruise or mark on our body; punches, scratches, kicks, slaps or bites. Reinforce to your child that giving hurtful touches are not a good way to show anger or frustration. It is also not okay for people that look after children to give them hurtful touches or for children to see other people getting or giving hurtful touches.

There is as another kind of hurtful touch to talk about with our children; abusive touch. This type of touch is never 'okay'. Try to come up with helpful definitions to put this type of touch into context; 'When someone bigger or older looks at or touches the private parts of a child's body for no good reason, or when someone bigger or older asks the child to look at or touch the bigger or older person's private parts'. With older children include: 'or when an older or bigger person talks to you in a sexual or inappropriate way or shows you pictures or sites on the internet of naked people or of people touching people's private or sexual parts of their bodies' (Alberta Health Services, 2009).

Ensure that you also explain that there are times when it would be necessary and even helpful for an adult to look at or touch a child's private parts. Have a chat about when that may be, if you can; as a family parents need to help their children in the bath, to change a baby's nappy. Adults that are not in the family may include the doctor or nurse. They may need to look at or touch a child's private parts if they are sick or hurt. At these times, you as parents would be there to support your child also.

Bringing the network of stakeholders together

Over the last 4 chapters, we have explored a variety of ways of getting the Relationships and Sex Education provision you want into your setting. I wish I could give you all the answers to the unforeseen questions you may have or will have in the future, all we can do is share and support each other. When you have the support of your whole school community and each know their roles and recognise the importance of what you all want to achieve for the life outcome of your special learners, it can only have a positive conclusion.

5 Relationships and sex education for those with profound and multiple learning disabilities and severe learning disabilities

Strategies and teaching ideas

Strategies and teaching ideas; how do we ensure all our special learners can access Relationships and Sex Education (RSE) when receptive communication is limited? I love Jo Grace's view on this; 'A person's ability to communicate is not dependent on their being able to master certain skills, it is dependent on our ability to listen and communicate responsively' (Grace et al., 2017).

I have chosen to embrace both PMLD and SLD 'descriptors' for our special learners within this chapter. There will be strategies and teaching ideas that could work for both; you will have learners that these specific descriptors merge for. As the term PMLD, used throughput this chapter, suggests our special learners have a multiplicity of disabilities, with profound intellectual impairment being the significant factor (Lacey, 1998). They require specialised teaching strategies, specialised environments and equipment and specialised support around them. In addition to very severe learning difficulties, these learners have other significant difficulties, such as physical disabilities, sensory impairment or a severe medical condition. These special learners require a high level of specialised adult support, both for their learning needs and also for their personal care. (Henderson et al., 2015)

> ....during our lives, we all, more or less, create our own narrative. The story of our lives. It's an unfinished story, but a story nevertheless, with many unpredictable twists and turns. Many joys and sorrows. Many successes and failures. Young people with PMLD don't often get the chance to do that. For practical reasons, they tend to be 'done to'. They are defined, analysed, restricted, contained, prescribed, followed and led.
>
> (Colley, 2013)

The term Profound and Multiple Learning Disabilities is not a clinical diagnosis, just a description of a diverse group of people with learning disabilities who have a complex range of difficulties. There are no definitive set of characteristics for PMLD. When you meet one person described as PMLD – you have met that one person (cf. Raising our Sights *How* to guide for Commissioners, 2013 cited by Doukas et al., 2017).

We have the drive, experience and knowledge of certain individuals that are determined in their advocacy of those with PMLD and thankfully we now have; 'Supporting People with Profound and Multiple Learning Disabilities: Core and Essential Service Standards' (Doukas et al. 2017). These standards are designed to be used by educational, health and social care providers – and commissioners of these services – to work together to ensure consistently good practice in all settings.

For schools, we know that our learners who carry the description of PMLD are likely to need a high level of sensory stimulation and a personalised curriculum tailored for their particular communication and learning style. Some learners will communicate by gesture, eye pointing or symbols, others by vocalisation or very simple language. Flo Longhorn used to use the words 'very special learners' when describing those with SLD and PMLD (Longhorn, 1997). Thankfully our very special learners have very special teachers and very special people to support them.

How can a RSE programme be designed to be accessible and relevant for our very special learners? How can a sensory based RSE programme develop our special learners' understanding of self and self-advocacy? Is it even a reasonable target? Within this chapter there will be shared strategies and teaching ideas that are currently being used by specialist teachers to deliver outstanding RSE across the county. We will also ask each other some challenging questions.

With the fabulous contribution by the always impressive and generous *Jo Grace* within this chapter we will also pose some thought provoking ideas for you to consider. The internal dilemma of our own self-doubt when supporting our learners to be individuals first in the face of their profound and multiple needs, encourages an on-going conversation about how we can be true advocates for those in society who find it difficult to get their own voice heard. How do we ensure dignity and privacy for those who require constant support and intimate care? How do we facilitate everyone's right to sexual expression and to be recognised not only as a person but also as a sexual being with human rights?

The minimum requirement of us as humans is basic, meaningful human connection and interaction, a sense of social belonging. It could be argued that to deny that interaction is an abuse of human rights if we fail to provide our colleagues with sufficient expertise for making human communicative contact with our special learners who are 'difficult to reach' (Article 21, United Nations, 2006). All of the rights and freedoms contained in the Human Rights Act must be protected and applied without discrimination; Article 14 requires there be no discrimination in the application of human rights on any ground, and this includes grounds such as disability (Children and Families Act (2014)). No person should remain isolated, everybody is reachable. It may take the dedicated, micro-tuned technique but everybody can have true social participation and relationships as of right (Hewett et al., 2019).

Simmons et al. (2014) are persuasive as they argue that developmental definitions of PMLD create a view that those with PMLD are somehow non-persons. They base their assertion on a variety of debates including an understanding within bioethics about what it means to be a person; the concepts of 'self-awareness', 'linguistic competence' and 'sociability'. Our special learners are often compared to infants with our PMLD learners being described as presenting at the earliest, preverbal stage of development. They cite a variety of literature where special learners with PMLD are described as being pre-volitional, because many lack the ability to move, being pre-contingency aware as they do not necessarily show awareness of cause-effect relationships and pre-symbolic because they do not intentionally communicate meaning to others. Simmons and Watson warn us that descriptions of this sort add to the societal view that those with PMLD can be dehumanised and 'potentially lead to their exclusion and degradation' (Simmons et al., 2014).

They conclude that there is a way to go before individuals with PMLD will be fully accepted as 'people' in their own right. They urge us all to take up the debate about what it means to be a person, and to 'challenge the developmental reductionism of the label "PMLD"' (Simmons et al., 2014).

I am so grateful that **Jo Grace**, who is a Sensory Engagement and Inclusion Specialist, author, trainer, TEDx speaker and founder of The Sensory Projects, agreed to add her considerable knowledge and experience to the conversation around whether all human beings are accepted as sensual and sexual beings.

These are Jo's words and I urge you to consider the views she eloquently shares with us here

People with Profound and Multiple Learning Disabilities 'have more than one disability, the most significant of which is a profound intellectual disability. These individuals all have great difficulty communicating, often requiring those who know them well to interpret their responses and intent. They frequently have other, additional, disabling conditions which may include for example:

- physical disabilities – that limit them in undertaking everyday tasks and often restrict mobility; risk to body shape
- sensory impairments
- sensory processing difficulties
- complex health needs (e.g. epilepsy, respiratory problems, dysphagia and eating and drinking problems)
- "coping behaviours" (to their communication or other difficulties for example) which may present as challenging
- mental health difficulties (Doukas et al., 2017).

In my work the definition above has been very useful in recognising the breadth and complexity of the challenges faced by people who have P MLD and by those who support them. However, I have felt uncomfortable using the terminology P M LD in association with the friends and consultants and I work with who are all classed under this umbrella, not because it is inaccurate, but because it fails to capture their strengths and brilliance. It is, as per the medical model of disability, a definition very much focused on the physical. It neglects things that are harder to define. That my friends have a light in their eyes, a joy and enthusiasm for life that shames my more cynical approach to my far less impinged life. My friends have a fantastic connection to this moment, this sensation and the wonder available in this moment. My friends live visceral exciting and accepting lives, they welcome me as a part of their now. In connecting with them, where they are, and how they are, right now I am shown, by them the beauty of humble things. I bring a handful of herbs from the garden, or a plastic bottle full of water and glitter, and they treat them as treasure and in doing so I feel how precious our world is. None of this ability is captured in the definition above.

In fishing around for a more comfortable term to use I coined the term Sensory Beings, it is not as comprehensive or as useful as the definition from Doukas et al. 2017, but I find it helpful, and so as I write here you will find me using this term over the term Profound and Multiple Learning Disabilities. A Sensory Being is a person who experiences the world, and meaning within it, in a primarily sensory way (Grace, 2018). Sensory Beings may not have the ability to lay down memories, or to anticipate a future, therefore I focus on the present when considering our interactions and the opportunities available to them.

I firmly believe the lives of Sensory Beings are equal to the lives of Linguistic Beings (those of us who use language to experience and frame meaning), something I and my friend Chloe spoke about on the TEDx stage (Grace & Salfield, 2017). This is an easy thing to say, and an easy thing for people to agree with. Of course all lives are equal. As my five year old said in response to reports of health inequalities faced by people with learning disabilities at the out-break of the COVID-19 pandemic 'But they are people, and I am a people, everyone should get the same help'. However, when you look at the nitty gritty reality of this claim to equal rights of access, people swiftly get uncomfortable. I have twice written articles advocating for the right for Sensory Beings to choose who attends to their personal care needs (Grace, 2020a).

You will notice only one reference in the brackets ending the previous paragraph, this is because the first article was so trolled online that its publishers no longer felt confident hav-ing it in the public realm and removed it. Never before have I written anything so controver-sial, I was even reported to a child protection agency as people saw my belief that Sensory Beings should be given the same rights to choose that I have as a threat to their wellbeing.

Of course, I did not mean that the consent of Sensory Beings should be sought in the same way as mine. I can report verbally who I would like to, for example, perform my smear test, I am not suggesting we seek verbal consent. Nor that we seek the sort of com-prehending consent that I can give. If you are living a life with a brain that cannot juggle abstract concepts then consent is going to be a different type of thing for you.

Where I differ from mainstream thinking is that I still think that the consent should belong to you, not to the well-meaning team that surround you who offer to perform their type of consent on your behalf. I wrote about how to listen to meaningful choices from peo-ple with profound disabilities in Observing Many 'Nows' (Grace, 2020b). In making these assertions, I always consider what I would wish for: as I approach the door of my smear test would I want my family to decide who wields that speculum? I love and trust my family enormously, and if I couldn't choose I'm sure they would do their best, but I can choose. I can choose and so I want to make the choice.

Sensory Beings can choose, and communicate that choice. Their ability to do this is not dependent on them mastering particular formal methods of communication; it is dependent on the abilities of those around them to listen to their pre-existing communication. Every-one is communicating, and should have their personal communication style respected and listened to. Sensory Beings have their own capacity to consent and people should respect their consent and hold it sacrosanct in the way we would wish our own consent to be held.

With all of the above in mind I want to offer an idea and request that you consider it with not just an open mind, but also with a mind that is happy to just consider the shape of this idea, without leaping to the implications.

A Sensory Being experiences life in this moment, the value of that life is found, by them, in the connection to the people and animals around them in those moments and in relation to the sensations available. Connection and sensation are what it boils down to.

If I want to provide for them a rich and meaningful lived experience then I will seek out deep connections and rich sensations. I will spend time allowing these to unfurl, to be explored, shared.

In my life sex is an activity that sees me connect deeply with a person I love enormously, and share some of the richest sensations I experience in life. Were someone say to me, that because of a definition associated with me, I was not allowed to have sex, that this fundamental experience of life was automatically off the table for me, I would have a lot of problems with that assertion.

Remember that I asked you to hold this thought in your head without launching into its implications, I ask: should having profound and multiple learning disabilities automatically disqualify you from the opportunity to experience sexual sensations?

It is impossible isn't it? My mind is already racing through the risks and dangers, but for a moment I think you can glimpse my point. I am not in any way suggesting that we should set about arranging sexual meet ups for people with profound disabilities. I am simply asking that in recognising their humanity, their equality to ourselves, we acknowledge that this can include sexuality. Sexuality is after all a fundamental biological characteristic, sitting alongside equivalents like the need to eat and the necessity of defecation. To deny it is to deny an aspect of a person's humanity.

Historically people with disabilities have been viewed as 'less than'. This is reflected in the language used around them, for example people with profound and multiple learning disabilities used to be referred to as 'severely sub-human'. People with disabilities have been viewed as being akin to children. Staff I have worked alongside advised me when I began my career that certain topics should not be spoken of in front of people with disabilities, for example, particular news items, or historical events such as the world wars. All of these things infantilise or 'other' the person with disabilities. Wrapping them in cotton wool is not a kindness, it is an act of exclusion.

From time to time in my work I meet wonderful examples of families or professionals who in recognising the whole of the person in their care include their sexual expression as a part of that. Helen Dunman's ground breaking work at Chailey Heritage Foundation School is a fabulous practical example of this, Flo Longhorn, one of my all-time heroes speaks of how she arranged for a young man to have a drawer in his bedroom resourced with items that helped him to masturbate independently and to clean himself afterwards. I am constantly on the lookout for more examples, keen to see people with disabilities recognised as wholly human.

(Grace, 2021)

Finding the balance

What I believe Jo would want is for those examples of great practice to be shared widely. We need to be open, honest and transparent in what we are doing, and why, to move the discussion along. When you consider the human rights and anti-discriminatory legislation that exists, that we adhere ourselves to with great enthusiasm and determination, we should ask ourselves why we continue to accept that equality cannot be for all. It appears some of us are not equal, that some of us should not attain the same rights as other humans, as other people, because we as a society are more comfortable with that social construct than any alternative.

It is the 'high-wire' balance that we have to find; between the absolute determination of keeping those we support completely safe, because we understand their vulnerability whilst also allowing them to have the same distinction we would have for ourselves. As Jo Grace so openly considers; it is not so much the practicalities of the consequences of this thought, it is being able to have the thought in the first place. Ultimately, if we believe that we are all equal and have equal rights as humans then we have to have difficult conversations. If these types of conversations never took place before, if those before us decided not to consider how we were treating other human beings, where would all our special learners be now? What would their lives be like, what futures would they have? Whilst it is true we have made progress within a societal view of equality rights for those with learning disabilities, we still have some way to go…

It is important that everyone understands that people with profound and multiple learning disabilities have the same rights as every other citizen. We must enable each individual to engage with their world and to achieve their potential so that their lives go beyond being 'cared for' to being valued for who they are as people.

(Mencap PMLD Link, 2016)

I stand by the equal rights declaration and the aim of enabling everyone to engage with the world and achieve their potential. We know that our special learners, our 'Sensory Beings' will always require care and will always be cared for, so going 'beyond cared for, to being valued' is also to value the care they receive and we provide.

For our learners, being part of the care and taking some control is the best way to have some sense of self and self-advocacy; fundamental elements within RSE. The always inspirational Peter Imray has some strong views on how the care we provide should be seen as far more than an inconvenience between 'formal' learning.

If we reduce care to the realms of a time consuming necessity because we see it as stopping education we are taking a blinkered view that can have unwanted consequences for the long-term safety of our learners 'because it assumes that there are more educationally important things to do than take control of one's own life' (Imray, 2015).

As Colley (2013) puts it at the start of this chapter; it is the 'doing to' rather than 'doing with' which leads to a view that care is taking away from learning. How many lost learning opportunities does that view create? Imray and Hinchcliffe (2014) argue that care is a crucial element of the curriculum, not an add-on. They suggest that we should recognise the pedagogical opportunities that these care activities offer. 'Ensuring the right approach to care and the increasing opportunities to work towards independence in care situations must be a priority if learners are to avoid becoming "helpless"' (Imray, 2015).

Bringing the idea of care as part of learning is not new of course. We spoke earlier in the book about staff using learning opportunities during personal care routines for body awareness; using mirrors that were attached to the ceiling of the changing area, but Imray and others stress this should be accepted practice that requires a structured, sophisticated approach which address the social and health care needs of learners with PMLD. This approach requires a continuous assessment cycle to ensure a holistic, person-centred focus. The thought being that symptomatic changes in behaviour are recognised and responded to ensuring poor care practices do not lead to the development of learned helplessness (Imray, 2015).

Education for our special learners with PMLD requires a very different type of learning map. Their learning is not just an intellectual or cognitive process; we must enable our learners to respond to their world in real time and as independently as possible. Imray reminds us that not all learners will naturally strive for independence and that we can have an impact on any learning taking place due to our willingness to take control of a given situation. As teachers we should be co-explorers but understand that we can dominate those with PMLD even if that is not our intention. We must facilitate our learners' engagement in the process of care in the same way that they must be actively engaged in the process of any learning experience. Care must become something the individual learns to take responsibility for, so that they 'do with us' and take control rather than merely having 'done to' and remain passive (Imray, 2015).

We must be very careful that the current obsession with measuring progress does not force us into only teaching what can easily be measured and does not blind us to the fact that education for those with PMLD is a holistic process. Measurement of progress for those with PMLD may well become a case of hitting the target but missing the point.

(Imray, 2015)

There are many PMLD curricula, many an assessment tool and routes connected to levels and many school leaders that would adhere us to a curriculum something akin to what our inspectors understand rather than our learners need. This is why it is so important that we have advocates for our special learners and understand that the learner dictates the content and direction of any PMLD RSE curriculum.

For relevant RSE provision for our PMLD learners we need to be thinking of our learners individually more than ever before. We also need the input and experience of all those around them, and there will be many, including parents and carers.

How can we use the knowledge and experience of external therapists to build on our RSE provision? As Kate Boot, a Speech and Language Therapist I know well, explains; 'Decent, differentiated RSE is a must for all, and area I believe Speech and Language Therapists have a key role to play and assist with. For example, ensuring language is pitched appropriately and the correct visuals are used based on understanding the speech, language and communication needs of the individual learners'.

If there is a will, and there is an understanding of the relevance of the Relationships and Sex Education we want to provide for our very special learners, then therapists can also take on a lead role for ensuring individual profiles and RSE targets within these profiles are as tailored as possible.

- Occupational therapist – Sensory 'diets' that focus on body awareness
- Speech and language therapist – see Kate's comments above
- Access technology profile, with teacher, ICT coordinator. OT and SaLT

- Eyegaze profile
- Powered mobility profile
- Functional skills profile, especially life skills
- Physiotherapist – interaction, relationships
- Physical profile, with hippotherapist and swimming coordinator
- Communication profile – interaction, relationships
- Eating and drinking next steps, which may come under various profiles
- Oral skills next steps, which may come under various profiles

'The child is the curriculum'

A thought from Chailey Heritage School about the nature of a relevant PMLD curriculum;

> *While we do, of course, take ideas from the many respected thinkers in SEND education (inspirational teachers such as Penny Lacey; Jo Grace; Peter Imray; Flo Longhorn; Dave Hewett and Melanie Nind, Barry Carpenter, Jean Ware and more) we still believe that there are no standard or uniform teaching techniques which meet all of these learners' needs or support them to overcome all of these barriers. There is not a single menu of interventions and approaches, and there is no one curriculum which could possibly fit all our pupils. Each needs a unique curriculum:* **'the child is the curriculum'**. *Above all, everything we do, and everything each learner experiences, must be meaningful, and we must all, as educators, know why we are doing what we are doing with our learners.*
>
> (Chailey Heritage School, 2020)

There are strategies and activities here that I am sure you can add to. These may be a vehicle for your holistic RSE learning; Sensology; Intensive Interaction; Music; Musical Interaction; Swimming and Hydro; Movement to Music; Sherborne; Physiotherapy; [Massage]; Art; Sensory Integration; Drama; Dance; Rebound Therapy; Sensory Cooking; ICT; Sensory Stories; Community Awareness; Inclusion; Meal times and Care times (Milestone School, 2016). If we are to ensure these activities are 'meaningful' then when we work with our learners we should focus on what was happening 'in the moment'. We need an acute awareness of the alternative influences on their interactions at three levels: within, around and beyond the learner but ultimately we need to be playful (Watson, 2014).

> *Play is an intrinsic part of learning where learning is the development of thinking (cognitive), emotional (affective) or physical (psychomotor) skills. Indeed, Piaget and Vygotsky both contend play, in its various forms, is central to development from birth to adulthood.*
>
> (Carlton, 2010)

We as co-explorers and play partners need to accept our learners learn best when they are actively engaged. Whilst our special learners may have difficulty staying focussed and sustaining a task, it is our role to provide an environment that enables them to learn in their own time and space, enabling the opportunity and environment to for active play. If we are able to stay mindful and adjust our behaviours and interactions to the functional level of our learners, we will strengthen our relationships with them; and RSE is all about relationships (Fountaindale School, 2015). To ensure that we offer appropriate facilitation of play we need to ensure the continual observation and assessment of that play. See Figure 5.1.

Mindful interdependence

Debby Watson from the University of Bristol undertook a study into play and playfulness for our learners with PMLD. The over-arching theme in the study became known as 'mindful interdependency'.

In order to encourage playfulness, learners with PMLD need us to focus on what is happening 'in the moment'. We need to be aware of alternative influences on their interactions at three

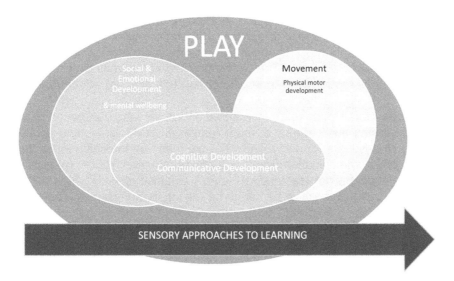

Figure 5.1 PLAY – A pre-formal curriculum.

levels: within, around and beyond the special learner. The study demonstrated that playfulness in learners with PMLD can be described as 'fragile and fleeting'. Watson reflects on the substantial barriers to playfulness that our learners experience and observes that it is remarkable that children with PMLD are playful at all. The study showed that our special learners emphatically are playful, with only very rare exceptions such as when a child is in a permanently sleepy state (Watson, 2014).

We must remember that the most effective play experiences are those directed by our learners. These play experiences incorporate and enhance self-esteem, social development, communication and concept development; all intrinsic elements of Relationship and Sex Education. 'It should not be designed to focus on limited, specific skills and concepts. It must not be one directional. It should be spontaneous. It should be active and fun' (Fountaindale School, 2015).

As Watson reassures us, there is no need to provide a manual for playfulness, it is just about us wanting to do it, finding our own playfulness and tuning in to our very special learners is usually enough! (Watson, 2014)

Strategies that could be a good fit for RSE learning

Sensory stories can be a way to combine playfulness and rich sensory experiences. We can use sensory stories to share a range of narratives with our learners. Jo Grace wrote about her delight of discovering the vehicle of social stories that enabled her to include learners with PMLD in shared time together. *'Using a sensory story was the first time that I, as a teacher, had been able to connect in a meaningful way with my students with PMLD. I was thrilled to discover ways sensory stories could be used to develop communication and understanding in my students'* (Grace, 2018).

Sensory stories can be the perfect vehicle for delivering whole school or class RSE topics in an interesting and exciting way that works for the developmental needs of our learners. Once written, the same story could be repeated daily or weekly for up to a term so that learners have an opportunity to become familiar with it and so practice their sequencing, turn taking, anticipatory and memory skills. Older learners can still enjoy and be involved in sensory stories. Sensory stories do not need to be childish – you can make them as gory, disgusting and rude as you like! (The Milestone School, 2016).

When it comes to Relationships and Sex Education, Chailey Heritage School have detailed and carefully considered teaching approaches, personalised for each learner, their needs and abilities. They source disability specific RSE resources, and deliver in-house RSE training for staff. They have Individual plans called My Next Steps for each learner and these will include RSE and PSHE targets as appropriate. These personalised targets will be overseen by the school's RSE and PSHE lead as well as class teachers. Reassuringly they plan the provision with input from parents and families. The drive is to help their learners understand how to keep safe, at whatever level and develop their self-awareness and self-advocacy skills (Chailey Heritage School, 2020).

Sensology is the work of Flo Longhorn and Richard Hirstwood. It embraces the importance of the theory of early learning through sensory stimulation, sensory experiences and multisensory environments. At its most simplest, Sensology is sensory stimulation or 'practising with the senses' (Hirstwood, 2005). 'The Sensology Workout: waking up the senses' (2008) by Flo Longhorn is a fantastic guide to implementing this sensory education (The Milestone School, 2016).

Intensive Interaction requires us to be responsive and observant, our reactions are the important factor in developing our learners' communication skills. Melanie Nind and Dave Hewett have done much to advocate for and refine what we mean by Intensive Interaction. We must be responsive to any communication from our learners, however subtle; by responding to the interaction and extending it our learners can learn fundamental skills. Again, this is all about relationships; with us as the sensitive person to be the interaction partner. The approach works by progressively developing enjoyable and relaxed interaction sequences between us and our special learners. These interaction sequences are repeated frequently and gradually grow in duration, complexity and sophistication. As this happens, the fundamentals of communication are what we would want from our RSE PMLD curriculum;

- Learning to give brief attention to another person
- To share attention with another person
- Learning to extend those attentions, learning to concentrate on another person
- Developing shared attention into 'activities'
- Taking turns in exchanges of behaviour
- To have fun, to play
- Using and understanding eye contact
- Using and understanding of facial expressions
- Using and understanding of non-verbal communication such as gesture and body language
- Learning use and understanding of physical contacts
- Learning to use and understand vocalisations

The RSE intensive interaction sessions should be frequent, quite intense, but also fun-filled, playful and enjoyable. Both should be at ease with enjoyment of the activity and that enjoyment will encourage motivation for our learners. A session could be highly dynamic. A session could involve physical contact. A session could also be peaceful, slow and quiet (Henderson et al., 2015).

For PMLD learners communication, however brief, will form the basis of your sessions, however, it can also be valuable to have a language focused or a 'SULP' group.

Social Use of Language Programme: Developed by Wendy Rinaldi, it aims to develop our learners' interpersonal and social skills from a communication and thinking perspective. It offers multisensory activities that encourage learning to develop from understanding and comprehension to use of skills. The sessions focus on elements of learning that sit perfectly within a RSE curriculum: eye contact, listening, turn taking, awareness of personal space and awareness of self and others, you and your body, interests and friendships, self-esteem-strengths and -weaknesses.

Language Group should reflect the needs of the learners within it. The group should follow a set format and focus on encouraging the following types of skills, which again can have an RSE focus: recognising and responding to adults, turn taking, initiating contact, imitation and social interaction. This is done through a variety of different activities and games.

Music and Music Therapy: Music can engage like nothing else. If we encourage our PMLD learners to make music for themselves rather than us imposing ourselves on to the music through hand over hand support it can allow play and interaction. It can also offer us another vehicle for our RSE provision. Music can allow our special learners to play and to develop an inner satisfaction at communicating with others, they may learn to tolerate the closeness of another person and hopefully enjoy being with another person. They could initiate social interaction, develop early communication, such as meaningful eye contact, body language, facial expression, anticipation and turn-taking exchanges. It could also lead to the development an understanding of cause and effect, both socially, how their behaviour affects others, and physically, how their behaviour affects the environment. Importantly, music can develop physical imitation skills and develop self-esteem from knowing that we are interacting with them because we are enjoying the interaction and we want to be there.

Massage: As we mentioned previously our special learners with PMLD are likely to have limited awareness of their own bodies. They may not know how their body parts are connected which is our proprioceptive sense. They may not know where their bodies are in relation to the space around them which is our vestibular sense. Self-awareness and body awareness are important areas of RSE and the two kinaesthetic senses of proprioceptive sense and vestibular sense need to have the same focus as the conventional five senses. Massage sessions might concentrate on a particular area of the body. Different areas could be the focus per week or half term.

Sherborne Developmental Movement was developed by Veronica Sherborne, and is based on Rudolph Laban's analysis of movement and movement qualities. Laban Movement Analysis (LMA) is a method and language for describing, visualizing, interpreting and documenting all varieties of human movement (Longstaff, 2007). Sherborne looks to extend the movement repertoire and vocabulary of learners; and explore the areas of body and spatial awareness, relationships and creativity. Again these are all solid RSE learning areas.

Rebound Therapy is the therapeutic use of trampolines to help encourage the development of body awareness, communication, motor skills, balance and coordination. The sessions are matched to our learners' individual abilities and disabilities and are informed by their previous experiences and likes and dislikes. This is hoped to lead to greater independence, lots of fun, enjoyment and the opportunity to succeed.

Creative arts: Activities such as drama, movement, dance, music, and art are fantastic opportunities for our learners to communicate without formal language. Through the arts we can promote teaching and learning across the school for all our special learners. Creative arts project also offer fabulous opportunities for truly inclusive RSE experiences for all of our learners to share together (The Milestone School, 2016).

The Mirror Project: Helen Dunman of Chailey Heritage School wanted to explore and develop the whole area of 'Body Awareness' for her learners. She understood that many of the special learners who use wheelchairs may have never seen their whole body and certainly may not ever have seen their own genitals. We talk at length about the importance of preparing and guiding our leaners through puberty yet our PMLD learners may never be able to see how their body is changing and developing during puberty.

For Dunman she felt that her learners were very unsure of what genitals they had. For some learners that may always be the case, but Dunman felt there was more she could do. Nearly all of the learners at Chailey Heritage School used incontinence pads and were changed on a bench in 'hygiene areas'. Along with a colleague Dunman re-enacted the view and movements of both learner and adult whilst personal care was taking place (Dunman, 2019).

> *When you're lying on your back even with your head propped, you can't see anything much. So it made sense to place large mirrors alongside the bench so that when a student is rolled they can really see themselves. This is a very simple idea but actually required a lot of work.*
>
> (Dunman, 2019)

The researching of suitable mirrors, writing a rationale and getting funding would have been a challenge it itself, but getting the staff on board and trained could have been the breaking point. Her colleagues were trained in giving really clear, short explanations of what they were doing and, importantly, why. They used sensory cues and used appropriate, anatomically correct language. Staffs were encouraged to say when they are enabling a learner to look in a mirror; *'"You're a girl, with a vagina" and to gently point in the mirror. For some staff this was a challenge and I needed to be really clear about why we need to use clear anatomically correct language, with no confusing euphemisms'* (Dunman, 2019).

As the learners reached puberty the staffs were asked to talk to the learners and show them the changes: *'You're growing some hair around your penis – yay, you're a teenager – you're growing into a man!'* (Dunman, 2019).

The impact of the Mirror Project saw some of the learners being able to correctly identify their gender and genitals by pointing on an anatomically correct doll. Learners throughout the school were able to really look at themselves and be part of their care, a very intimate activity that they could feel quite distanced from. As Imray (2015) stressed, care can be a learning opportunity that our learners can take a full part in so that they 'do with us' and self-advocate and gain understanding of self rather than merely having 'done to'.

It is perhaps too obvious to point out, but projects such as this may not have the impact on some of our learners due to the profound nature of their needs, but should that mean that they should not have the experience?

Learners at Chailey Heritage School were encouraged to take part in their care and to really look at themselves; 'some smile, there is definitely increased engagement. It's learning in context' (Dunman, 2019).

Guidelines on the use of touch

- Changing is part of the curriculum. The process of changing offers opportunities for interaction with learners which should be exploited.
- Gloves must always be worn when removing and replacing pads and using wipes and changed for each learner.
- Changing beds should be washed every day and wiped down after each learner has been changed.
- Students, student nurses and volunteers can only assist in changing.
- When hoisting a learner onto the changing bed ensure the learner's head is nearest the door. This is to ensure the learner's respectability is maintained should anyone enter the room unexpectedly.
- During activities involving touch, for example, physio and rebound, a pillow/cover should be placed over intimate areas to avoid uncomfortable situations when necessary.
- When hoisting learners always inform them of what you are doing and offer them the standardised object of reference for 'toilet'/'changing'.
- The wishes of the parents and carers, their religious beliefs and otherwise, should be respected, particularly regarding of the sex of the member of the staff doing the changing (Marquez, 2016).

It goes without saying that we should welcome any ideas and involvement that we can encourage from the parents and carers of our learners. In the development of any collaborative work we do around sexuality and sexual identity we should view the link we can develop with parents and carers as a crucial factor towards the outcomes that we are trying to develop and build on.

For many schools RSE provision for learners with PMLD will have this type of look;

- Identity
- Responding to others
- Co-active work and engagement with peers and familiar adults
- Participating in self-care
- Developing independence skills

(Waverley School, 2016)

Of course, Relationships and Sex Education for our very special learners with PMLD will focus on the relational and self-awareness element of RSE rather than on the 'sexual' element but this should not stop us considering our learners as sexual human beings. Sexual identity formation should be an area that we facilitate and promote within the developing personality of all our learners. Within all of the specialised RSE provision we offer our learners with PMLD we should focus our support on our learners' creating positive connections with others, developing meaningful relationships, encouraging self and body awareness and enabling them to be part of what we do together within a playful environment. What we offer as far as the particulars of RSE provision is only hampered by our own limited imagination or an unwillingness to challenge ourselves and others.

It is vital that we understand the distinctive needs of people who are often excluded from society. That's because, in doing so, we are respecting their right to be included. It is only by focusing on their needs and rights, and working to remove the barriers they face, that people with profound and multiple learning disabilities will achieve their rightful place in society. It also acknowledges that while many barriers can be challenged and even removed, ultimately we cannot change the nature of people's disabilities. In doing so we are not being discriminatory, rather we are respecting people's differences and valuing them for who they are. At the same time, we can continue to fight for equal rights.

(Mencap/PMLD Network, 2016)

6 Relationships and sex education for those with Down's syndrome

Strategies and teaching ideas

We are all unique, and there is not be one teaching strategy that works for us all, irrelevant of our preferred learning style. Rightly, many individuals with Down's syndrome do not see themselves as having additional needs; 'Having Down syndrome means nothing to me, I'm special like everyone else. I do not let people judge me for having Down syndrome. The important thing is how I feel about myself. On the inside, I feel beautiful' (Barbanell, 2020). I know my nephew, Lewis, feels equally as beautiful, even if he is unable to communicate as eloquently.

Our special learners with Down's syndrome often have moderate learning difficulties, some have more severe learning difficulties and some have complex needs including autism. Strategies mentioned in other chapters could also be used successfully for these special learners.

It was believed that those with Down's syndrome who displayed autistic traits were thought to be exhibiting these traits due to their severe learning disabilities. It is now universally recognised that autistic spectrum disorders can coexist with Down's syndrome. Some people, such as the great Lorna Wing, believed that as many as 10% of children with Down's syndrome also have autistic spectrum disorder and more recent research projects tend to reinforce that view (Down Syndrome Education International, 2020). Nevertheless, there are often problems in diagnosing autism and there may still be a failure to recognise the dual diagnosis except in the most obvious of cases.

There could be a range of potential reasons for the difficulty of dual diagnosis; those working with autistic learners may be unaware of the developmental profile that children with Down's syndrome typically present. When certain developmental delays that are atypical in those with Down's syndrome are attributed, potential symptoms of autism may be overlooked.

Those special learners who do have a dual diagnosis may display a range of behaviours not typically found in children with Down's syndrome alone and this could hamper progress that is based on particular teaching strategies.

- They may be overly sensitive to sound, light, touch or pain or fail to respond at all.
- They may have pronounced food fads and resist the introduction of anything new into their diet.
- They may lack imaginative play.
- They may react negatively to changes in people or routines.
- They may become angry or distressed if their routines are interrupted or their personal space is invaded.

Well practised approaches appropriate for special learners with Down's syndrome may simply not work with a learner with a dual diagnosis. These strategies may even adversely impact on their developmental progress. With our special learners with a dual diagnosis, it is the autism which must be considered as the primary focus. It is this which gets in the way of the learning and the progress we would expect of learners with Down's syndrome (Down's Syndrome Association, 2014).

We accept that it is not only good practice, but the right thing to do, in getting to know the individual you are supporting as well as you can. We all have our own personalities and all with different individual levels of interest and need. We cannot begin to think that because someone has Down's syndrome then we can pull a strategy of the shelf that will work for that individual. However, through significant research findings and the development of our understanding through neuroscience, we are offered a better insight into how we may be best prepared to support our learners. The strategies offered here are painted with fairly broad strokes, but they could support in your planning for relevant RSE learning for those with Down's syndrome.

Human sexuality encompasses an individual's self-esteem, interpersonal relationships and social experiences relating to dating, marriage and the physical aspects of sex. Sex education, appropriate for the developmental level and intellectual attainment of individuals with Down syndrome, adds to life quality by engendering healthy sexuality, reducing the risk of

sexual abuse, avoiding sexual misunderstandings, preventing disease transmission, preventing unwanted pregnancy and alleviating other problems related to sexual function.
(National Down Syndrome Society, 2002)

In the past, sexuality was not considered an issue for those with Down's syndrome because of the ill-informed belief that their intellectual disability produced permanent childhood. In fact, all people with Down's syndrome, like all people, are sexual beings and have sexual feelings and intimacy needs. Children with Down's syndrome experience the same sequence of physical and hormonal changes of puberty as other children in their age range. The sometimes dramatic emotional changes of adolescence will also present themselves, and may be intensified by their particular circumstances and access (or not) to community activities.

As adolescents, we are influenced by our community, our school environment and the wider media so we inevitably develop an awareness of sexuality. However, for our special learners with Down's syndrome, there may be a lack of input from certain areas of influence. Often there is some delay in the development of social maturity, emotional self-control, social communication, abstract thinking and problem solving skills. (Wood, 2004; National Down Syndrome Society, 2002)

These changes may bring on anxiety and confusion if our special learners have not been prepared for them in advance. Almost all young women with Down's syndrome ovulate, with menstruation beginning between 11 and 13 years of age. Leaving preparation for menstruation until Key stage 3 is too late for girls who need to be prepared for signs of puberty. When prepared, most girls with Down's syndrome cope with menstruation well, looking after their own needs independently. Again, the leaflet 'I Change my Pad' by Me-and-Us publishers may be worth using as part of your sessions.

Historically young women with learning disabilities were often sterilised without their consent to prevent pregnancy (Garbutt, 2008). Thankfully it is now accepted that young people with Down's syndrome should have access to contraceptives when they choose to be sexually active. There are limited options for males, with the condom being the obvious choice for protection, but fine motor skills issues may make the use of condoms problematic. For females the range of choice is that of the general population. As young adults those with Down's syndrome are often supported by appropriate practical advice on the use of chosen contraception. Depending on the young person's level of learning ability, some contraceptives may be more suitable than others. As always, this should be a matter of consultation between the young adult, school staff and parents and carers; always respecting the young person's rights to have their voice heard (Beadman, 2005),

Most males with Down syndrome are sterile (Rogers and Coleman, 1992; Sheridan et al., 1989 cited by Heaton, 1995). Males with Down's syndrome may also have an increased incidence of genital abnormalities (Beadman, 2005). Any concerns should initiate a referral for paediatric urologic evaluation. Routine reproductive health maintenance; the examination of the male genitalia should be part of every routine physical examination. Some men with Down syndrome, depending on individual cognitive status and level of personal support, may be able to learn testicular self-examination (Heaton, 1995).

Around the start of adolescence young people with Down's syndrome will often become more self-aware and struggle to come to terms with their perceived differences. They may see their school friends and siblings doing things that they are not, appreciating a more independent lifestyle than they can enjoy. This can obviously be a frustrating and confusing time for a teenager with Down's syndrome.

As with all adolescents, those with Down's syndrome will want to explore their sexual feelings, some of which may be quite confusing to them. It is essential that we as educators, along with their family, explore ways of teaching appropriate public and private behaviour such as shows of affection, masturbation or seeking consent in relationships. This is a time when careful guidance and support will be needed (Beadman, 2005).

D'aegher et al. (1999) used the term 'teachable moments' to describe how supportive it can be to take the opportunity to chat about certain situations as they arise in our everyday life.

When children or other family members take a bath, whilst sorting various clothing for the laundry, unpacking items such as toiletries, condoms, sanitary towels or tampons from the shopping or whilst watching various storylines unfold in the family's favourite television soaps and dramas.

(Beadman, 2005)

As already discussed it is vital that parents are aware of what their child is learning within Relationships and Sex Education at school in order to seek out opportunities to reinforce the learning further at home, as those chances present themselves. RSE is the obvious vehicle to use when planning for adulthood as it applies to independence in educational, social, residential and vocational settings (D'aegher et al., 1999). However, RSE resources suited to the general population often do not meet the particular needs of individuals with Down's syndrome, who may benefit from focused role play opportunities and actively practicing skills through play and through repetition, with unambiguous resources that reinforce new concepts. The content and issues around RSE should be the same for all of us. '*However...the way we provide the information should look a bit different - not so much content, but process*' (Couwenhoven, 2007 cited by Barrett-Ibarria, 2018).

Those with Down's syndrome can experience the most significant delays with their speech and language, with expressive speech often developing behind receptive comprehension.

Special learners with Down's syndrome are often visual learners; as well as learning by doing, they can also learn and retain more from seeing the information than from just listening to us. This can be through the use of drama, film, objects and pictures and symbols. There are a range of useful sources of images for use in our RSE sessions, which will help in supporting new vocabulary. Makaton have RSE signs and images, Proloquo have RSE and body part images, there is 'Picture This' (both 1 and 2) that have an extensive array of photos and line drawings of almost everything you could wish for in RSE images. With well-planned and resourced RSE sessions with suitable images to help develop a vocabulary for thinking about emotions and their bodies we can prepare our special learners with Down's syndrome for growing up and their future relationships.

Our learners with Down's syndrome can be particularly perceptive to our non-verbal social cues and our emotional tone. If we can be mindful of our physical and verbal confidence when discussing growing up and changes to our body, and always using accurate language and imagery that suits the learner's level of understanding, we will encourage their engagement and a deeper understanding (Wood, 2004).

The learning profile of children with Down's syndrome

- Children with Down's syndrome are not simply developmentally delayed, but have a specific learning profile with characteristic strengths and weaknesses. For example, Wang (1996, cited by Down's Syndrome Association, 2014) showed physical differences in the brains of youngsters with Down's syndrome that can help to explain specific weaknesses in certain verbal skills and activities and relative strengths in visual-motor skills.
- When planning and differentiating programmes of work, the characteristic learning profile, together with individual needs and variations within that profile, must be considered and matched to the subject matter.

How Down's syndrome affects learning

The following factors are typical of many, certainly not all, special learners with Down's syndrome. All factors will have implications for learning.

- Strong visual awareness and visual learning skills. The ability to learn and use sign, (Makaton) gesture and pictorial/symbol support. The ability to learn to read and to use the written word.
- Ability to learn from others, especially their peers. The ability to copy their modelled behaviours.
- Delayed fine and gross motor skills due to poor muscle tone and loose ligaments which can affect cognitive development.
- Visual impairments. Up to 70% of learners with Down's syndrome are prescribed glasses before the age of seven.

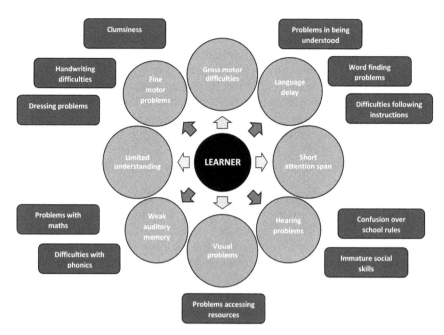

Figure 6.1 How Down's syndrome affects learning.

- Auditory impairments. Up to 20% of learners with Down's syndrome have a sensorineural loss, caused by developmental defects in the ear and auditory nerves. Over 50% of learners with Down's syndrome are likely to suffer from a conductive hearing loss due to glue ear. Clarity in hearing due to glue ear can fluctuate daily.
- Speech and language delay. The receptive skills of our learners are greater than their expressive skills. The depth of thinking and reasoning skills can make it more difficult to make generalisations, to transfer skills or to make decisions and choices. Understanding abstract concepts and problem solving abilities may also be affected.
- Poor short-term auditory memory which can cause difficulties with processing and retaining verbal information. This lack of short-term auditory memory will impact on our learners' ability to respond to or learn from the spoken word.
- Learners with Down's syndrome can have short concentration spans; they need time to learn and to consolidate new skills and can be passive learners with low motivation and well developed avoidance strategies. I am sure your own observations back up research (Down's Syndrome Association, 2014) that has shown learners with Down's syndrome can make poor use of their skills and have higher levels of ability than they generally choose to share with us.
- Many of our special learners with Down's syndrome are sensitive to failure and can be unwilling to tackle new tasks in case they do not succeed. In addition, some may have particular difficulty in correcting wrong responses once a mistake has been made and highlighted (Down's Syndrome Association, 2014).

Although it may be assumed by many that children with Down syndrome are less motivated and persistent than typically developing children, research suggests that this may not be the case.

One recent study by Down Syndrome Education International, matched 33 learners with Down's syndrome, aged 10–15 years, with 33 typically developing learners with similar vocabulary comprehension, aged 3– 8 years. A number of tasks were used to evaluate aspects of motivation; curiosity, preference for challenge and persistence at seemingly difficult tasks. This study reported no significant differences between the groups on these tasks – learners with Down's syndrome were as motivated as typically developing learners at a similar stage of cognitive development.

Interestingly, this study included learners with Down's syndrome who attended special schools and also learners in mainstream schools. The study found no differences in motivation between the two groups even though the children with Down's syndrome in the mainstream settings are perceived to be challenged more, experience more failure and be more aware of the differences between their achievements and those of their peers.

This study also offered us the thought that learners with Down's syndrome who were more interested in social interaction performed less well than other learners with Down's syndrome on one measure of persistence. This could have been because those learners were more likely to seek adult help quicker and be more adult dependent. When no adult help was available they chose to give up rather than persist with the task. I guess the message is that we as parents and teachers need to understand that too much attention and providing our help too quickly may actually undermine a learners' motivation. Probably better to leave them to it for longer than we would normally do.

It is also important that parents and teachers understand that learners with Down's syndrome are not less motivated or less persistent in problem solving or learning situations than other learners at the same cognitive level. Cognitive level is the relevant guide to their performance not chronological age (Down Syndrome Education International, 2020).

Why is relationships and sex education particularly important for learners with Down's syndrome?

- They are less likely to learn effectively from indirect, subtle sources.
- They may be at greater risk of developing low self-esteem and RSE may be helpful in raising this.
- Opportunities to learn from social situations and peers may be more limited.
- Risk of abuse and exploitation is greater for people with intellectual disabilities than their typically developing peers (Wood, 2004).

For our special learners with Down's syndrome; they can be cast as eternal children and asexual (Garbutt, 2008) at the same time others see people with Down's syndrome as having a heightened and pathological hyper-sexuality (Couwenhoven, 2007).

> *Any socially inappropriate expressions of sexuality in people with Down Syndrome, stem from a lack of information about their bodies, about boundaries, about relationships, but are not innately linked to the condition as is often believed.*
>
> (Couwenhoven, 2007)

They, like the vast majority of their special learner peers, have just not had the RSE they deserve and have a right to receive.

To be effective, RSE must be individualised and therefore understandable, with a strong focus on self-advocacy, decision-making, peer pressures, relationships, social skills and opportunities. An ideal RSE curriculum will ensure that individuals with Down's syndrome understand their bodies, their emotions, their behaviours and their relationships.

> *Creating an environment conducive to healthy sexual expression must be considered in designing educational, vocational, social, recreational and residential programs. Positive sexual awareness can only develop through personal empowerment, self-esteem, understanding of social relationships and personal interaction/communication skills. All these factors influence how intimacy needs are met.*
>
> (National Down Syndrome Society, 2002)

The information that we share should be factual, realistic and stress the importance of personal responsibility and a shared appreciation of adult behaviour (National Down Syndrome Society, 2002). Some RSE delivery examples to use;

- Drama and role play
- Discussion of case studies/real-life scenarios: possibly from TV or magazine photo-stories.
- Story-telling, poems and songs
- Use of puppets and dolls (anatomically correct dolls for RSE teaching)
- Pictures, comics and story-boards
- Videos and photographs: including TV adverts, clips from soap operas
- Art activities including collage and poster making
- Games - team and individual
- Peer massage

Wood (2004) offers differentiation examples for our learners with Down syndrome and these are as important for teaching Relationships and Sex Education as any other topic area. It should go without saying it is important to ensure that our learners are motivated to learn about RSE by carefully choosing teaching strategies that the individual learner enjoys and which have previously been successful. Making the information feel familiar and grounded in the learners' experiences will help them to use their previous knowledge to understand concepts on a deeper level. We could choose characters from the learner's favourite books, films or TV programmes or create stories that focus on various RSE scenarios.

> *With any new information taught through reading activities, it is important however, to build in activities to ensure that the child understands what he or she has read, i.e. through acting out the information with puppets, dolls or in role-play or through re-ordering sentences or retelling the story.*

(Wood, 2004)

Books can tell a story which also illustrates a play sequence to follow. We can include models for language use, RSE theme vocabulary and specific social communication strategies. The adapted books can be read to a small group of learners so all peers are learning how to play more effectively and support one another as well. The play sessions that follow can be observed and supported by teachers. Time spent in solitary play can decrease and time spent in social play for our learners can increase over time, especially important if we want to engage a range of learners with a range of special needs.

This matters as learners who spend more time in solitary play are more at risk for behaviour problems and social difficulties later (Down Syndrome Education International, 2020).

If we simply focus on the learner's level of attainment and then make the content of the lesson easier to access, have we taken into account how our learners learn most effectively? When differentiating our RSE curriculum for our special learners with Down's syndrome, how the content is delivered and the methods used are as important as the content itself. Use the learner's strengths and learning styles, understand their areas of weakness and developmental stage. A flexible approach on our part is, therefore, required (Down's Syndrome Association, 2010).

John Visser (1993) defines differentiation as '*the process whereby teachers meet the need for progress through the curriculum by selecting appropriate teaching methods to match an individual child's learning strategies, within a group situation*'

Repeat, repeat and reinforce

The one-off chat about the birds and the bees will not be helping anyone, certainly not our special learners. We know that individuals with Down's syndrome benefit from seeing, doing and discussing concepts over an extended time scale; through play or roleplay. Our RSE provision needs to be a process not kept to a session or two. Plan for reinforcement and revisiting of previous content and always be on the lookout for opportunities to repeat and reinforce information that make sense for our learners; at break time when they are interacting, or when sharing a lunch. Remember, during a planned RSE session, avoid the temptation to jump in with support too early.

Proper names, facts and boundaries

All our body parts have names; the embarrassment around calling a vulva a vulva and a penis a penis is ours, not our learners'. Think about it. Do we have a nickname for our arms? It is an arm. Our special learners struggle with the sometimes ambiguous social rules and boundaries surrounding the words we prefer to use. These are our issues and we really should use the real names and definitions. Teach the facts, teach the proper names and define the boundaries to develop understanding and appropriate social behaviour.

Masturbation is touching or rubbing the genitals for pleasure. That is a fact. Masturbation is private. If you want to touch or rub your penis and testicles, or your vulva, vagina and clitoris, you need to go to your private place. That is the boundary. We are never saying 'no', we are perhaps saying 'not here, but your private place'.

We should never focus on stopping masturbation, but on directing this natural activity towards appropriate times and private places. Most individuals with Down's syndrome can be supported to identify which times and places are appropriate. Supporting parents and carers with this concept may be more difficult, particularly if they view their children as asexual.

Flirting means using your body or words to let another person know you are attracted to them or interested. Another fact. What are the boundaries around flirting? Who is it okay to flirt with? When? Have a chat with your learners, what do they understand? *(Check out fig 7.1 in Chapter 8 for a handy visual learning aid for understanding flirting).*

A date is a planned get together between two people who might like to be a couple or are already a couple. That is what we understand a 'date' to be. What are the boundaries around who is an appropriate dating partner? Have a chat.

In their book 'Count Us In: Growing Up with Down Syndrome' co-authors Jason Levitz and Mitchell Kingsley talk with openness about the issues they faced, like; 'having a date, missing girlfriends, sexual stuff, and being in love with a girl' (Kingsley et al., 1994). Within the book, Levitz remembers the important role a school counsellor had in helping him to understand appropriate physical boundaries with female learners. He learnt from that chat and was able to apply what he had learnt in his social interactions.

As demonstrated so well by many others, maybe the social and interpersonal skills needed for dating can be taught and hopefully understood. Over time and repeated often, with many opportunities to practice the interpersonal and social skills that we all need, we may see that opportunity for that 'chat'. Keep these opportunities alive as part of your long-term life-skills-based RSE curriculum, through role-play, through play activities that may be based on your learners' individuals book adaptations – and hopefully well in advance of any actual dating experience.

Use you individual learner's assessment to identify immediate needs

The range and scope of Relationships and Sex Education topics and potential issues can be overwhelming. To narrow the scope begin with your learner's most immediate needs. More often than not the most immediate individual needs addressed through RSE revolve around healthy relationships, safety, social appropriateness, and independence. There may not be a need to go into depths where you feel uncomfortable initially (Couwenhoven, 2007).

The use of social stories

Using social stories involves regular reading of books that have been made personal to that particular learner with illustrations or photographs that help guide our learners through a range of social situations and demonstrating socially acceptable behaviours. Social stories offers us a helpful strategy of supporting our special learners with Down's Syndrome about a variety of Relationships and Sex Education areas of learning; healthy relationships, friendship, bullying, public and private, good, bad and necessary touch, personal hygiene, periods, wet dreams or who to talk to when we are worried. As mentioned before, this can also be done with small groups and have play sessions opportunities attached to the stories.

The reinforcement of the social story bookwork with other activities that encourage our learners to re-enact the story with dolls or puppets can also support that understanding. Our older learners may engage with creating their own photo story using pictures of themselves or favourite characters. Again, role-playing opportunities that develop from these activities should not be missed (National Down Syndrome Society, 2002).

The familiar issues with providing RSE for our learners with Down's syndrome

Because of their often poor working memory, learners with Down's syndrome find it harder than their peers to process and retain spoken words. Their understanding and ability to respond appropriately to spoken language, to follow verbal instructions, in learning abstract or unfamiliar vocabulary and remembering rules and routines are all significantly compromised. Words just disappear too quickly from the memory. Think about that in context of your typical Relationships and Sex Education session. It will be full of abstract and unfamiliar words, and, if we are not careful without relevant context. We have stressed the importance of having a shared group agreement for our RSE sessions, how are we visually referring to our agreement? How are we reinforcing new words, new concepts, new routines around personal hygiene and interpersonal skills through both imagery and practice?

A learner struggling to process and remember what was said can quickly become overloaded if given unfamiliar vocabulary or long complicated sentences. If that happens, they will either switch off completely or retain only parts of what they have heard, typically the beginnings or ends of sentences. Chances are you will have a group of special learners with a range of needs, abilities and primary diagnosis that you will need to plan your RSE programme around. I am not for one minute telling you how to do your job, but there are a lot of RSE 'off the shelf' programmes of study that do not always have all the particular learning profiles considered. This is where your knowledge of your learners and your teaching talents will shine.

Specialised Relationships and Sex Education resources for people with Down's syndrome are increasingly in demand, but can be incredibly difficult for individuals and their caregivers to access. How can we offer our support to their families? (Couwenhoven, 2007) Parental anxiety can be a significant barrier to our learners being properly prepared for adult life. As our special learners with Down's syndrome grow into adulthood, many will require lifelong support from their parents and extended family. Even with access to the most specialised RSE, living at home does not always allow space for much privacy. Parents and carers may have to confront their own attitudes and biases toward sexuality. (Sofia Barrett-Ibarria, 2018) We looked in more detail about how to encourage parent and carer involvement in Chapter 3. This really is a vital relationship to develop as you advocate for your learners and their futures.

"I cannot tell you how judged I have been by my own community," says Mary Erickson, whose 26-year-old daughter, Marissa, has Down's syndrome. She tells of the backlash she received from other parents of adults with Down's syndrome for discussing sexuality openly with her daughter. Maryanne and Tommy, who both have Down's syndrome, have been happily married for over twenty years and living independently for fifteen. According to Maryanne's sister, the two also have a happy and healthy intimate relationship, though immediate family and friends have not always been supportive. The immediate family received a lot of criticism and was told it was 'disgusting' that they were being allowed a sex life (Sofia Barrett-Ibarria, 2018).

When parent and carers are unwilling or unprepared to discuss safe sex, boundaries, and consent with their children, they are just putting off the inevitable and perhaps unwittingly placing their children in more harmful situations. Individuals with Down's syndrome run similar risks associated with sex as do their non-disabled peers, like unwanted pregnancy, sexually transmitted disease, and sexual exploitation. They also run a higher risk for sexual abuse (Down Syndrome International, cited by Sofia Barrett-Ibarria, 2018).

This is vital to share and be clear about, but the message needs to be put into a perspective of best interests, the right to a relationship, and the law. At 18 years of age, when many of our special learners are still with us in post-16 provisions, they have the right to make choices, including choosing a partner, even if other people, including their parents do not believe this person is the ideal candidate. People with Down's syndrome can choose to engage in sexual relationships, as long as that choice was informed by understanding and consent and the person was not pressured or coerced in their decision. We are all free to make choices that are not always agreed with. Can anyone reading this say they have always made the wise and correct decisions about their relationships?

Informed consent is the key concept

To consent to a sexual relationship means that both individuals understand what it is that they are consenting to. People are allowed to make risky decisions, though if the person's decision places them or others at serious risk of harm, and they do not show an understanding of the possible consequences of their choice, then the person's ability to give informed consent may come into question.

With all of these factors coming into play, dating with Down's syndrome can be a complicated prospect. Many people with Down's syndrome are *"pretty much on track with almost everything related to sexuality; physical development, experiencing sexual feelings and crushes, desire to date… and current aspirations to have a serious, long-term relationship as an adult"* (Couwenhoven, 2007).

Evan as younger learners, individuals with Down's syndrome often have a keen interest in marriage and family. One young man I worked with for years had the same vision for his future throughout his secondary and post-16 education. During each EHC plan review, his hopes for his future were; get a job, find a girlfriend and a have house of their own. The two young authors of 'Count Us In' share their ideas of commitment and marriage; *"… you need to be able to understand how important and how you are going to support yourself and your wife… Part of my future plans is to marry and have a wife, but I need more skills."* (Kingsley et al., 1994)

> *Though sex and disability are still considered taboo, a quest for love, self-actualization, pleasure, and happiness lie at the centre of sexual expression - these are universal desires and deserves, regardless of whether or not an individual can fully grasp the 'true meaning' (which is actually relative, right?) of love or relationships.*
>
> (Sofia Barrett-Ibarria, 2018)

7 Relationships and sex education for autistic learners

Strategies and teaching ideas

If you have met one autistic person…you should meet some more, we are pretty awesome.
(Unknown)

What words do people prefer to use to describe those who identify as neuro divergent and are diagnosed 'with' ASD? On the autism spectrum? 'Autistic'? 'with autism'?, 'has autism'? The National Autistic Society (NAS), the Royal College of GPs and the University College London (UCL) Institute of Education, published research in the Autism journal (2015), which asked people on the autism spectrum, their families, friends and professionals about the preferred language used to describe autism.

The findings, perhaps unsurprisingly, confirmed that there is no one term that we all like. The research found that all groups like the terms 'on the autism spectrum' and 'Asperger syndrome'. Autistic adults like the identity-first terms 'Autistic' and 'Aspie'. Professionals also like the term 'autism spectrum disorder' and because of the changes to the main diagnostic manuals, 'autism spectrum disorder' (ASD) is now likely to become the most commonly given diagnostic term.

The language we use is important because it embodies and can therefore help change attitudes towards autism. To reflect the findings of this research, the NAS has begun to gradually increase the use of the term 'autistic' – particularly when talking about and to adults in that group. We will also use 'on the autism spectrum' as the default way of describing people on the autism spectrum.

(NAS, 2020)

The National Autistic Society believe that this research shows that language preferences are evolving, and that they will continue to research and test how different groups prefer to speak about autism.

These findings, and informal conversations, show me that there is not one way of describing autism that is going to be accepted, let alone universally liked. The autistic community are, at times, understandably divided in their preferences and some disagreements appear deeply entrenched. With some hesitation, I will adopt the term 'autistic' to describe our special learners within this chapter. However, and whatever way, I choose to describe our autistic learners it will not be accepted by some. I apologise for any antagonism my words cause, I will promise to keep learning also.

An individual autistic learner may present with a diverse range of needs and skills. To produce a single chapter and a range of RSE resources to meet the needs of all our special autistic learners is simply not feasible. There are many autistic/ASD specific RSE Schemes of Work out there for you to gauge and adapt for your specific needs. However, I will try to use this chapter to paint some helpful pointers and strategies, even though the brush may appear to be particularly wide.

RSE for our autistic learners will ideally increase their knowledge and understanding of their changing bodies and growing into adulthood, gender differences and similarities, public and private places and activities, relationships, sexual health and parenthood. This is not exhaustive but we should think about empowering our learners to develop relationships as well as keeping them safe from harm. RSE provision would include exploring different types of relationships, the development of our sexuality, puberty and reproduction. We would develop skills to identify risks associated with unhealthy relationships, unsafe sexual practice and understanding how to protect from sexually transmitted infections. RSE would also offer ways to prevent pregnancy as well as developing our understanding of the responsibilities that come with parenthood whilst considering attitudes and values regarding relationships and sexual health (Organization for Autism Research, 2020).

Ideally, RSE would develop a depth of knowledge and a range of skills to enable our learners to make their own informed decisions about their own sexuality and sexual behaviour. These skills would include communicating with others, assertiveness, assessing and avoiding risks, accessing information and advice and respecting themselves and others. That could seem daunting to many of us, in terms of designing learning opportunities, but that is what many of our special autistic learners require.

Autistic individuals, parents and professionals agree that issues related to sexuality, sexual health and understanding different types of relationships can be particularly confusing and stressful, because the subtleties of relationships are challenging in themselves. Any Relationships and Sex Education programme for our autistic learners must take autism into account. That seems a particularly obvious statement to make, but I have fallen into the trap of providing RSE that I *thought* would be understood only to have frustrated learners and the difficulty of reengaging and reimagining my teaching.

We often make assumptions as to the understanding of our learners, believing that certain social concepts that neurotypical learners would understand at a young age would also apply to them. For our special autistic learners, sometimes the social concepts are not intuitively learned. Our learners are often confused by 'public' and 'private' definitions and boundaries. Understanding who is a 'stranger' and who may become a 'friend' can understandably be confusing. This confusion can lead to a risk of abuse and exploitation if not dealt with sensitively (Organization for Autism Research, 2020).

Whatever the cognitive level our learners are accessing, being academically able does not mean a greater understanding of all things social. Consent, reading signals, uninvited physical touch, social boundaries, how our tolerance of certain behaviours change as we get older, may not be organically consumed by our autistic learners (Centre for Autism, 2016). We need to find ways of helping our learners to understand social norms and accepted societal rules. We also need to help the wider society understand that we do not all think the same way; and that fact is to be celebrated.

Some autistic learners often need longer to understand any changes in their lives. This is vitally important when considering when and how to introduce the concept of puberty. Puberty is a time that has long been associated with feelings of stress and anxiety, particularly for those with autism (Centre for Autism, 2016). We need to explore how and when to introduce certain aspects of puberty within RSE and how to deliver these difficult concepts. With our autistic learners often having literal interpretations of language we use they may take everything you say on face value and be confused by the information we share; 'periods', voice 'breaking' or 'wet' dreams for instance. For some of our learners understanding the appropriate and inappropriate touching of self and others during puberty exploration and beyond, including the where and when, can also be a difficult concept to navigate (Raising Children Network, 2020).

Why relationships and sex education is important

A report in 2015 by the BBC showed that over a period of just two years 4,748 reports of sexual abuse against adults with disabilities were reported in England. The data showed that 63% of the reported cases were against those with learning disabilities. Research from the US has also indicated that there are higher rates of abuse amongst autistic children than those without disabilities.

Kiranpreet Rehal, Department for Education (DfE) safeguarding project manager at the National Autistic Society details three reasons why this may be the case.

- Our special learners are more dependent on others to meet personal and intimate care needs.
- Our special learners are not always aware that what is happening to them is even wrong.
- Communication difficulties that prevent our special learners from expressing concerns about what is happening to them (Big Talk Education, 2020).

There are unfortunately far too many frightening reasons to see RSE as needing to be protective with a focus on our special learners' ability to understand and identify unwanted and inappropriate sexualised behaviour presented by others toward them, and of course it is essential we do so. We also need to rethink the content and strategies of our RSE provision to help keep our learners engaged and not simply frightened, in the hope that they can have the type of relationships they may want in the future. We need to find the balance between protecting and safeguarding our vulnerable special learners and upholding their human rights as sexual beings that will lead them to a future as fulfilled as we would wish for ourselves.

Our RSE provision for our autistic learners will obviously need to be designed to give them a clear framework of what is right and wrong; good touch, bad touch and necessary touch. It will need to cover the language they will need to tell a trusted person if something happens to them. We will also need to allow them the time to develop an understanding of the peculiarities of non-verbal communication. The social interaction and the subtleties of non-verbal communication that drive our relationships is often beyond what our special autistic learners can imagine. They can find it harder to understand other points of view, they also may not be able to identify when someone is interested in them or when someone is taking advantage of them (Organization for Autism Research, 2020).

When we were younger, trying to navigate what is appropriate and what is not, we may have relied heavily on our friends and their experiences; I know I certainly did. However, our autistic learners may not have access to an unsupervised friendship group to support them. They may not have the backing and support from family either, which means they are even more dependent on us as advocates to help them navigate this area of their life.

Some teaching tips

Consider where and when to begin. Our teaching which underpins Relationship and Sex Education should start as early as possible, be constantly reviewed, revisited and be part of life-long learning if it is to have the impact we would want. RSE does not have to be delivered as a planned 'session'. It is delivered in what we do and how we do it every day.

It is *all* about relationships.

Social stories are a good way to navigate and explore concepts of relationships with our learners. These stories can be adapted to the individual learners' need and level of understanding and can be used to support learning at home as well as school and residential environments. Other strategies and learning aids to support RSE for autistic learners, such as schedules and visual reminders that support the understanding of how to behave and respond in a given situation will also have their place.

We can help our autistic learners interpret social situations where they may be vulnerable through these Social Stories, outlining 'risky' and 'safe' scenarios. The information should be presented in a literal way, with no ambiguities, offering some understanding of a previously difficult situation or scenarios that may occur. By providing information about what might happen in a particular situation, and also providing some guidelines for behaviour, our hope is to reduce anxiety at these times and for our autistic leaners to have strategies to manage these situations (Big Talk, 2020). Roleplay, scripted, set situations, the use of T.V. and film clips of different scenarios can all be used to discuss appropriate responses.

How?

Our autistic learners are more likely than most to take things literally. We cannot rely on the usual talk to the class group and expect our learners to remember it, process what you have said, understand it and be able to put it into practice after one session. How can we show things visually and interactively, revisiting often, using a variety of interactive resources to make it more personal?

Social rules

Reading body language is often tricky for our autistic learners, as is understanding social norms and guidance that seem implicitly understood by most other young people. Our special learners need to gain experience of practicing social situations, even within role play sessions in the reassuring, safe school environment. We will need to offer on-going commentary and a narrative about peoples' body language, the social clues offered and how we can interpret them. Offer strategies, offer context.

For some of our autistic learners who are at a very early stage of development, more intensive individual support may be required to enhance awareness of others and develop joint attention. This may be through approaches such as Intensive Interaction, Floor time or Arts therapies.

When appropriate, elements can be integrated into our RSE provision. Strategies explored within the chapter on PMLD and SLD learners can also be adapted and used successfully (NAS, 2008).

Keeping safe

We know our autistic learners are more vulnerable than most to being exploited and encouraged to engage in unsuitable and unsafe sexual behaviours. However, sexual curiosity, sexualised talk and behaviour is entirely natural. We need to be aware of what normal behaviours are and what may be concerning behaviours. We cannot interpret every sexualised behaviour as a sign that a learner is doing something dangerous. Brook's 'Sexual Behaviours Traffic Light Tool' is helpful for these discussions and for some reassurance. However, privacy and consent do need to be regularly revisited and we need to refer to these terms in different contexts.

Another helpful resource is the NSPCC's 'P.A.N.T.S.' rule; Privates are private, Always remember your body belongs to you, No means no, Talk about secrets that upset you, Speak up, someone can help you.

There is also the 'Growing Up Safe' programme form Big Talk. This goes beyond the NSPCC's pants rule, as abusers may not only target this area of the body. It is particularly important to teach our autistic learners, who communicate in a literal way, that other areas of their body are also private.

> To do this we classify the four private areas of the body which we use to teach about good and bad touches, these include the chest and mouth area, in addition to the genital area and the bottom.
>
> (Big Talk, 2020)

Public, private and boundaries

We will need to explain the difference between private and public that is clear for our learners. Unfortunately, this is not as simple as it first appears. The distinction needs to be taught very early on and it needs to be consistent, despite occasional conflicts that may arise.

Be wary of using absolute examples; 'we do not take our clothes off in public' then take your learners to the public baths and expect them to change for swimming. 'Your bedroom is where you can touch yourself' then find out your learner shares a bedroom with a sibling. This subject of privacy could also extend to conversations about how to keep safe. We can teach which things are public and which are private, in terms of our bodies, places, actions and words through social stories, pictures and role play to build a strong concept of the two categories and what to do if someone else does something we do not like. We may also need to provide some guidelines about who to talk to when we are worried and have any concerns; for example, our parents and carers, our teacher or our support staff.

To deprive our learners of private and public boundaries is to leave them clueless as to what sorts of behaviour would be acceptable as an adult. Most of the incidents which lead to trouble for our autistic learners are 'boundary violations' that they do not fully understand (NAS, 2008).

If our learners start to touch other people (particularly private body parts), this needs to be addressed by the school and parents in a co-ordinated way. Some young people grow in to adults without this knowledge and some behaviours like exposing private body parts in public or touching other people's private body parts without consent, can lead to being charged under the Sexual Offences Act. And all because our learners have not been given opportunities to grasp the concept of boundaries.

There are also 'virtual' boundaries that some of our learners will need some support around. I know there are a lot of autistic learners blissfully sharing their numbers, their Facebook details and trying to gain 'virtual friends'. They will need to know that inappropriate social networking, certain mobile phone and internet use can also lead to risky situations and perhaps legal intervention if rules are not followed.

We understand our learners may want more privacy and independence as they grow up and their bodies change. We can develop the understanding of boundaries through explaining that that in order to give them more privacy, we will respect closed doors and that they should too

(Moxon, 2011). We will also need to offer clarity about 'private' and 'public' rooms and places and how they should restrict masturbation to private rooms only and to 'home' (school is a public place and we do not masturbate in public).

To clarify this you may encourage parents to put a 'private' sign on the door of their child's private place in the house, for example their bedroom. This will establish a rule within our learners' home that people should knock on all bedroom doors before entering. Everyone who visits the home need to be made aware of these rules. This concept can be reinforced at school, without giving our learners the message that masturbating at school is fine.

Both parents and teachers need to ensure that our learners understand that if a room says 'private' on it, it does not necessarily mean that this is a suitable place for any sort of sexual activity (National Children's Bureau, Sex Education Forum, 2004).

Puberty, or the start of adolescence, is now taking place earlier than for previous generations, and is earlier in girls than boys. As already accepted, many of our special learners are not taught about puberty until it happens. This can lead to fear, misunderstanding and sometimes harmful behaviour. Autistic girls and boys may find the mood swings and physical changes at this stage very hard to manage (Moxon, 2011).

Our learners need to learn about their body parts, including private body parts and their correct names to enable a better understanding about their own body, how it feels, how they change, how they grow and the differences between boy's and girl's bodies.

Our autistic learners should be learning about body parts from a very early age. If they learn 'penis', 'testicles' and 'vulva', 'vagina' at the same time as 'hands, feet and head', they will not see these words as any different. The words are not sexual or embarrassing to any child, they are just the correct biological terms. If our special autistic learners know the correct words it is easier for them to communicate in a matter of fact way that they are sore, or where someone has touched them. If a learner has limited vocabulary, or communication difficulties, too many words can be confusing. It is then better to just have the one correct name (NAS, 2008; Big Talk, 2020; Organization for Autism Research, 2020).

If we support an autistic learner who has profound learning difficulties we can employ sensory games to enable body and self-awareness; using silk scarves and items that make a certain sounds. When they move, each body part can make a different sound; for example, feet on gravel, side on 'whoopee cushion', head on foil, arms in shells, bottom on bubble wrap (National Children's Bureau, Sex Education Forum, 2004).

Puberty and change

Many autistic learners have a fear about changes generally, so changes to their body can cause a lot of anxiety if they are not prepared. We are all different and we all change. Prepare our learners for inevitable changes and normal differences. We can work with parents and carers to develop their child's understanding. Parents and carers can carry out one-to-one work, encourage their son or daughter to explore their own bodies in a safe environment in their own home. In their bedroom, in front of a mirror. At bedtime or at bath time. Parents can also use this time to check understanding of the RSE topics being discussed in school (Moxon, 2011; Autism Victoria, 2006).

Understanding about differences between people, including noticing changes in themselves and others, can provide some foundation for learning about gender, age and body awareness. It is perfectly normal for us to have similarities as well as differences. Use family photos, even photos of yourself at different stages of your life, use visual timelines and photos of your learners when they were younger. If a learner shows an awareness of how older people are physically different to them, this is another good starting point for discussion. Noticing a beard, breasts or underarm hair is a very tangible, visual sign for our autistic learners and can present clear differences or similarities of others to themselves (NAS, 2008).

An activity we can do both at school and at home is to produce a visual basic body outline and label all of the various body parts. Some learners will relate better to realistic images of bodies and body parts rather than cartoons and line drawings, so use photographs if we need to. In each area, we could highlight the various changes that will occur; from increases in height and muscle tone to growth of genitals, breasts and pubic hair. This can also start conversations about when we get older we will have to be aware of the importance of personal hygiene.

Personal hygiene

With changes to our bodies, we need to understand our personal hygiene routines are important. Young men and women need to take extra care with their hygiene. If our autistic learners are prepared for the changes that will happen they can also be introduced to new items they will use, like a shaver, deodorant or sanitary products. Hopefully as our special learners approach puberty they will already have an established routine for washing themselves, their clothes and their bedding. They may already use a tick-list or schedule that they work through to ensure they have completed each stage in their morning routine schedule. If this is the case then perhaps it can be adjusted to include the use of deodorants and shower gels, showering every day, shaving every other day (NAS, 2008; Moxon, 2011).

Early introduction to the variety of personal care items, before they become necessary, may allow our autistic learners to explore and identify any unwelcome sensory issues. Some autistic learners will have heightened sense of smell or touch which can make some aspects of personal hygiene unwelcome. The feel of water from a shower, the pressure, the temperature, the smell of particular shower gels or shampoos and the texture of some towels may all have an impact on their sensory wellbeing (Autism Victoria, 2006).

Not only will the actual processes of personal hygiene need to be explained, for example, how to shave, but the reasons behind them will also need to be made clear. Sometimes our autistic learners have difficulties understanding the social rules behind certain activities. A morning shower may be seen as a part of a normal, well-practiced daily routine. Therefore, if this routine changes in anyway, like introducing a shaver, shaving foam or hair conditioner, they may choose not have a shower. This could obviously have an impact on their personal hygiene and possibly their relationships with their peers. It will help if our autistic learners know *why* keeping clean is important (NAS, 2008).

We sweat more when we reach puberty. Most people don't like the smell of sweat, so we wash regularly. This will help to keep us healthy. It is also a good thing to do for others.

Masturbation

Firstly, to be clear; masturbation is natural and a normal activity for all sexual beings. We should not have a 'no masturbation' policy, but we can have a 'not here' view. The touching of oneself and masturbation in public are issues for many autistic boys and girls. Yes, it can be embarrassing for other people, but that is not an excuse to highlight this particular behaviour as 'bad' or 'unacceptable'.

Issues concerning masturbation normally occur around the time of puberty, but younger learners also masturbate and adults who have not been taught about boundaries may also masturbate in public. Now, we understand that it is a natural behaviour and that our special learners require support around the 'where and when' but for the general society that understanding is not there. It can be classed as an offence to masturbate in public and can have serious consequences for the individual involved (Moxon, 2011). It is not just the legal consequences that should concern us though. If we have reinforced the concept that our learners can us the toilets at school to masturbate, what have we inadvertently promoted? What are the usual visual cues we are offering when directing our learners to the toilet? A toilet sign that is the same, or very similar, to the signage used for public toilets? The truth could be that seeing that sign in public means that it is okay to masturbate there.

For some of our learners masturbation has never been discussed, some are ashamed to talk about masturbation, some have the impression reinforced that it is somehow wrong. Some even think it is against the law. Information about private touching and masturbation needs to be available to all our learners as part of Relationships and Sex Education so they know it is normal and not wrong. This area of learning will crossover the aspects of public and private and will need to be reinforced and revisited as often as possible (Bennie, 2018).

Again, support from home and school will encourage and enhance the understanding of where and when.

- Social stories can help teach about appropriate behaviour in appropriate places.
- Use pictures, photos and symbols to show public places where it is not okay to masturbate and private places at home where it is okay to masturbate.

- Use consistent signs, symbols and responses from school staff and parents to say 'not here' when it occurs.
- Allowing the young person private time at home to explore their bodies during bath time or bedtime and removing restrictive clothing or pads.

(NAS, 2008; Raising Children Network, 2020)

Again, we will need to reinforce the messages about the importance of personal hygiene and how to keep ourselves and our environment clean after masturbation.

Periods

Many of our special autistic learners are not taught about periods until they happen. This often leads to confusion, misunderstanding and real fear. Previously we have spoken about young learners believing that they were bleeding to death.

We all cope better when we have some awareness of what will be happening. This may not always help with certain deep laid anxieties, but if we know in advance and have the support of others we trust it certainly makes life easier. Before puberty, and periods start, girls should gain an understanding that their bodies will change as they grow and they will bleed once a month. This is nothing to worry about, it is normal. For some autistic girls the knowing of *why* will certainly help (see Chapter 4).

- Introduce information about periods before they happen.
- Social stories can be developed about how to manage a period. Also 'I Can Change My Pad' by Me-and-Us publishers can be helpful.
- Keeping a diary or calendar to show when a learner has her period.
- Our learners have their own instructions to remind them when and how to change their sanitary wear.
- Keep a container in the toilet at home and one in a toilet at school with sanitary wear and the same instructions.

Sensory sensitivities can be overwhelming for our autistic learners; tags in clothes, socks too tight, certain smells, variety of lighting can all have a significant impact on their wellbeing. Sensory sensitivities can have a dramatic impact on relationships. Sometimes that means certain touch, intimacy and sexual sensations can be deregulators and unmanageable.

Our learners may actively seek or avoid intimacy, they be over-aware or unaware of personal space, body language and their body odour and personal hygiene. Some of our learners may have strong reactions to perfume and deodorant. By understanding and being aware of this we can support our learners with their individual personal and interpersonal needs; and all will be different (McCann, 2017).

Build up confidence – self-esteem

Helping our special learners to feel positive about themselves and their abilities is a crucial aspect of supporting them through their school life and especially through puberty (Hartman, 2013). Having support to create an individual style, of whatever kind, can help to develop resilience and make it easier to cope with the ups and downs of moving through puberty into adulthood.

A Relationships Circle (or Relationship Target) can be drawn and developed to help our learners to map which people are in their lives, what their relationship is, and what would be appropriate or inappropriate behaviours with each person. From this they can identify different people in their life and the various roles they play; 'who can I tell about my period?' 'Who can I talk to about having an erection?' 'Who will help explain the differences between public and private?' (Moxon, 2011).

Sexual orientation

Some of our autistic learners may not be aware of sexual orientation. Some will be unsure of their sexual orientation. Others may know that they are lesbian, gay or bisexual but worry about this. They may be transgender but do not have the vocabulary or awareness to express that view. Awareness of our sexual orientation usually starts during puberty and teenage years but can begin earlier. It can be difficult for all of us. Many of our special learners have never been taught that people can be lesbian, gay, bisexual or transgender (Löfgren-Mårtenson, 2011).

We need to be aware of the importance of addressing this aspect of sexuality so that our learners understand that whatever their sexual orientation, it does not change them as individuals.

A high percentage of our special learners, autistic or otherwise, for whatever reason, are sheltered from the fact that same sex relationships exist. This information needs to be part of their learning about people and the make-up of their own community.

Different relationships are okay, and there are many different relationships in any community. If a learner decides that they are lesbian, gay, bisexual or transgender, or are uncertain, they need to have the confidence to know that they do not need to be worried or frightened; we are there for them.

Co-occurring autism spectrum disorder and gender dysphoria

The topic of Gender Dysphoria (GD) and its connection to autism is gaining focus. Dr. Mark Stokes from La Trobe University in Melbourne, Australia completed one of many research projects examining this topic. The results from the international study found a higher percentage of those with autism have gender distress, ambivalence and/or neutrality.

When compared to controls, autistic individuals demonstrated significantly higher sexual diversity, reported gender-identities incongruent with their biological sex, and higher gender-dysphoric symptomatology (Bennie, 2017).

There are a number of other research projects that conclude that there is a link between being autistic and having gender confusion (Strang et al., 2018; Van Der Miesen et al., 2016). Does that link mean that our autistic learners who are confused over their gender are either females trapped in male bodies or males trapped in female bodies? Is the conclusion that there needs to be appropriate Gender Dysphoria related treatment provided; even if it requires surgery?

Dr. Kathleen Levinstein who has a daughter who went through surgery to reassign her gender wrote; *'A movement telling young people on the spectrum that the identity issues they will struggle with as they grow-up can be solved through sex change or "gender questioning" is cruel. Surface changes in clothes and pronouns will solve nothing and only exacerbate their suffering. What they need is not biological alteration, but greater acceptance and understanding of their neurobiological differences'* (Levinstein, 2016).

In 'Initial Clinical Guidelines for Co-Occurring Autism Spectrum Disorder and Gender Dysphoria or Incongruence in Adolescents' (Strang et al., 2018), one conclusion is that the diagnosis of ASD should not exclude an adolescent from also receiving a Gender Dysphoria diagnosis and, when agreed, appropriate Gender Dysphoria related treatment. The research goes on to state that clinicians and parents sometimes dismiss Gender Dysphoria as a trait of autism; as an over-focused interest.

Although in some cases GD symptoms appear to stem from ASD symptoms, many autistic youngsters have persistent Gender Dysphoria independent of their ASD. Similarly, an undiagnosed ASD can be missed if a clinician or parents view an adolescent's social difficulties as stemming from GD-related challenges alone. The concern is that parents or clinicians may resist further assessments after receiving one diagnosis, whether it would be ASD or GD, if they view all symptoms through the lens of the initial diagnosis (Strang et al., 2018).

Between 8 and 10 percent of children and adolescents seen at gender clinics around the world meet the diagnostic criteria for autism, according to studies carried out over the past five years, while roughly 20 percent have autistic traits such as impaired social and communication skills or intense focus and attention to detail. Some seek treatment for their gender dysphoria already knowing or suspecting they are autistic, but the majority of people in these studies had never sought nor received an autism diagnosis (Bennie, 2017).

As previously stated, I would advocate for anyone to be who they wish to be, and need to be, to feel complete. As already confessed, I do not have the knowledge to come to any conclusion; in fact I am not the only one; in 'Gender dysphoria and autism spectrum disorder: A narrative review' (Van Der Miesen et al., 2016) the research states that Gender Dysphoria and ASD were found to co-occur frequently – sometimes characterised by atypical presentation of Gender Dysphoria, '*which makes a correct diagnosis and determination of treatment options for Gender Dysphoria difficult'*.

Despite these challenges there are several case reports describing gender affirming treatment of co-occurring Gender Dysphoria in autistic adolescents. Various underlying hypotheses for the link between Gender Dysphoria and ASD were suggested, but almost all of them lack evidence. So, not a lot of solid evidence to back up any or either side of the 'argument'; in time I am sure there will be, but whatever the drive, the decisions need to be convinced by clear knowledge.

As psychiatrist Martin L. Kutscher writes in 'Kids in The Syndrome Mix' (2007), '*Many women who have Asperger's syndrome have described to psychologists and in autobiographies how they sometimes think they have a male rather than a female brain, having a greater understanding and appreciation of the interests, thinking, and humour of boys during their early school years'.*

Let us as professionals, with a Duty of Care to do what is in our learners' best interests, not make hasty decisions, or allow others to do so. Let us build relationships with other professionals, with families, let us build trusting relationships with our special learners.

Relationships

For most students the best part about coming to school is seeing and spending time with friends. For students who struggle to make social connections, however, going to school can be a lonely and frustrating experience'

(Kluth et al., 2003)

Throughout our lives we are involved in and develop many different relationships with the vast number of people that cross our paths. Some of these will be short-lived and perhaps superficial, others may grow into lasting friendships or loving relationships. For many of our autistic learners they will want to have a 'boyfriend' or 'girlfriend' but they can find that aspect of their life difficult to navigate. Going back to the social skills aspect of RSE, in all situations communication is the key to linking people and developing relationships.

Those of us working in schools can provide an environment where the development of relationship and communication skills can be explored in a safe way. Through Social Stories, through role play and drama activities we can discover the variety of social situations that our autistic learners have to adapt to over time.

The social and emotional skills associated with our relationships have direct influence on our outcomes as adults. We should appreciate the need of providing a social curriculum as well as an academic one, especially for our autistic learners. The fact that Relationships and Sex Education is now statutory subject will help; the next step will be to have Personal Social and Health Education (and the other variants) become statutory subjects in all schools.

Exploring our sexuality can be a very positive experience and autistic people have sexual feelings, needs and behaviour just like everybody else. As previously mentioned, I have spoken to many autistic adults who wished they were given opportunities to understand the 'rules of relationships' during their school life. Hatton et al. (2010) interviewed autistic learners at school, many of whom also said they would have benefited from being taught more about how relationships work when they were younger.

Providing helpful relationship education at the right time is crucial for making sure our autistic learners are prepared for this aspect of adult life, prepared and safe. When we reach the legal age of consent to sexual activity, which is 16 in the UK for both homosexual and heterosexual sex, we may choose to be sexually active; so perhaps will many of our special learners. It is not possible for others to stop young men and women from being sexually active by ignoring the fact it may happen.

Surely better as an informed choice, based on the knowledge of staying safe within a healthy relationship. By denying privacy, not discussing sex or relationships, we will just encourage distrust and confusion for our autistic youngsters.

We become sexually mature approximately up to five years before we reach the emotional maturity to make important decisions. I am sure we can all remember making some very unwise decisions at that point in our life. Or am I the only one?

Making friends and developing relationships that may become intimate is a key developmental life stage for us all. Social understanding and development is based on our ever expanding experience, and our autistic learners have fewer opportunities for social interactions than their typically developing peers (Moxon, 2011).

Our special learners are growing up at a time where information is easily accessible, a culture in which most media offer images and messages suggesting that everybody is having sex. It is not only accepted, but expected behaviour. We need to demonstrate to our special autistic learners that engaging in sex is not compulsory; it is a choice, a decision. One that is hopefully based on sound knowledge.

Relationships are exciting, so how can we support our autistic learners to overcome the confusion and enjoy the experience? Our autistic teenagers have the same desire as the rest of us have at that time in our lives. Some will have an urge to find intimacy and companionship, others may not.

Some of our learners will find it difficult to understand and interact appropriately to the many different types of relationships.

What is flirting?

The Birds and the Bees project was designed by Dr. Sarah Curtiss, who is an assistant professor specializing in special education, to support autistic learners to socially interact and understand the unwritten social rules and potential social pitfalls. It enables our learners to gain a better understanding of the consequences of their actions and to control impulses when faced with unfamiliar situations or changes in routine.

Our learners need to gain a deeper understanding that other people have thoughts, feelings and intentions that are different to their own. Just because we may feel deeply for someone else, it does not mean the feeling is reciprocated. How do we show to our learners that a strong interest in another person can be unwanted and interpreted as intimidating?

It is important to support our autistic learners to develop the necessary skills and strategies that will support them as they develop relationships and understand their own sexuality, this includes how to:

- Understand the value of friendships and how some friendships can evolve into more intimate relationships
- Reduce confusion and uncertainty

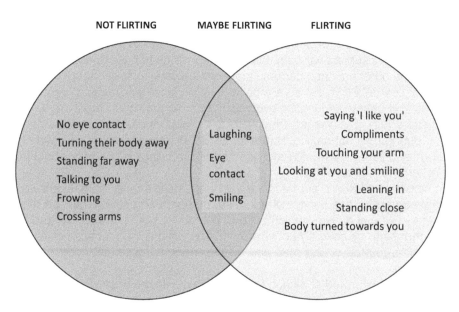

Figure 7.1 Signs of flirting.

- Increase knowledge, self-advocacy and assertiveness
- Develop confidence, self-esteem and self-worth
- Be aware of and enjoy their sexuality
- Behave safely, responsibly and appropriately within relationships
- Promote health and safety
- Communicate about feelings, relationships and sexual matters
- Understand sexual health and associated risks
- Be able to access help and support
- Have an awareness of what abuse may look like and develop the skills to enable them to protect themselves against abuse and against abusing others (Curtiss et al., 2014)

Awesomely autistic

A final word on this chapter from my friend Tigger Pritchard. He is an Autism and Pathological Demand Avoidance advocate, trainer and consultant. He is also 'awesomely autistic.'

If a Neurodiverse individual is to have a happy, intimate, close and wonderful relationship with someone who is Neurotypical, some core relationship areas must be paramount. Every relationship needs certain areas which have to be at the core, and then built upon these as time goes by and the relationship continues.

However, if you are in a relationship with someone who is awesomely Neurodivergent, Autistic let's say, you need to have some very strong shared core areas, and to continually revisit them, carefully, lovingly, again and again.

Communication; gain an understanding of the Autistic person from themselves, not necessarily from a book or film! Understand their sensory issues, and communication style, oh have I said that already?

Communication is key; talk, write, video, sing, post it notes, text, sign, whatever you both agree upon at certain times, but please do communicate. This is not easy, but it is so important. It offers the chance for an Autistic person to really say, "This is me", openly and with vulnerability.

Then to have an open, receptive partner to listen, learn and to understand, and to accept you as you. Oh it is wonderful, not easy at all, but so worth it.

With an agreed process of communication, (don't be afraid to think outside the box here), then other areas can be discussed, sensory issues, physical intimacy. A misunderstanding in these areas could lead to great anxiety, for both. With communication, the ability to learn, to compromise, to understand, to reduce anxiety and from there to support the growth of the relationship is hugely possible, positive and achievable.

There is sadly a misconception that Neurodivergent individuals cannot form relationships; yet another add to a very long list of other misconceptions. All these misconceptions need to be addressed and accepted views changed. As ever, approaches and ideas from the neurodiverse world, when applied to all, can pay huge dividends...

Every individual, regardless of race, religion, sexuality, culture, beliefs and neurotype, has the right to love and to be loved.'

8 Planning ahead

*Securing sustained development
in relationships and sex education*

It will not necessarily be a quick fix; it may very well be a struggle to have introduced quality Relationships and Sex Education (RSE) into your establishment. It can be easy to get disheartened and frustrated with others who do not 'get it' though. We need to keep encouraging, keep demonstrating and keep positive; this is all for our learners.

'We can improve our relationships with others by leaps and bounds if we become encouragers instead of critics' (Meyer, 2020).

How can we ensure that the outstanding Relationships and Sex Education provision that we have put in place will survive changes of staff, RSE leadership responsibilities or a schools' status? We have developed shared RSE responsibility with other stakeholders within school and our wider community and this has ensured continuity and progression of quality of our RSE provision.

Creating a working party of staff, governors, parents, learners and external partners has ensured RSE is an integrated, natural part of our school life. Reviewing and adapting the parents' RSE courses constantly has ensured relevance and manageability. Planning ahead so that parental involvement eventually leads to the workshops being delivered by the parents and carers themselves will be our long-term aim.

The conclusion has to be that if we had a 'wish list' of stakeholder engagement, tailored staff training, quality resources, relevant long term planning and parental support in place then we will see measurable progress in the skills and knowledge of our special learners when it comes to Relationships and Sex Education. This would include; understanding themselves as sexual beings, understanding different types of relationships, including what constitutes a healthy relationship, growing from children to adults and the changes to their emotional and physical self and, of course, self-advocacy and keeping themselves safe.

Is that where our job ends though? Is our job to ensure our special learners have the knowledge and skills to have the best future they can achieve? Ultimately what we do is strive to ensure that our special learners will have the best life that they can; to be who they aspire to be. The real key to securing sustained development in RSE is to see the long-term goal, the big picture, if you will. Relationships and Sex Education needs to start as early as possible, for it to be based on rights and responsibilities and for it to be understood that for our special learners it will be lifelong learning.

Our learners will eventually leave their schools, possibly head to a college and maybe attend a day centre. If they are really lucky they may gain a supported work placement.

Transition from school to college

Further Education colleges, sixth form colleges, 16–19 academies and independent special schools in England, approved under Section 41 of the Children and Families Act 2014, have duties under the Equality Act 2010. In particular, they must not discriminate against disabled children or young people and they must make reasonable adjustments to prevent them being placed at a substantial disadvantage.

> *This duty is anticipatory – it requires thought to be given in advance to what disabled young people might require and what adjustments might need to be made to prevent that disadvantage.*
>
> (DoE and DoH Social Care, 2014)

For our special learners their future study programmes should focus on opportunities, which prepares them well for independent living, being healthy adults and participating in society.

...support to prepare for independent living, including exploring what decisions young people want to take for themselves and planning their role in decision making as they become older. This should also include discussing where the child or young person wants to live in the future, who they want to live with and what support they will need...
This also includes support in developing and maintaining friendships and relationships.

(DoE and DoH Social Care, 2014)

Relationships and Sex Education must continue as an integral part of our special learners' further education. The legislation is clear. If RSE is not part of the curriculum I would suggest that the college is working against the SEN Code of Practice (2014, updated 2020) as well as The Equality Act (2010).

And what would this RSE curriculum look like for our special students and young adults?

Relevant RSE for our special learners has a number of additional, unforeseen, benefits that include delaying the onset of first sexual experience and increasing the likelihood of contraception use. In addition, RSE, when done well, can help to generate a positive sexual identity and foster respectful relationships. (Blanchett et al., 2002) It can also develop knowledge and understanding of reproductive and sexual health, sexual development, gender identity and relationship formation. It is easy to show a film clip made for SEN learners about the biology of sex, but is that what our learners really need?

FPV [Family Planning Victoria] regularly sees clients with intellectual disabilities for one-to-one education programs, who have sexualised behaviours of concern deemed to be in part, or wholly, as a result of a lack of adequate sexuality education. Individuals with intellectual disability are over-represented as victims and offenders of sexually-based crimes in the justice system, primarily because of knowledge-deficits regarding sexually appropriate behaviour and consent.

(Meaney-Tavares et al., 2012)

By denying our special learners quality RSE, we are *knowingly* allowing them to become vulnerable within a society that will not see RSE as important for our special learners, because they are seen to be different to us (Craft, 1987; Rohleder, 2010). However, when it comes to behaviour that may be classed as sexually inappropriate, they are then punished the same as us; '*Labelling of some acts as sexually abusive, which plainly were not, and to the labelling of some people as sexual abusers, who plainly were not*' (Fairbairn, 2010). I do not apologise for using that quote twice.

Despite the social isolation that many of our teenaged special learners face, unsurprisingly repeated studies have shown that many of them would like to have a sexual life, get married and have children. Our learners have fewer opportunities to socialise, let alone live with their peers, making it difficult to achieve their life goals.

The undeniable truth is that many of our special learners will become isolated from society, making it almost impossible to find partners. This stigma can lead individuals to internalise concepts of asexuality which could negatively impact on their confidence, desire, and ability to find a partner while distorting their overall sexual self-awareness (Darry et al., 2010).

Many are excluded or may feel excluded from social activities, therefore, as a way to overcome these barriers, they may develop behaviours that could heighten risk. Behaviours such as seeking out sexual activity without being prepared or with insufficient protection or even non-consensual. For some of our learners, sexual relations may signify being attractive, loved, chosen, even if affection is not involved (Bononi et al., 2009).

Any Relationships and Sex Education curriculum needs to move from focussing on the biological aspects of sexuality to a curriculum that focusses on developing a healthy sexual identity, respectful relationships, safer sexual practices, informed decision-making, protective behaviours and sex in the context of intimacy, desire and pleasure (Family Planning Victoria, 2015).

"When we love and respect people, revealing to them their value, they can begin to come out from behind the walls that protect them." Jean Vanier

There are professionals who advocate for a completely different way of focusing on RSE. Those that believe in the equal rights of our special learners to make and break relationships, to have a sexual life, and a 'sexual voice'.

> *There is limited consideration of the importance of pleasure in published discussions of sexuality and intellectual disability. The literature is dominated by conversations about the need for sex education, vulnerability to sexual exploitation, capacity to consent, and protection/safeguarding. Of course, this is essential and necessary, but there is plenty of room for more discourse about pleasure, sensuality, and feeling good.*
>
> (Alexander et al., 2017)

These conversations can be hard for professionals to have within public services. Parents and carers may feel uncomfortable about raising these issues with other people within the support system. Sexuality as an integral part of all our lives, denying these conversations prohibits sexual expression for our special learners as they grow into adulthood (Alexander et al., 2017).

Pleasure

Pleasure is connected to the richness of our sensual self. The connection to our sense of touch, taste, sight, hearing, smell and proprioception. We experience pleasure in eating good food, smelling freshly cooked bread, walking along a beach between sand and sea on a sunny, clear day, listening to our favourite music, socialising with our favourite people, and taking in the picture of a sunset. These connections are essential to us being human. Sexuality and sexual expression are connected to our humanness, and integral to the experience of pleasure. For our special learners pleasure may not be seen as important to anyone but them. In their daily lives, there is a distinct lack of talk and encouraged understanding about pleasure and that fact can lead to an 'experiential poverty' (Alexander et al., 2017).

Mental capacity and sex

The five principles of the Mental Capacity Act (MCA) and how they could relate to sex:

- Assume capacity: people with learning disabilities can have sex and relationships;
- Support people to make their own decisions: provide sex education;
- People can make unwise choices: a bad relationship is a mistake we can all make;
- If someone lacks capacity the decision must be in their best interests: assess capacity to consent to sex;
- Try to limit restrictions on the person's rights and freedom: where an individual lacks capacity to consent to sex it may not always be in his or her best interests to stop opportunities for sexual contact.

I am in no way pretending to know the details of the law when it comes to The Mental Capacity Act and Sex, however I feel should share the eloquent view of Lorraine Curry, who is both a social worker and professional lead for the MCA, on the changes to law in light of recent judgements and legislative changes.

Of all cases involving the decision to consent to sex, which has required that the relevant information that the individual should be able to understand, retain and use or weigh is:

- the mechanics of the act;
- the possibility of pregnancy in heterosexual sex;
- the possibility of sexually transmitted infection and
- that the person could say yes or no to sex (Currie, 2020).

Considering the other person's consent

However, the decisions were not based on mutual capacity and did not include consideration of the other person's consent. The new ruling was that all of the above is considered – as well as;

- the fact that the other person must have the capacity to consent to the sexual activity and must in fact consent before and throughout the sexual activity.

Whether it is as easy for us mere mortals to grapple with capacity to consent to sex versus capacity to engage in sex I don't know. But I do know this: all social workers will have been driven to distraction by an assessment of capacity for sex, where the bar is so low and rights are so high that they can't not find the person to have capacity and yet they know the risks of acting on that capacity are huge.

(Currie, 2020)

The court has to balance three principles, in relation to sex and capacity:

1. Autonomy; defined in article 1 of the United Nations Convention of the Rights of Persons with Disabilities as 'to promote, protect and ensure the full and equal enjoyment of all human rights and fundamental freedoms by all persons with disabilities, and to promote respect for their inherent dignity'.
2. Protection; people do require protection when they are placed in particularly vulnerable circumstances and situations.
3. That sexual relations between two people can only take place with the full and ongoing consent of both parties.

The principals of autonomy and protection have challenged social workers like Curry for 13 years. The question she poses is, '*does it help to now make the decision active rather than abstract? No longer to assess capacity to consent to sex, but to assess capacity to engage in sex which clearly involves the consent of the partner*' (Currie, 2020).

Rights and responsibilities

How does our RSE provision highlight our special learners' rights or their responsibilities? If our RSE is not rights-based we will not give our learners the skills they need to be part of any community.

They will pass an age milestone and acquire rights they didn't have the day before and that they do not know how to utilise, benefit from or put into practice safely. By starting our RSE provision from the earliest possible age, with a rights-based approach, is the only way forward. To do this differently for our special learners than we would with any other young people is unacceptable (Currie, 2020).

Capacity within intimate relationships is about consenting to engage in sex; it is about respecting the rights of others and knowing our responsibilities. How do we demonstrate this when the other person may say 'no' or say 'stop'?

Most of all I hope there will be much better education and training and preparation for life.

(Currie, 2020)

Transition to adulthood

The special learners you are supporting now will eventually become adults. They will remain special, as we all do, hopefully they will remain lifelong learners. Some are going to be extremely close to that milestone. What will their adult life be like I wonder?

Thankfully there are examples of residential care settings that actively advocate for their residents' human rights and right to privacy. Like those beacons of quality RSE providing schools, one would hope the best practice demonstrated in these homes could be shared more widely.

Things are changing for adults with learning disabilities, we are told. I wonder how quickly? Seven years ago 80% of adults with learning disabilities were living in independent sector residential care, with smaller numbers living in adult placements, local authority residential care homes or nursing care (Emmerson, 2013). The level of residential care provided varied in different areas. The report 'Transforming Care' (2013) that investigated abuse in a large residential homes, reported that over 3,000 people were still living in larger medical units or hospitals known as 'Assessment and Treatment Units' (DoH, 2013 cited by SEAD, 2015).

In 2001, 'Valuing People', a government White Paper called for an end to long stay hospitals. However, the last long stay hospital did not close until 2009 and in some areas, new private sector hospitals have opened. In 2009, another White Paper, 'Valuing People Now, an update on progress' said that people with learning/intellectual disabilities should be able to choose where they live. The report also stated that like everyone else, people with learning/intellectual disabilities 'want and need personal and sexual relationships' (SEAD, 2015).

Our special learners have the right to respect for private, home and family life [Human Rights Act 1998, Article 8 (1); United Nations 2006, Article 22]. The Convention on the Rights of Persons with Disabilities (United Nations, 2006) directs organisations to

> *Take effective and appropriate measures to eliminate discrimination against persons with disabilities in all matters relating to marriage, family, parenthood and relationships, on an equal basis with others'*
>
> (Article 23)

Does that play out in the homes where all our special learners now live? Many residential group settings for people with learning difficulties do not provide individuals with the private space in which they can explore their sexual relationships in a safe and dignified manner (Choice Support, 2020). This smacks of a lack of 'appropriate measures' to eliminate discrimination. Not respecting private spaces, due to our choices or our embarrassment, is to deny our fellow sexual beings their human rights.

Many individuals with learning disabilities who lack privacy, venture to isolated public or semi-private spaces to be sexually active. This obviously places the already vulnerable at considerable risk. Surely a self-advocacy driven policy guidance must be developed which requires residential services to review their practice to ensure that they accommodate residents' need – and human right – for privacy, whilst supporting them to lead safe sexual relationships (Hollomotz, 2009).

Supported Loving is a human rights-based campaign hosted by the simply wonderful *Choice Support*. They believe people with learning disabilities and/or autism should be able to enjoy the same sexual and romantic freedoms as everyone else.

Supported Loving started by highlighting the importance of good support for our special learners and adults with additional needs to form and maintain close relationships. They want to make changes to legislation, to society's views and develop opportunities to help make love a reality for everyone. Supported Loving's goals are to ensure that

- sexuality and relationships are a mandatory focus in Care Quality Commission (CQC) inspections in the Key Lines of Enquiry
- training on sexuality and relationships is provided to all social care staff
- people with learning disabilities and/or autism are aware of their sexual rights

Dr Claire Bates, who is an honorary research associate at the University of Kent's Tizard Centre, set up Supported Loving in 2017, as a response to her PhD exploring relationships for adults with learning disabilities. She found that relationships were important to people, but often they relied on staff support to start and continue. Claire continues to research relationships and sexuality, identifying the barriers many people with learning disabilities and/or autism face in this area (Choice Support, 2020).

> *Supported Loving isn't about glib answers to simple issues – it's about having an open discussion about how to provide good support in complex situations.*
>
> (Choice Support, 2020)

Our special learners must be acknowledged as sexual human beings, and have access to education, information and resources to make informed choices about their sexuality and reproductive and sexual health. In short we all need to gain an understanding of the given rights of our special learners to be able to exert their human right to be able to have fulfilling relationships as sexual beings.

We should all support the principles that our special learners have the right to:

- respect for their human worth and dignity as individuals
- realise their individual capacities for physical, social, emotional and intellectual development
- services support their attaining a reasonable quality of life in a way that supports their family unit and their full participation in society
- participate actively in the decisions that affect their lives, including the development of policies, programs and services
- any necessary support, and access to information, to enable them to participate in decisions that affect their lives
- receive services in a way that results in the minimum restriction of their rights and opportunities

Our homes have rules that do not allow our partners to sleep in our bedrooms. But there should be ways around them. Especially couples who have been together for a long time are upset by those rules. We want to do in our home whatever we like to do. That is what other people do. We want privacy and a right to sexual lives.

(Hollomotz, 2009)

From the perspective of adults with learning disabilities, there are obviously mixed experiences and messages, with some having positive experiences of being able to experience dating and supported relationships while others feel confused about what constitutes 'acceptable' behaviours and what would be considered 'acceptable' within a random range of set boundaries.

Adults with learning disabilities want access to education regarding the expression of their sexuality, advocacy, and support to understand their rights and responsibilities; this also includes protection from exploitation and abuse (Schaafsma et al., 2015). Families and paid carers also require access to education and training regarding the sexuality of their family member with learning disabilities (Ward et al., 2014).

Whereas some small changes have taken place, the prevailing experience is of restriction. There is a need for greater discussion of the complex issues regarding relationships and sexuality at a societal and policy level. '*Societal attitudes and perceptions are driven by education and knowledge, if there is no exposure to sexuality and disability, it follows suit that society would have a narrow understanding of these*' (Darry et al., 2010).

Is it simply down to a lack of exposure I wonder, or down to our society's attitude and ambivalence? (Rohleder, 2010)

Choosing to hide from our societal duties, by ignoring the attitudes of many in our own communities towards our special learners; hiding from our duty of care as professionals by choosing to ignore the parts of the curriculum and parts of legislation that we deem unnecessary, is shameful.

I started my Relationships and Sex Education journey looking at how we could improve RSE within my school at that time. I have ended this part of the journey unfortunately convinced that this is a larger issue than simply not having suitable resources for our special learners; it is all about attitudes and the lack of will to address relationships and sex for our special learners and those with learning disabilities. The ambivalence that Rohleder writes about appears to lie heavy.

Perhaps there is something much deeper here that might help in explaining this continued devaluing of people with learning disabilities. One might be forgiven for thinking that the more things change the more they stay the same, and that it may just be that one of the Emperors new items of clothing - the policy of inclusion - is gradually unwinding - laying bare some of its naïve assumptions. Perhaps it is timely to ask whether we will ever see a national debate in the UK as to a need for a fundamental review into current central social policy to establish whether the current agendas for people with learning disabilities and their families are serving their best interests or the interest of those who purport them.

(Gates, 2012)

So, nine years on from Professor Bob Gates' reflections, we still await that national debate. Other organisations, like 'Choice Support' and 'Supported Loving' and certain individuals are choosing not to wait though; they are generating change through action.

Two groups; the Tizard Centre at the University of Kent and the National Development Team for Inclusion (NDTi) working with My Life My Choice, undertook detailed research looking at relationships for people with learning disabilities. The findings were not too much of a surprise as it confirmed that many people did not know their rights around sex and relationships. With the help of the Supported Loving Network, they created;

'Sexuality and relationships – my rights charter' (2020)

The charter is just brilliant and I will use the uncomplicated, easy read, words here to highlight the messages;

The Human Rights Act (1998) is an important law that makes sure everyone has the same rights so they can live their life as they want and to have privacy. This law includes things like:

Your sexuality
- We mean the way we feel about our own body and what makes us feel good. It is also about whether we fancy men or women, both or neither
- Your body
- How you look/dress – What clothes you like to wear or how you like look
- Your relationships with other people – it might be with friends, family, or someone you feel more strongly about

Your rights
- I have the right to make my own decisions about my relationships, sexuality or sex life
- There might be some decisions I need help with
- If this happens a meeting called a 'capacity assessment' might be needed to see if I can make this decision
- If I need a capacity assessment, I have a right to be there and be as involved as possible
- **If I have a capacity assessment** and it is decided that I am unable to make a decision around sex or relationships
- It is my right to have support and education to help me to understand and be able to make my own decision
- This might need to be tried several times
- I must have this to be able to make a decision
- If I am still unable to make the decision myself (this is called lacking capacity) I need help to keep myself safe
- It is my right that any decision made must help me to have as much choice and freedom as possible

I have the same rights to a relationship as anyone else
- I have the right to have sex if I choose to, whether I am in a relationship or not (as long as both people agree)
- I have the right to get married or have a civil partnership
- I have the right to not be in a relationship

I have the right to be taken seriously
- Everyone should respect me and take my relationships or sexual life seriously
- I may need help to meet people who I might like as a partner
- I have the right not to talk about my relationship with others if I choose not to
- My supporters should meet my on-going needs and any needs I may have as part of a couple, as this may change over time (e.g. as part of a couple we may need different help the longer we are together-like help to move in together)

I have the right to privacy in my home with a partner
- I have the right to shut my bedroom door
- I have the right to a double bed
- I have the right to private space and a lock on my bedroom door
- I have the right to have someone to stay over in my room
- I have the right to keep any texts, phone calls and messages private

I have the right to sex and relationships support that I understand

- I have the right to ongoing relationship support and information on how to keep safe
- This could be practical and emotional support
- I have the right to make mistakes in my relationships
- I have the right to say no or change my mind about what I do, just like anyone else can
- I have the right to sex education in a way I understand

I can choose the contraception that is right for me

- I have the right to information I understand about contraception
- I have the right to choose what contraception is best for me
- I have the right to have information about having children, about avoiding pregnancy and getting an abortion if I choose
- I have the right to information about sexually transmitted infections and how to stop myself from getting sick
- If a doctor suggests long term contraception, like the injection or implant, or something that lasts forever like sterilization, then it is especially important that I get good information and support to help me make an informed decision

I have the right to express my gender and sexuality

- I have the right to masturbate, and use legal pornography and sex toys if I want
- I have the right to dress in any way I choose to express my sexuality
- I have the right to express my gender I any way I choose

My Responsibilities

- I need to understand what consent means – that both me and a partner agree to anything sexual that we do together
- My partner must be able to tell me that they agree using either words or signs
- I must understand about sexually transmitted infections and how to not spread them to a partner – usually by using a condom
- I need to make sure anything sexual I do, either alone or with a partner, is in done in a private place – usually in mine or a partner's bedroom
- I must make sure anyone I do anything sexual with is over 16 years old – this is the law
- I must understand that having sex between a man and women can make women pregnant. I must use contraception if I do not want this
  This charter was made to help people know what their rights are around sexuality and relationships. People need to know so they can speak out if they are being stopped from having the same rights as everyone else. We want you to share this charter with people you know so everyone knows their rights.

Where can I share the charter?

- With your friends and family
- With your advocacy group
- With your college/day service
- With your staff

What If My Rights Are Being Ignored?

If your sexuality and relationship rights are being restricted you can talk to someone about this. You could speak to:

- Your Support Staff or the manager of your support
- Your Social Worker (if you have one)
- An Advocate
- A Self Advocacy Group
- Someone you trust like a tutor at college
- Your Family
- Care Quality Commission
- A Solicitor

(The Tizard Centre, NDTi & My Life My Choice, 2020)

What next?

Together the partners; the Tizard Centre, NDTi, My Life My Choice and Supported Loving are calling on all organisations providing support to people with learning disabilities to share the charter widely and to pledge to uphold and respect the rights of people they support around their sexuality and relationships.

They want the charter to be used in several ways, to:

- Start having conversations with the people we support to help them understand their rights.
- Start conversations about how people might want to learn or get information about sex or relationships.
- Help people think about their relationships and how they could develop more meaningful relationships and friendships.
- Ask organisations to review how they support people's sexuality and relationships. Are human rights always upheld and respected?
- Ask how can we support people to have more meaningful relationships or friendships?
- Question whether other professionals are acting lawfully, or do they need to be challenged? Remember best interests' and decisions surrounding sex need to be referred to the Court of Protection. No one else has the authority to take these decisions.

(National Development Team for Inclusion, 2020)

We have plenty still to do; I will take a step back to the opening chapter. Our job of supporting our special learners is challenging on many levels and equally as rewarding. When we have the pleasure of witnessing real progress that will impact on our special learners for the rest of their lives, it gives us perspective and encouragement to continue to learn ourselves.

The challenge of providing quality Relationships and Sex Education for your special learners will be one that will reward you like no other. We are enabling our special learners to become as independent as possible as they journey through life, engaging in healthy relationships and hopefully finding love.

Sam Sly, who is a Health & Social Care Consultant, wrote a fantastic blog in 2018 for the wonderful Choice Support organisation, part of which I would like to end on…

So, if like me you believe in love and think love is the right of every citizen I would like you to reflect and consider in whatever job you do with people with learning disabilities, or whoever's life you touch.

Can you put your hand on your heart and say that you strive to increase the love in someone's life every day? Do you ensure people understand relationships, develop new ones, nurture important ones, explore sex and their sexuality and have opportunities to give and receive love?

Life is not worth living without love.

Appendix 1

Self-evaluation audit tool

5 Excellent/Exceeds Standards

4 Satisfactory/Meets Standards

3 Some Progress Made/Approaching Standards

2 Must Address and Improve/Standards Not Met

1 Standards not applicable to our learners

KEY FOCUS 1 – LEADERSHIP AND MANAGEMENT

Table A1.1

Target Standards	Why are these Standards Important?	Evaluation					Observations and Actions required. Who? What? Reason for standard not being applicable.
		1	2	3	4	5	
1(a) There is an identified RSE Lead, with appropriate status (ideally SLT member) time, CPD training and senior leadership support.	1(a) An identified RSE Lead will be able to coordinate the self-evaluation and action plan. With confidence and SLT support they will be able to lead by example.						
1(b) A RSE policy is in place which mirrors best practice and meets (and ideally exceeds) DfE guidance.	1(b) The policy will commit the school and stakeholders to improving RSE provision, following best practice.						
1(c) The RSE policy reflects a process of consultation with all stakeholders.	1(c) With all stakeholders involved there will be a sense of shared ownership.						
1(d) The entitlement of all learners to RSE is guaranteed through policy and planned provision for RSE across the whole age range and various cohorts.	1(d) The policy and RSE provision should involve all learners, irrelevant of individual needs or age. All learners are entitled to quality RSE.						
1(e) RSE is taught following best practice through the suitable curriculum area. (PSHE, My Body, Independent Living Skills etc.)	1(e) If RSE is to work in reality then it needs to be evident throughout the curriculum and throughout the school culture of positive relationships.						

KEY FOCUS 2 – THE RSE PROVISION TEAM

Table A1.2

Target Standards	Why are these Standards Important?	Evaluation					Observations and Actions required. Who? What? Reason for standard not being applicable.
		1	2	3	4	5	
2(a) Quality Continuing Professional Development (CPD) relating to RSE in a SEN setting is completed by all staff who contribute to learners' progress in RSE; including teachers and all teaching assistants.	2.a We know that confidence in providing RSE is low across the teaching profession. Without the relevant training and support confidence levels will remain low, as will the quality of RSE provision.						
2(b) Support and RSE workshops are available for **parents and carers** so they can gain a better understanding and contribute to the RSE programme.	2(b) Training and/or workshops for parents is as important as staff training. With the parents' understanding and backing of the type of provision you want to develop you have every chance of real success.						
2(c) Good internal and home/school communications ensure teachers are aware of personal issues that may affect the issues addressed in sessions or pupils' responses to them. Appropriate referral pathways for pupils are established if necessary.	2(c) If you have a working partnership with parents in providing RSE then you will gain a better understanding of any issues that some learners may have. By developing a close working relationship with external partners the relevant support will be available.						
2(d) Teachers of RSE are willing and committed to the teaching of this subject, and are supported as they gain knowledge and experience.	2(d) Training and support can have a limited influence on some staff who oppose RSE for special learners due to fear or moral beliefs. These need to be addressed.						
2(e) Teachers of RSE have the necessary confidence, subject knowledge and skills to provide RSE, understanding the sensitive and personal nature of RSE.	2(e) Through a programme of training and support teachers will develop the confidence to adapt sessions or groupings to reflect any difficulty an individual may have. As above, the partnership with parents will certainly help overcome any problem.						

(Continued)

Table A1.2 (Continued)

Target Standards	Why are these Standards Important?	Evaluation					Observations and Actions required. Who? What? Reason for standard not being applicable.
		1	2	3	4	5	
2(f) All teaching staff have the confidence, knowledge and skills to deal with sensitive matters concerning puberty, emotional changes and inappropriate behaviour. Additional support for those learners identifying as transgender, homosexual or bisexual is accepted and sought.	2(f) Preparing our learners for puberty and the physical and emotional changes that will take place is vital. An understanding and acceptance that certain behaviours need to be treated with sensitivity will better support our learners. If we accept the fact that we humans do not conform to gender and sexual 'stereotypical' norms then we need to have an awareness of potential support needs for learners and staff.						
2(g) School nurses, LD nurses and/or Health Promotion Service contribute to the RSE programme. *This links with 2.f*	2(g) Having the resources and knowledge of your various health teams to support your provision is important for the confidence in learners and the health teams as the learners transition from school. *(2.f)*						
2(h) There is whole school awareness of the RSE policy and programme in order that all staff (including governors) may respond appropriately to questions or issues raised by outside agencies or individuals.	2(h) Demonstrating a shared understanding and commitment of the RSE provision (and process) to those who may not be part of the stakeholder group will generate greater confidence of your wider community.						
2(i) Whole setting knowledge and understanding in place that all stakeholders have a safeguarding responsibility to all learners.	2(i) With our learners being three times as likely to suffer from all types of abuse; understanding the signs and having a safeguarding awareness of child protection shared by all stakeholders is paramount.						
2(j) The teaching of RSE is effectively monitored and supported, and all members of the team share in self-evaluation and development of the RSE provision.	2(j) There need to be a culture of learning from each other. No one has all the answers. Through shared self-evaluation and shared input into development plans RSE provision will continually improve.						

KEY FOCUS 3 – LEARNING AND TEACHING

Table A1.3

Target Standards	Why are these Standards Important?	Evaluation 1	2	3	4	5	Observations and Actions required. Who? What? Reason for standards not being applicable.
3(a) The structure of RSE provision is planned to ensure progress over time (long term, whole school planning). The assessment of individual learner's progress informs future planning and the re-visit of certain elements of RSE.	3(a) Where possible we need to ensure that our learners have the access to a wide ranging RSE curriculum, covering all areas. If we agree the content at different stages of a long term plan then required coverage will be secured.						
3(b) All RSE learning groups agree 'ground rules'. Staff creates a safe and positive learning environment for RSE sessions.	3(b) RSE group agreements are important to ensure that both learners and staff are clear on expectations, the process and content of the sessions.						
3(c) Appropriate RSE resources are sourced with regard to the learners' age, cognitive levels and background. Resources reflect the diversity of the settings community. Where appropriate, single sex groups are formed.	3(c) As with all learning experiences we plan, relevant RSE resources suitable for the needs of your learners is important. Your Health Promotion Team will be a good source of sexual health resources.						
3(d) Where possible the single sex groups share knowledge with each other, demonstrating the importance of understanding the differences between the sexes and those that identify as homosexual or transgender as we grow and change.	3(d) If you choose to have separate single sex groups for particular sessions, having the opportunity for the groups to share their learning is a good way of extending learning of the opposite sex that also includes those who identify as homosexual or transgender.						
3(e) RSE sessions are wide ranging and address all agreed areas of learning; (e.g. This is Me, My Changing Body, Gender, My Emotions, Being Healthy, Staying Safe, Public & Private, Relationships, Consent, Sexual Expression).	3(e) As for **3(a)** the areas of RSE learning need to be accessed by all learners throughout their time at your setting. Some areas may seem difficult to address; but as with a jigsaw, learners will not see the bigger picture if we only select comfortable areas of learning to focus on.						
3(f) Strategies are in place to ensure the learning programme is responsive to the real needs of learners, including issues raised by families and the school nurse.	3(f) The individual assessments and parental questionnaires will give you an idea on individual RSE 'learning gaps'. If you can be responsive to changing needs it may have a lasting positive effect.						

(Continued)

Table A1.3 (Continued)

Target Standards	Why are these Standards Important?	Evaluation					Observations and Actions required. Who? What? Reason for standards not being applicable.
		1	2	3	4	5	
3(g) RSE lessons support learners to develop confidence when exploring sensitive issues and to appreciate a range of views people may hold about them.	3(g) We are all different; we are all unique. Strong relationships start with strong self-esteem; therefore, we need to encourage learners to reflect on what makes them great.						

KEY FOCUS 4 – THE WIDER LEARNING COMMUNITY

Table A1.4

Target Standards	Why are these Standards Important?	Evaluation					Observations and Actions required. Who? What?
		1	2	3	4	5	Reason for standards not being applicable.
4(a) All staffs are trained and know the safeguarding/child protection procedures and what to do in the event of a disclosure or behaviour that raises concerns.	4(a) With our learners being three times more likely to suffer from all forms of abuse than their mainstream peers it is vital that safeguarding procedures are understood. Your RSE sessions will bring a better understanding of inappropriate behaviours and therefore the chance of disclosures.						
4(b) Learners are involved in all stages of the planning, evaluation and development of their RSE provision wherever possible.	4(b) Having all stakeholders; including learners, involved in the whole process will give them ownership. It may also offer some surprising topic areas for you to plan for.						
4(c) Parents and carers are informed, and listened to, in the consultation process through information drop-ins and are invited to RSE workshops to support them in continuing the learning with their children at home.	4(c) Getting parents and carers on board is an obvious standard to reach for. This may not be as straight forward as one would like, but it is worth the time spent on encouraging parental involvement form the start of the process.						
4(d) External partners (Social Care, LD Health teams, Family Support teams) are invited to join with consultation process and add their on-going support to individuals and their families.	4(d) If we are to see the outcomes quality RSE can provide for our learners then we need to be working in partnership with all interested parties. This will have positive long-term implications for our learners.						
4(e) A working partnership is established with similar schools and colleges, which serves to promote cross-phase continuity and progression in children's experience of RSE (particularly during transition if applicable).	4(e) A partner school could support you in the self-evaluation process and act as your quality assurance as you support them. As for learners who will be transitioning to colleges it is important that colleges are able to build on your work and develop the knowledge and confidence built by the learners.						

KEY FOCUS 5 – RSE PROVISION CONTENT

Table A1.5

Target Standards	Why are these Standards Important?	Evaluation					Observations Actions required, scope for development, reason for standards not being applicable to the setting.
		1	2	3	4	5	
5(a) What makes us all unique. Things learners enjoy and are good at. Sharing qualities and likes with peers. Peers identify qualities in others.	5(a) Strong relationships are built on strong self-esteem. It is important that our learners identify what makes them who they are and build confidence.						
5(b) Relationships. How our relationships with family and friends can change as we get older. What makes a good friend? (see 'Relationship target game')	5(b) Understanding that our relationships are different (family, friends, school staff, peers, loved ones) and that these relationships can change is significant learning. Identifying the traits of a good friend will support choice making and keeping safe for our learners as they get older.						
5(c) Demonstrate the link between positive self-esteem and being able to develop healthy friendships and relationships.	5(c) Strong relationships are built on strong self-esteem. It is important that our learners identify what makes them who they are and build confidence.						
5(d) Knowing the proper names for the main parts of the body, including both male and female genital names and internal sexual/reproductive anatomy where appropriate.	5(d) Vital learning. Without the ability to use proper names for genitals our learners become more vulnerable and have been classed as unreliable witnesses in abuse cases.						
5(e) How boys' and girls' bodies, feelings and emotions change as they approach and move through puberty. What to expect and how to manage periods. What to expect and how to manage wet dreams.	5(e) Vital learning. The least we can do for our learners is to prepare them for the inevitability of puberty; both the physical and the emotional changes they will encounter.						
5(f) Public/Private. What is a public place? What does it mean to be in a private, safe place? What can we do in private that we cannot do in public?	5(f) Not as straight forward as one would initially think. The interchanging, contradictory definitions are difficult enough for us. Our special learners will benefit greatly if this area of RSE gets the attentions it needs.						
5(g) Public/Private. What parts of our bodies are private to us?	5(g) Vital learning. With some complications and contradictions for some of our learners who rely on personal and intimate care.						
5(h) The importance of personal hygiene and understanding how to keep ourselves clean and healthy.	5(h) For our learners be as independent as possible in personal care routines should be a shared aspiration.						

(Continued)

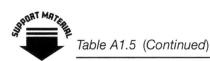

Table A1.5 *(Continued)*

| Target Standards | Why are these Standards Important? | Evaluation | | | | | Observations Actions required, scope for development, reason for standards not being applicable to the setting. |
		1	2	3	4	5	
5(i) Good and bad touch. Consent. Learners are given opportunities to advocate for themselves; Learners practice asking for permission and respecting others' decisions.	5(i) Vital learning. Having knowledge about what constitutes good or bad touch, and our individual preferences, supports our learners to keep safe; as is consent and respecting others views.						
5(j) The ways in which the media and peer group may influence individuals' behaviour and choices.	5(j) Giving our learners the tools to identify and reject unwanted pressure to behave in ways that may be harmful.						
5(k) Keeping Safe. Who do we talk to if we are concerned about a situation or behaviour?	5(k) If our learners feel unsafe or worried, the fact they know who they can approach can give them confidence.						
5(l) How to identity and access sources of help, support and information (including online, if appropriate) independently whilst keeping themselves safe.	5(l) Knowing how to ask for help, and the different ways to access support, will develop confidence and self-help skills.						
5(m) The influences that lead to early sexual activity, and the issues, including physical and emotional risks, associated with this	5(m) With many of our learners being trustful, and keen to please others, they need to recognise the risks of the decisions they make.						
5(n) Where appropriate, an understanding of the law in relation to consensual sexual activity and mental capacity.	5(n) A number of our learners will go on to develop sexual relationships. If appropriate, they need to know the facts about their rights as sexual beings.						
5(o) Conception and reproduction in humans. Sex for pleasure.	5(o) Building on learning done through statutory science, expanding on the 'biology' of reproduction - and looking at why people have sex (sex for pleasure) will give our learners a better understanding.						
5(p) Contraception. The personal and social implications of teenage pregnancy. The realities of parenthood.	5(p) Keeping safe and making decisions around safe sex and contraception will be an important part of RSE for your older learners. Understanding the realities of parenthood can support learners to make appropriate decisions.						

Individual learner assessment

Table A1.6

Name:	Evaluation			Observations
RSE Individual Assessment Areas	**NO**	**WITH HELP**	**YES**	
Can identify own gender*				** A learner may not iden-tify their own gender due to genuine confusion. We humans do not neces-sarily assimilate to the gender, sexuality or role that we were 'assigned'. Obviously this is as true for our special learners as anyone else, so we should stay creative and open in our interpreta-tions of answers to RSE related questions as we would with any other area of learning.*
Can identify similar peers (gender & age) from a range of ages and genders				
Can identify differences between male and female bodies (clothed and naked)				
Can identify differences between adult and child bodies, both male and female				
Understands that these changes (at puberty) hap-pens to all of us – and will happen to them				
Can identify and name body parts, including proper names for sexual body parts				
Can identify their own body parts that are private to them*				**contradictions may apply to those learners that rely on intimate care – under-stand that permission should be sought and received before intimae care routines take place*
Can identify the body parts of others that are private (male and female)				
Can offer examples of personal care routines and why it is important that we keep our bodies clean				
Can identify public and private places from a range of examples				
Can identify certain activities that are private and those that are not				
Can identify the difference between good and bad touch and offer examples				
Understands that we should all ask permission (consent) before physical contact (relate to peer massage)				
Understands that friends can make you feel that you should do things for them (peer pressure) but it is okay to say no				
Can explain that even if they may like to hug or kiss someone, it is wrong unless the other person wants a hug or kiss				

(Continued)

Table A1.6 (Continued)

Name:	Evaluation			
RSE Individual Assessment Areas	**NO**	**WITH HELP**	**YES**	*Observations*
Can identify who or where to go for help if feeling unsure of the behaviour of someone else				
Can offer examples of different types of relationships people have; family, friends, romantic and sexual				
Can identify different type of romantic relationships (e.g. heterosexual, homosexual)				
Understands what periods are and that it is females that have periods				
Can give examples of how to manage periods ('I change pad' routine)				
Understands what 'wet dreams'* are and that this happens to some males when asleep				*certainly for ASD learners, this need to be expressed clearly. 'Wet dreams' are not necessarily wet or dreams.*
Understands what masturbation is and where this should happen (link to 'private places' and 'keeping clean')				
Can offer a reason why people enjoy masturbation (an understanding of arousal and orgasm)				
Understands that when two people want to be close and then hold each other, then there are changes to our bodies that make us feel aroused (e.g. penises becoming erect, vaginas becoming lubricated and there is increased heart rate)				
Understands that sex does not have to penetrative and there are different ways that people can enjoy each other safely				
Understands that sex should be pleasurable for both, and that people have sex for pleasure as well as (heterosexual sex) for pregnancy				
Can give a description of pregnancy and how pregnancy occurs				
Can give examples of how pregnancy can be avoided (methods of contraception)				
Can give examples of how mothers and fathers take care of babies and some examples of the care needs of a baby				
Understands that people can get sexually transmitted infections (STIs) from having unprotected sex				
Can give examples of how to keep safe and healthy when two people are planning/wanting to have sex				

Appendix 2

Staff questionnaire

Please complete this questionnaire as honestly as you can. Your honesty will really help us to assess how we are doing as a school and identify the areas that may need development. It will also help us to target our support more efficiently. Thank you.

Please circle/highlight the answer that best answers the question. Some questions will require a written answer.

Table A2.1

How often do you teach planned RSE lessons?	Once a week	Once every two weeks	1–2 times a term	Never
How often do you carry out 'spontaneous' RSE to respond to issues that arise in the class or school environment?	Once a week (or more, depending on need)	Once every two weeks	1–2 times a term	Never
If you are not teaching much RSE, what causes this?	Lack of time to plan and teach?	Unsure of how to teach it?	No suitable resources	Other (please specify)
How important do you think it is to teach RSE?	Very	Quite	Not very	Not at all
Do you feel confident teaching RSE?	Very	Quite	Not very	Not at all
Have you noticed a positive impact on children's behaviour and learning as a result of RSE lessons?	A lot	Some	Not much	Not at all
What subjects and topics have you taught in the last term that had a link to RSE? (please specify)				
What do you view to be the main benefits of teaching RSE to the learners across the school?				
What areas of RSE have you become more confident in during the last year?				
What areas of RSE or learner cohort would you like more support with?				
Any other comments/ questions:				

Bibliography

Alberta Health Services (2009). Sexuality and Disability: A Guide for Parents. Nova Science Publishers. ISBN: 978-1-60876-628-4, © 2010 Nova Science Publishers, J:\Parent Packages and Labels\sexuality and disability, 2009 7.

Alexander N and Taylor Gomez M (2017). Pleasure, sex, prohibition, intellectual disability, and dangerous ideas, Reproductive Health Matters, 25(50), 114–120. Accepted author version posted online: 23 May 2017, https://www.tandfonline.com/doi/full/10.1080/09688080.2017.1331690

Allen M and Seery D (2007). The Current Status of Sex Education Practice for People with an Intellectual Disability in Ireland. The Sexual Health Centre Commissioned by Irish Sex Education Network, Dublin and Cork.

Apple M (1993). The politics of official knowledge: Does a national curriculum make sense? Teachers College Record, 95(2), winter. Copyright © by Teachers College, Columbia University 0161-4681-93/9502/222$1.25/0

Association of Christian Teachers (2014). Christian Doctrine (2014) Evangelical Alliance (2014). http://www.parliament.uk/business/committees/committees-a-z/commons-select/education-committee/inquiries/parliament-2010/pshe-and-sre-in-schools/?type=Written#pnlPublicationFilter [accessed 02/09/2014]

Atkin Hussain Y K and Ahmad W I U (2002). South Asian Disabled Young People and Their Families. Policy Press, Bristol.

Autism Speaks (2018). Autism in Teens: Helping Your Child through Puberty, September 5, 2018. https://www.autismspeaks.org/expert-opinion/autism-teens-helping-your-child-through-puberty

Autism Victoria (2006). Information Sheet Autism Spectrum Disorder, Reviewed April 2011. http://capacity-resource.middletownautism.com/wp-content/uploads/sites/6/2017/03/fact-sheet-sharing-the-diagnosis-of-asd.pdf

Barbanell E (2020). https://loveexpands.com/quotes/edward-barbanell-285128/?c=down-syndrome [accessed 2020]/

Barker (2010). The Curriculum Challenge. http://networks.ssatuk.co.uk/thinkpiece/2010/02/18/think-piece-4-the-curriculum-challenge/ [accessed 03/06/2014].

Barnard-Brak L, Schmidt M, Chesnut S, Wei T, and Richman D (2014). Predictors of access to sex education for children with intellectual disabilities in public schools. Intellectual and Developmental Disabilities, 52(2), 85–97. doi: 10.1352/1934-9556-52.2.85

Barrett-Ibarria Sofia (2018). People with Down Syndrome Need Healthy Sex Lives, Too. https://tonic.vice.com/en_us/article/ne49mk/sex-dating-and-down-syndrome

Bartholomaeusa C (2017). The capacity of South Australian primary school teachers and pre-service teachers to work with trans and gender diverse students. Teaching and Teacher Education, 65, 127–135.

Beadman J (2005). Adolescence and Sexuality – Information Sheet. By Jane Beadman, DSA UK Education Consortium 2005, Down's Syndrome Association.

Beemyn G and Rankin S (2011). The Lives of Transgender People. Columbia University Press. E-ISBN: 978-0-231-51261-9

Bennie M (2018). How do I Teach Sexuality to a Person with ASD? https://autismawarenesscentre.com/teach-sexuality-person-asd/

Bennie M (2017). Autism and (Trans)Gender: Dysphoria, Ambivalence, and Gender Fluidity in ASD. https://autismawarenesscentre.com/autism-transgender-gender-dysphoria/

Big Talk Education (2020). https://www.bigtalkeducation.co.uk/parents/parents-of-children-with-autism-your-questions-answered/

Blacker C P (1950). The control of population. Eugenics Review, XLM(8).

Blake S (2007). There's a Hole in the Bucket: The Politics, Policy and Practice of Sex and Relationships Education. Brook, London, UK.

Blake S (2014). http://www.huffingtonpost.co.uk/simon-blake/sex-education_b_4673884.html [accessed 08/08/2014].

Blake S and Muttock S (2004). PSHE and Citizenship for Children and Young People with Special Needs: An Agenda for Action. National Children's Bureau, London.

Blanchett W and Wolfe P (2002). A Review of Sexuality Education Curricula: Meeting the Sexuality Education Needs of Individuals with Moderate and Severe Intellectual Disabilities. https://journals.sagepub.com/doi/10.2511/rpsd.27.1.43

Bononi B M, Carvalho Sant'Anna M J, Vasconcellos de Oliveira A C, Renattini T S and Pinto C F (2009). Sexuality and persons with Down syndrome. A Study from Brazil. https://uknowledge.uky.edu/cgi/viewcontent.cgi?article=1075&context=pediatrics_facpub

Brantlinger E A (1992). Sexuality education in the secondary special education curriculum: Teachers' perceptions and concerns. Teacher Education and Special Education, 15, 32–40. https://doi.org/10.1177/088840649201500106

Bray P (2015). Sex and relationships education for special educational needs – an exploration of the quality of provision. Advance. Preprint. https://doi.org/10.31124/advance.12826382.v1

Brighton & Hove City Council (2018) Trans Inclusion Schools Toolkit Version, 2018.

Brill S and Pepper R (2008). The Transgender Child: A Handbook for Families and Professionals. Cleis Press San Francisco, CA: (first published June 3rd 2008), 1573443182 (ISBN13: 9781573443180).

Cajani L, Harnett P, Fulop M and Johansson R (2009). Discerning Bias in Research: Challenging Epistemological Assumptions. Children's Identity & Citizenship in Europe, London Metropolitan University, London.

Calgary Communities against Sexual Abuse (2008). Educating Your Child about Child Sexual Abuse. http://www.calgarycasa.com/

Calgary Health Region (2009). Sexuality and Disability: A Guide for Parents; Sexual and Reproductive Health Education and Health Promotion. Alberta Health Services.

Care Management Group, CHANGE and Choice Support (2020). Transgender: An Easy Read Guide. https://www.choicesupport.org.uk/uploads/documents/Transgender-easy-read-guide-For-Web.pdf

Carley (2015). Educational Theories You Must Know: Maslow. St. Emlyn's. https://www.stemlynsblog.org/better-learning/educational-theories-you-must-know-st-emlyns/educational-theories-you-must-know-maslow-st-emlyns

Carlton (2010). http://playwithlearning.com/2010/12/07/where-play-meets-learning/

Carson G (2017). https://www.communitycare.co.uk/2017/08/17/man-learning-disabilities wins-damages-human-rights-breach/Adults. Learning Disability, August 17.

Catholic and Loving It (2014). http://www.lovingit.co.uk/2012/07/the-acceptable-face-of-child-sex-abuse.html [accessed 03/09/2014].

Centre for Autism (2016). Relationships and Sexuality Education, Volume Two, Research Bulletin Issue No. 22.

Chamba R, Ahmad W, Hirst M A, Lawton D and Beresford B (1999). On the Edge: Minority Ethnic Families Caring for a Severely Disabled Child. Policy Press, 1st edition.

CHANGE (2010). Talking About Sex and Relationships: The Views of Young People with Learning Disabilities. The Final Report of the Sexuality Project by CHANGE 2007–2010, University of Leeds.

Chapman C and Gallannaugh F (2008). School Self-Evaluation: a Resource Pack. SSAT, London.

Chapman C and Muijs D (2014). Does school-to-school collaboration promote school improvement? A study of the impact of school federations on student outcomes. School Effectiveness and School Improvement: An International Journal of Research, Policy and Practice. doi: 10.1080/09243453.2013.840319

Chapman C, Muijs D and MacAllister J (2011). A Study of the Impact of School Federation on Student Outcomes. National College for School Leadership.

Chapman C and Sammon P (2013). School Self-Evaluation for School Improvement: What Works and Why? CfBT Education Trust.

Children and Families Act (2014). https://www.legislation.gov.uk/ukpga/2014/6/contents/enacted

Chailey Heritage School (2020). https://www.chf.org.uk/rse-training.html

Choice Support (2020). https://www.choicesupport.org.uk/about-us/what-we-do/supported-loving/what-is-supported-loving

Colley A (2013). Personalised Learning for Young People with Profound and Multiple Learning. Jessica Kingsley Publishers, London. ISBN: 978-1-84905-367-9

Colley A (2016). To what extent have learners with severe, profound and multiple learning difficulties been excluded from the policy and practice of inclusive education? International Journal of Inclusive Education. Downloads/To_what_extent_have_learners_with_severe_profound_.pdf

Community Care (2020). https://www.communitycare.co.uk/2020/06/17/capacity-consent-sexual-relations-latest-case-may-help-social-workers-navigate-challenges/

Couwenhoven T (2007). Teaching Children with Down Syndrome about Their Bodies, Boundaries and Sexuality: A Guide for Parents and Professionals. ISBN: 978-1-89062-733-1

Craft A (Ed.) (1987). Mental Handicap and Sexuality: Issues and Perspectives. Costello. ISBN 0710400608

Craft A (2010). Living Your Life. 3rd edition. In: Bustard S and Stewart D (Eds.). The Ann Craft Trust, Brook.

Curfs L M G, Kok G, Schaafsma D, and Stoffelen J M T (2013). Exploring the development of existing sex education programmes for people with intellectual disabilities: an intervention mapping approach. Journal of Applied Research in Intellectual Disabilities, 26(2), 157–166.

Currie L (2020). https://www.mentalcapacitylawandpolicy.org.uk/capacity-and-sexual-relations-trying-to-make-it-personal/

Curtiss S and Burns (2014). The Birds and the Bees Project, Assistant Professor of Special Education at the University of Delaware. https://asdsexed.org/2014/11/19/signs-of-flirting/

Cusitar L (1994). Strengthening the Links: Stopping the Violence: a Guide to the Issue of Violence against Women with Disabilities. Disabled Women's Network, Toronto.

D'aegher L, Robinson P and Jones S (1999). Talk to Me: A Personal Development Manual Down Syndrome. Association of NSW Inc., Parramatta Blue Tower Solutions, Parramatta.

Daily Mail Reporter (2011). Sex Education Should Not Be Taught in Schools, Say More Than Half of Parents. http://www.dailymail.co.uk/news/article-1383930/Sex-education-taught-schools-say-half-parents.html [accessed 02/09/13].

Darry K, Esmail S, Knupp H and Walter A (2010). Attitudes and perceptions towards disability and sexuality. Disability and Rehabilitation, 32(14), 1148–1155. NARIC Accession Number: J59153.

Department for Children, Schools and Families (2009). Customer Voice Research; Sex and Relationships Education. Sherbert Research Published Department for Children, Schools and Families.

Department for Education (2013). Consultation on PSHE education. Summary Report. March 2013. www.nationalarchives.gov.uk/doc/open-government-licence DFE-00031-2013 [accessed 26/08/2013].

Department for Education (2018, 2019). Relationships Education, Relationships and Sex Education (RSE) and Health Education: Statutory Guidance for Governing Bodies, Proprietors, Head Teachers, Principals, Senior Leadership Teams, Teachers. DfE.

Department for Education and Department of Health and Social Care (2014). Published June 2014, SEND Code Of Practice: 0 to 25 Years Guidance on the Special Educational Needs and Disability (SEND) System for Children and Young People Aged 0 to 25, from 1 September 2014. Last updated 30 April 2020.

DfES (2004). Sex and Relationship Education – Schools Responsibilities pdf

Dhejne C, Van Vlerken R, Heylens G and Arcelus J (2016). Mental health and gender dysphoria: a review of the literature. International Review of Psychiatry, 28(1), 44–57. doi: 10.3109/09540261.2015.1115753

Dickman B J and Roux A J (2005). Complainants with learning disabilities in sexual abuse cases: a 10-year review of a psycho-legal project in Cape Town, South Africa. British Journal of Learning Disabilities 33(3), 138–144. Wiley Online Library.

Dixon H (2006). Sexual Health Skills a Manual for Trainers on Sexual Health and Sex and Relationships Education Hilary Dixon Me-and-Us MU005, published 2006 by Me-and-Us.

Dixon H (2010). Confident in SRE sex and relationships education for young people with learning disabilities. A Guide for Trainers and Educators' Sheffield, published 2010 by Me-and-Us.

DO RSE (2018). https://www.dosreforschools.com/

Doughty S (2013). High Court Judge Makes Legal History after Sanctioning Sterilisation of a Disabled Man, 36, Because It Is in His 'Best Interests'. https://www.dailymail.co.uk/news/article-2395596/British-legal-history-sterilisation-sanctioned-man-severe-learning-difficulties.html

Doukas T, Fergusson A, Fullerton M and Grace J (2017). The Core and Essential Service Standards for Supporting People with Profound and Multiple Learning Disabilities. http://www.thesensoryprojects.co.uk/PMLD-service-standards [accessed 25/7/20].

Down's Syndrome Association (2010). Down's Syndrome Association Publication 2010. https://www.downs-syndrome.org.uk/about/campaigns/parliamentary-work/equality-act/

Down's Syndrome Association (2013). Sexual Health a Guide for Parents and Carers.

Down's Syndrome Association (2014). Education Support Pack for Schools; Special Schools. Down's Syndrome Association Publication 2014.

Down's Syndrome Education International (2020). https://www.dseinternational.org/en-gb/

Dunman H (2019). Moods, sweats and sex: A sensory approach to teaching SRE. PMLD Link, 31(1), 92.

Emery H (2013). Sex Education Matters. http://www.sec-ed.co.uk/blog/sex-education-matters [accessed 23/07/2013].

Emmerson L (2013). Sex Education Forum response to Public Consultation on the Draft National Curriculum Proposals. www.sexeducationforum.org.uk [accessed 21/08/2013].

Emmerson L and Lees J (2014). SRE Policy Guidance: A Step-by-Step Guide to Updating Your School Sex and Relationships Education Policy. Published by NCB for the Sex Education Forum.

Equality Act (2010). http://www.legislation.gov.uk/ukpga/2010/15/section/11 [accessed 09/07/2013].

Esmail S, Darry K, Walter A and Knupp H (2010). Attitudes and Perceptions towards Disability and Sexuality. Disability and Rehabilitation, 32(14). Department of Occupational Therapy, University of Alberta, Edmonton, Alberta, Canada.

Fairbairn G (2010). Can There Bullying without a Bully? In: Interdisciplinary Net Conference: Making Sense of Suicide. Prague, 8–10 November 2010. Leeds Metropolitan University Repository. http://repository.leedsmet.ac.uk/ [accessed 16/07/2014].

Family Planning Association (2007). Speakeasy. Facilitator's Handbook. FPA, London.

Family Planning Association (2011). Sex and Relationships Education Factsheet. http://www.fpa.org.uk/factsheets/sex-and-relationships-education [accessed 28/08/2013].

Family Planning Victoria (2015). Current levels of access and attainment for students with disability in the school system, and the impact on students and families associated with inadequate levels of support. Submission to the Senate Education and Employment References Committee, August 2015.

Fountaindale School (2015). The Pre-formal Curriculum a Creative Curriculum for Learning. July 2015 Updated 2016, 2019. https://www.fountaindale.notts.sch.uk/wp-content/uploads/2019/11/Pre-Formal-Curriculum-handbook-2019-2.pdf

Fullan M G (1993). Why teachers must become change agents. Educational Leadership, 50(6).

Fullan M G and Hargreaves A (1991). What's Worth Fighting for in Your School? Toronto: Ontario Public School Teachers' Federation. Andover, Mass.: The Network; Buckingham, U.K.: Open University Press; Melbourne: Australian Council of Educational Administration.

Fyson R (2007). Young people with learning disabilities who sexually abuse: understanding, identifying and responding from within generic education and welfare services. In: Calder M C (Ed.), Working with Children and Young People Who Sexually Abuse: Taking the Field Forward, Lyme Regis, Russell House.

Gadd M and Hinchliffe J (2007). Jiwsi A Pick 'n' Mix of Sex and Relationships Education Activities. https://www.fpa.org.uk/sites/default/files/jiwsi-sre-activities-english.pdf

Gant J (2019). For Mail Online. https://www.dailymail.co.uk/news/article-7273793/Now-protest-appears-outside-Nottingham-primary-school-against-sex-education-LGBT-lessons.html

Garbutt R (2008). Sex and relationships for people with learning disabilities: a challenge for parents and professionals. Mental Health and Learning Disabilities Research and Practice, 5(2), 266–277. ISSN 1743-6885

Garbutt R, Tattersall J, Dunn J and Boycott-Garnett R (2009). Accessible article: involving people with learning disabilities in research. (CHANGE, SHINE. Blackwell Publishing Ltd) British Journal of Learning Disabilities, 38, 21–34.

Garner R (2015). https://www.independent.co.uk/news/education/education-news/sex-education-tories-snub-puts-teenagers-risk-pregnancy-sexually-transmitted-diseases-and-exploitation-10050179.html

Gates B (2012). Plus ça Change, Plus c'est la même Chose: Reflection on Access to Health Care in Mainstream Services by People with Intellectual Disabilities in England. UK The Centre for Learning Disability Studies, The University of Hertfordshire, England, UK.

Glasier A, Gülmezoglu M, Schmid G, Garcia Moreno C and Van Look F A P (2006). Sexual and Reproductive Health: A Matter of Life and Death. http://www.thelancet.com/journals/lancet/article/PIIS0140-6736(06)69478-6/abstract [accessed 13/06/14].

Goldman J (2012). A critical analysis of UNESCO's International Technical Guidance on school-based education for puberty and sexuality. Sex Education, 12(2).

Grace J (2018). Sensory-Being for Sensory Beings. Routledge, Oxon, New York.

Grace J (2020a). I Decide – Consent and Personal Care. Nasen. https://www.facebook.com/JoannaGraceTheSensoryProjects/media_set?set=a.2596111790708307&type=3 [accessed 25/7/20].

Grace J (2020b). Observing Many 'Nows' to Infer Choice for People with Profound Learning Disabilities. Special Needs Jungle. https://www.specialneedsjungle.com/observing-many-nows-to-infer-a-choice-for-people-with-profound-learning-disabilities/ [accessed 25/7/20].

Grace J and Salfield C (2017). Inclusion: For Pity's Sake? TEDx. https://www.youtube.com/watch?v=_PbWFcVcaWQ [accessed 25/7/20].

Grieve A, McLaren S and Lindsay WR (2006). An evaluation of research and training resources for the sex education of people with moderate to severe learning disabilities. British Journal of Learning Disabilities, 35(1), 30–37. BILD Issue, Blackwell Publishing; Oxford.

Hall C and Noyes A (2009). School self-evaluation and its impact on teachers' work in England. Research Papers in Education, 24(3), 311–33.

Harflett N and Turner S (2016). Supporting People with Learning Disabilities to Develop Sexual and Romantic Relationships. National Development Team for Inclusion, Bath.

Hartman D (2013). Sexuality and Relationship Education for Children and Adolescents with Autism Spectrum Disorders: A Professional's Guide to Understanding, Preventing and Responding to Inappropriate Behaviours. Jessica Kingsley Publishers. ISBN-10: 1849053855

Hatton S and Tector A (2010). Sexuality and relationship education for young people with autistic spectrum disorder: curriculum change and staff support. British Journal of Special Education, 37(2).

Heaton C J (1995). Providing reproductive health services to persons with Down syndrome and other mental retardation. In Redfern D E (Ed), Caring for Individuals with Down Syndrome and Their Families, Report of the Third Ross Round Table on Cultural Issues in Family Medicine, in press.

Henderson E and Dumont J (2015). Three Ways School Profound and Multiple Learning Difficulties (PMLD) Curriculum from an Original Idea Created by Vale of Evesham School. https://www.argyll-bute.gov.uk/sites/default/files/Unknown/pnld_example_curriculum.pdf

Hewett D, Calveley J, McKim J and Mourière A (2019). Communication, human rights and Intensive Interaction. PMLD Link, 31(1), 92.

Hirstwood (2005). Practicing the Senses https://www.thomaswolsey.com/parents-zone/supporting-learning-at-home/37-curriculum/504-curriculum-home-page-new-3

Hollomotz A (2009). 'May we please have sex tonight?' People with learning difficulties pursuing privacy in residential group settings. British Journal of Learning Disabilities, 37. doi: 10.1111/j.1468-3156.2008.00512.x.

Hopkins D, Ainscow M and West M (1994). School Improvement in an Era of Change. Continuum International Publishing. ISBN-10: 0304326089

Howard-Barr E M, Rienzo B A, Morgan Pigg R and James Jr D (2005). Teacher beliefs, professional preparation, and practices regarding exceptional students and sexuality education. Journal of School Health, 75(3).

Human Rights Act (1998). https://www.legislation.gov.uk/ukpga/1998/42/contents

Hussain F and Cochrane R (2004). Depression in South Asian women living in the UK: a review of the literature with implications for service provision. Transcultural Psychiatry, 41(2), 253–270.

Imray P (2015). What does care have to do with education? PMLD Link, 27(2), 81.

Imray P and Hinchcliffe V (2012). Not fit for purpose: a call for separate and distinct pedagogies as part of a national framework for those with severe and profound learning difficulties. Support for Learning, 27(4).

Imray P and Hinchcliffe V (2014). Curricula for Teaching Children and Young People with Severe or Profound and Multiple Learning Difficulties: Practical Strategies for Educational Professionals. David Fulton/Nasen Routledge/Taylor & Francis Group. ISBN-10: 0415838479

Jigsaw (2018). Relationship and Sex Education in the Primary School: A Guide for Parents and Carers. https://www.jigsawpshe.com/

Kember D, Tak-Shing Ha, Lam Bick-Har, Lee A, NG S, Yan L and Yum J C K (2006). The diverse role of the critical friend in supporting educational action research projects. Educational Action Research, 5(3), 463–481. doi: 10.1080/09650799700200036

Kenny L, Hattersley C, Molins B, Buckley C, Povey C and Pellicano E (2015). Which Terms Should Be Used to Describe Autism? Perspectives from the UK Autism Community. http://www.altogetherautism.org.nz/wp-content/uploads/2015/10/2015-Kenny-terms-to-describe-autism.pdf

Kingsley J and Levitz M (1994). Count Us In: Growing Up with Down Syndrome. Mariner Books, ISBN-10: 0156031957

Kluth P and Straut D (2003). Do as we say and as we do: teaching and modeling collaborative practice in the university classroom. Journal of Teacher Education, 54(3), 228–240.

Kovic V, Plunkett K and Westermann G (2009). Eye-tracking study of inanimate objects. Psihologija, 42(4), 417–436.

Kutscher M D, Attwood T and Wolff R R (2005). Kids in the Syndrome Mix of ADHD, LD, Asperger's, Tourette's, Bipolar, and More!: The One Stop Guide for Parents, Teachers, and Other Professionals. Jessica Kingsley Publishers, 1st edition.

Lacey P (1998). People with Profound & Multiple Learning Disabilities: A Collaborative Approach to Meeting Complex Needs. Routledge, 1st edition. ISBN-10: 1853464880

Lancashire County Council (2013). Transgender Guidance: Supporting Gender Diverse and Trans-Identified Students in Schools. Lancashire County Council.

Laming W H (2003). The Victoria Climbié Inquiry: Report of an Inquiry by Lord Laming (Cm. 5730). https://www.gov.uk/government/publications/the-victoria-climbie-inquiry-report-of-an-inquiry-by-lord-laming

Levinstein K (2016). LMSW. https://4thwavenow.com/2016/05/06/social-work-prof-speaks-out-on-behalf-of-her-ftm-autistic-daughter/

Locket J (2019). The Sun. https://www.thesun.co.uk/news/9979466/kids-as-young-as-six-sex-education-shock/

Löfgren-Mårtenson L (2011). "I want to do it right!" A pilot study of Swedish sex education and young people with intellectual disabilities (Published online: 3 December 2011, Springer Science + Business Media, LLC). Sexuality and Disability, 30, 209–225. doi: 10.1007/s11195-011-9239-z

Longhorn F (1997). Sex Education and Sexuality for Very Special People: A Sensory Approach. Catalyst Education Resources Ltd. ISBN-10: 1900231204

Longstaff J S (2007). Overview of Laban movement analysis & Laban notation. Laban Analysis Reviews, Consultation, Research, Publication.

MacBeath J (1999). Schools Must Speak for Themselves: The Case for School Self-Evaluation. Routledge. ISBN 9780415205801

MacBeath J (2005). Leadership as distributed: a matter of practice. School Leadership & Management, 25(4), 349–366. doi: 10.1080/13634230500197165. https://warwick.ac.uk/fac/soc/ces/postgrads/teachfirst/1/induction2015/macbeath_2005_leadership_as_distributed.pdf

Manning S and Hookham M (2019). The Mail on Sunday. https://www.dailymail.co.uk/news/article-7490415/Children-young-SIX-given-compulsory-self-touching-lessons.html

Marquez Solera M (2016). Relationships and Sex Education Policy Ickburgh School. https://s3-eu-west-1. amazonaws.com/production-eu-west-1/user_store/1310780/user/rYMPKqlKr8?AWSAccessKeyId= AKIAXSFB2UMTNFUBN2F7&Expires=1607574370&Signature=lXoxJzJQ0Riq4lRHiOUggL2N2N0%3

Maslow A H (1943). A theory of human motivation. Originally Published in Psychological Review, 50, 370–396. An Internet Resource Developed by Christopher D. Green (http://www.yorku.ca/dept/psych/ classics/author.htm) York University, Toronto, Ontario. ISSN 1492-3713

McCall C and Straw F (2013, updated 2018). Puberty, Adolescence and Sexual Health. A Down's Syndrome Association Publication.

McCann L (2017). Eight Ways to Make Sex Education Autism-Friendly, 17th January TES. https://www.tes. com/news/eight-ways-make-sex-education-autism-friendly

McCarthy M (1999). Sexuality and Women with Learning Disabilities. Jessica Kingsley Publishers, London. ISBN 1 85302 730 8

McLeod S (2020). Maslow's Hierarchy of Needs, Simply Psychology. https://www.simplypsychology.org/ maslow.html

Meaney-Tavares R and Gavidia-Payne S (2012). Staff characteristics and attitudes towards the sexuality of people with an intellectual disability. Journal of Intellectual & Developmental Disability, 37(3), 269–273.

Mencap (2001a). Raising Our Sights How-to Guide to Commissioning Services for People with PMLD. Mencap, London.

Mencap (2001b). No Ordinary Life: the Support Needs of Families Caring for Children and Adults With Profound and Multiple Learning Disabilities. Mencap, London.

Mencap & PMLD Network (2016). About Profound and Multiple Learning Disabilities. https://www. mencap.org.uk/sites/default/files/2016-11/PMLD%20factsheet%20about%20profound%20and%20 multiple%20learning%20disabilities.pdf

Meyer J (2020). https://www.treasurequotes.com/quotes/we-can-improve-our-relationships-with-others-b [accessed 2020].

Mia N (2018). Promoting Healthy Sexuality in Adults with Down Syndrome, Surrey Place Centre. https:// www.dsrf.org/media/Nadia%20Mia%20Promoting%20Healthy%20Sexuality%20in%20Adults%20 with%20Down%20Syndrome.pdf

Middletown Centre for Autism (2011). Autism Spectrum Disorder Relationships and Sexuality Research Bulletin Issue No. 5. https://www.middletownautism.com/files/uploads/d025395b6bc81ccff53f90757e3f9235.pdf

Mitchell W and Sloper P (2002). Quality Services for Disabled Children, Research Works, 2002–02, Social Policy Research Unit, University of York, York. https://www.york.ac.uk/inst/spru/pubs/rworks/sept2002-2.pdf

Mitchell W and Sloper P (2003). Quality indicators: disabled children's and parents' prioritisations and experiences of quality criteria when using different types of support services. The British Journal of Social Work, 33(8), 1063–1080. doi: https://doi.org/10.1093/bjsw/33.8.1063

Moore S (2011). Controlling passion? A review of recent developments in British sex education. Health, Risk & Society, 14(1), 25–40.

Moxon L (2011). Autism Spectrum Disorder Relationships and Sexuality. Consultant Psychologist at Education and Services for People with Autism (ESPA). https://www.middletownautism.com/files/uploads/ d025395b6bc81ccff53f90757e3f9235.pdf

National Autistic Society (2008). Sex Education and Children and Young People with Autism Spectrum Disorders. NAS. https://edm.parliament.uk/early-day-motion/35037

National Autistic Society (2020). Relationships and Sex Education. https://www.autism.org.uk/our-schools/ church-lawton/latest-news/relationships-and-sex-education

National Children's Bureau, Sex Education Forum (2004). Sex and Relationships Education for Children and Young People with Learning Difficulties. https://www.ncb.org.uk/about-us/our-specialist-networks/ sex-education-forum

National Confederation of Parent Teacher Associations, National Association of Head Teachers and National Governors Association in partnership with Durex (2010). Sex and Relationship Education: Views Form Teachers, Parents and Governors. http://www.durexhcp.co.uk/news-article/sex-and-relationship-education [accessed 06/08/2013].

National Development Team for Inclusion (2020). https://www.ndti.org.uk/resources/publication/sexuality-and-relationships-my-rights-charter

National Down Syndrome Society (2002) https://www.ndss.org/resources/sexuality/

National Rehabilitation Information Center (NARIC) (2016). Revisiting Sex, Sexuality, & Disability: The Past 10 Years Volume 11, Issue 2. https://naric.com/sites/default/files/reSearch%20Vol.%2011%2C%20 Issue%203_1.pdf

National Working Group on Child Protection and Disability (2003). https://assets.publishing.service.gov.uk/ government/uploads/system/uploads/attachment_data/file/190544/00374-2009DOM-EN.pdf

NEU and The NSPCC (2019). NEU and NSPCC Survey into School Readiness for RSE Lessons 2020. https://neu.org.uk/press-releases/neu-and-nspcc-survey-school-readiness-rse-lessons-2020

NSPCC (2011). Response to the Green Paper, Support and Aspiration: A New Approach to Special Educational Needs and Disabilities. http://www.nspcc.org.uk/Inform/policyandpublicaffairs/consultations/2011/support_aspiration_wdf83141.pdf [accessed 19/07/2013].

NSPCC (2014). 'We Have the Right to be Safe' Protecting Disabled Children from Abuse. https://www.nspcc.org.uk/globalassets/documents/research-reports/right-safe-disabled-children-abuse-report.pdf

NSPCC (2015). Spotlight on Preventing Child Neglect. An Overview of Learning from NSPCC Services and Research. https://learning.nspcc.org.uk/media/1069/spotlight-preventing-child-neglect-report.pdf

Ofsted (2002). Sex and Relationships: A Report from the Office of the Chief Inspector of Schools. (HMI 433), From the Office of Her Majesty's Chief Inspector of Schools. http://www.ofsted.gov.uk/publications/docs/67.pdf

Ofsted (2010). The Special Educational Needs and Disability Review. https://dera.ioe.ac.uk/1145/1/Special%20education%20needs%20and%20disability%20review.pdf

Ofsted (2011). Ages of Concern: Learning Lessons from Serious Case Reviews, A Thematic Report of Ofsted's Evaluation of Serious Case Reviews from 1 April 2007 to 31 March 2011. https://assets.publishing.service.gov.uk/government/uploads/system/uploads/attachment_data/file/526976/Ages_of_concern_learning_lessons_from_serious_case_reviews.pdf

Ofsted (2013). Not Yet Good Enough; Personal, Social, Health and Economic Education in Schools, Ofsted, May 2013. http://www.ofsted.gov.uk/resources/not-yet-good-enough-personal-social-healthand-economic-education-schools

Organization for Autism Research (2020). OAR's Sex Ed. for Self-Advocates. https://researchautism.org/sex-ed-guide/

Parritt S and O'Callaghan J (2000). Splitting the difference: an exploratory study of therapists' work with sexuality, relationships and disability. Sexual and Relationship Therapy, 15(2), 151–169. doi: 10.1080/14681990050010745

Parveen N (2019). https://www.theguardian.com/education/2019/may/24/lgbt-lesson-protests-hijacked-religious-extremists-mps-say

Potter D, Reynolds D and Chapman C (2002). School improvement for schools facing challenging circumstances: a review of research and practice. School Leadership & Management, 22, 243–256. doi: 10.1080/1363243022000020381

Press Association (2015). Judge Authorises Sterilisation of Mother-of-Six with Learning Disabilities. https://www.theguardian.com/society/2015/feb/04/judge-sterilisation-mother-learning-disabilities-pregnant

PSHE Association (2014). Briefing on Teaching about Puberty. https://www.pshe-association.org.uk/system/files/PSHE%20Association%20briefing%20on%20teaching%20about%20puberty%20June%202014.pdf

Raising Children Network (Australia) (2020). Down Syndrome Victoria and Down Syndrome NSW Members' Journal 14 Voice, December 2012 Limited Raising Children Network.

Roberts (2014). http://www.pinknews.co.uk/2014/03/20/pledge-ed-miliband-compulsory-sex-education-welcomed-youth-health-charity-brook/ [accessed 03/05/2014].

Rohleder P (2010). Educators' ambivalence and managing anxiety in providing sex education for people with learning disabilities. Psychodynamic Practice, 16(2), 165–182. ISSN 1475-3634 print/ISSN 1475-3626

Rohleder P and Swartz L (2009). Providing sex education to persons with learning disabilities in the era of HIV/AIDS: tensions between discourses of human rights and restriction. Journal of Health Psychology, 14(4), 601–610. doi: 10.1177/1359105309103579. PMID: 19383660.

RSE Hub (2015). https://www.rsehub.org.uk/about-rse/statutory-requirements/

Schaafsma D, Kok G, Stoffelen J M T and Curfs L M G (2015). Identifying effective methods for teaching sex education to individuals with intellectual disabilities: a systematic review. Journal of Sex Research, 52(4), 412–432. doi: 10.1080/00224499.2014.919373

School of Health and Social Care, Edinburgh Napier University People with Learning Disabilities in Scotland (2017). Health Needs Assessment Update Report Sam Sly. https://www.choicesupport.org.uk/about-us/blog/all-you-need-is-love

SEAD (2015). Sex Education for Adults with Learning/Intellectual Disabilities in the UK. https://www.autismeurope.org/sead-project-sex-education-for-people-with-learning-disabilities-2012-2015/

SEN News Team (2009). Pupils with ASD Should Celebrate Sex. https://senmagazine.co.uk/content/specific-needs/autism-asd/674/asd-pupils-should-celebrate-sex/

Sex Education Forum Survey (2008). Sex Education Forum. NCB, London. https://www.sexeducationforum.org.uk/sites/default/files/field/attachment/SRE%20-%20the%20evidence%20-%20March%202015.pdf

Simmons B and Watson D (2014). Challenging the developmental reductionism of 'profound and multiple learning disabilities' through academic innovation. PMLD Link, 26(3), 25–27.

Sobsey R (1994). Violence and Abuse in the Lives of People with Disabilities: The End of Silent Acceptance? Paul H Brookes Publishing.

Stewart D (2009). Sex and relationship education and pupils with additional needs. SEN, The Journal for Special Needs, 41, 38–39. https://www.senmagazine.co.uk/articles/529-sex-and-relationship-education-and-pupils-with-additional-needs [accessed 12/07/2013].

Strang J F, Meagher H, Kenworthy L, et al. (2018). Initial clinical guidelines for co-occurring autism spectrum disorder and gender dysphoria or incongruence in adolescents. Journal of Clinical Child & Adolescent Psychology, 47(1), 105–115. doi: 10.1080/15374416.2016.1228462. Epub 2016 Oct 24. PMID: 27775428.

Swaffield S and MacBeath J (2005). School self-evaluation and the role of a critical friend, Cambridge Journal of Education, 35(2), 239–252.

Swango-Wilson A (2009). Perception of Sex Education for Individuals with Developmental and Cognitive Disability: A Four Cohort Study, Published online: 24 October 2009, Springer Science + Business Media, LLC [accessed 05/05/2014].

Swango-Wilson A (2011). Meaningful sex education programs for individuals with intellectual/developmental disabilities. Sexuality and Disability, 29, 113–118. doi: 10.1007/s11195-010-9168-2

The Milestone School Curriculum Document for Pupils with Profound and Multiple Learning Difficulties (PMLD) (2016). https://themilestoneschool.co.uk/files/1714/7919/9262/PMLD_Curriculum.pdf

The Tizard Centre, NDTi and My Life My Choice (2020). Sexuality and Relationships – My Rights Charter. https://www.choicesupport.org.uk/uploads/documents/Sexuality-and-Relationships-My-Rights-Charter-Final-15-06-20.pdf

Transgender Trend (2018). Supporting Gender Diverse and Trans-Identified Students in Schools. https://www.transgendertrend.com/wp-content/uploads/2019/08/Transgender-Trend-Resource-Pack-for-Schools3.pdf

UNESCO (2009). International Guidelines on Sexuality Education: An Evidence Informed Approach to Effective Sex, Relationships and HIV/STI Education. https://reliefweb.int/sites/reliefweb.int/files/resources/8556521DD9D4A9E64925762000240120-UNESCO-Aug2009.pdf

United Nations (1989). UN Convention on the Rights of the Child. Defence for the Children International and the United Nations Children's Fund, Geneva http://www.unicef.org.uk/Documents/Publication-pdfs/UNCRC_summary.pdf [accessed 13/07/2013].

United Nations (2006). Convention on the Rights of Persons with Disabilities. https://www.un.org/development/desa/disabilities/convention-on-the-rights-of-persons-with-disabilities.html

Van Der Miesen A I R, Hurley H and De Vries A L C (2016). Gender dysphoria and autism spectrum disorder: a narrative review. International Review of Psychiatry, 28(1), 70–80. doi: 10.3109/09540261.2015.1111199

Visser J (1993). Differentiation: Making It Work: Ideas for Staff Development. National Association for Special Educational Needs, Letts, ISBN-10: 0906730562.

Ward H, Brown R and Hyde-Dryden G (2014). Assessing Parental Capacity to Change When Children Are on the Edge of Care: An Overview of Current Research Evidence Research Report, June 2014, Centre for Child and Family Research, Loughborough University.

Watson D (2014). Go-getters' and 'clever little cookies': findings from a multimethod study on playfulness and children with PMLD. PMLD Link, 26(3), Issue 79. ISSN 2042-5619, Graduate School of Education, University of Bristol. http://www.themultisensoryartproject.co.uk/wp-content/uploads/2016/05/PMLD-link.pdf

Waverley School (2016). Relationships and sex education policy. http://waverley-school.com/wp-content/uploads/2017/05/RelationshipsandSexeducationPolicy.pdf

Wells (2009). http://www.telegraph.co.uk/comment/personal-view/5879177/Sex-education-must-not-be-statutory.html [accessed 19/06/14]

Weyman A (2004). Putting sex in context: sex and relationships education in schools. Education Review, 17(2).

Wood A (2004). Sexuality and relationships education for people with Down syndrome. Down Syndrome News and Update, 4(2), 42–51. doi: 10.3104/practice.330

World Health Organisation (2002). The World Health Report 2002. Reducing Risks, Promoting Healthy Life. https://www.who.int/whr/2002/en/whr02_en.pdf?ua=1

World Health Organisation (2006). Sexual and Reproductive Health and Research Including the Special Programme HRP. https://www.who.int/teams/sexual-and-reproductive-health-and-research/key-areas-of-work/sexual-health/defining-sexual-health

Index

Italicized and **bold** pages refer to figures and tables respectively.

Lightning Source UK Ltd.
Milton Keynes UK
UKHW051948030622
403975UK00004B/11

9 781138 487475